WILDERNESS OF MIRRORS

WILDERNESS OF MIRRORS

David C. Martin

Skyhorse Publishing

Skyhorse Publishing books may be purchased in bulk at special discounts for sales promotion, corporate gifts, fund-raising, or educational purposes. Special editions can also be created to specifications. For details, contact the Special Sales Department, Skyhorse Publishing, 307 West 36th Street, 11th Floor, New York, NY 10018 or info@skyhorsepublishing.com.

Skyhorse® and Skyhorse Publishing® are registered trademarks of Skyhorse Publishing, Inc.®, a Delaware corporation.

Visit our website at www.skyhorsepublishing.com.

10 9 8 7 6 5 4 3 2

Library of Congress Cataloging-in-Publication Data is available on file.

Cover design by Rain Saukas
Cover photo credit iStock

ISBN: 978-1-5107-2218-7
Ebook ISBN: 978-1-5107-2219-4

Printed in the United States of America

For E. D., Cate, and Zach

Contents

In tragic life, God wot,
No villain need be! Passions spin the plot:
We are betrayed by what is false within.

—GEORGE MEREDITH

Preface to the 2018 Edition

More than thirty-five years have passed since I wrote *Wilderness of Mirrors*. The two main protagonists, James Angleton and William Harvey, are dead, and so is my most important source, Clare Edward Petty.

By the time I met Ed, I had been working on *Wilderness* for about a year, collecting pieces of the puzzle without being able to see the big picture. I went to his home in Annapolis more out of thoroughness than with any expectation of a revelation. If he had lived farther away from Washington, I probably would have decided that my budget couldn't handle the expense. About halfway through our second session, Ed's hints finally registered. "Wait a minute, are you saying . . . ?" Indeed he was, but to understand it we had to go back to the beginning. Over the succeeding months, we would meet about once a week as he recounted, with almost total recall, the saga of the hunt for a KGB mole inside the CIA. I never saw him refer to any documents or notes, but I don't know of a single fact he told me that turned out to be wrong.

The last time I spoke to Ed, he was weeping. His grandson, Army Captain Christopher Paul Petty, had just been killed in Iraq. Ed, who had landed in one of the follow-on waves at Normandy and fought across France into Germany, passed away not long after. They are both buried at Arlington National Cemetery.

In the foreword to the original edition, I wrote that the secret war between the CIA and KGB was devious and the outcome ambiguous. Since then, of course, the outcome of the Cold War has been decided, and it is only fair to point out that Angleton, Harvey, and all the other CIA officers who come in for criticism in this book were on the winning side. Whether that justifies what they did is for the reader to decide.

—David C. Martin

Foreword

This book begins and ends in mystery, with precious few solutions in between. Such is the history of the secret war between the American and Soviet espionage services—the only arena in which the two superpowers actively and continuously confront each other regardless of chills and thaws in the Cold War. The battle is devious and the outcome ambiguous. Complexity and perplexity abound. The record is abstruse and, above all, obscure. Although the exposés and investigations of the 1970s have made it possible to examine the CIA's files with a fair degree of thoroughness and precision, the vaults of the KGB remain as tightly sealed as ever. Until they are opened we shall never know with certainty how the war is going. We can, however, study the dispatches sent from behind the American lines, and from there the message is that the war has been going badly. The CIA's defeats have been resounding and its victories Pyrrhic. What the KGB has not done, the CIA has managed to do to itself.

That distressing report is personified in James Jesus Angleton and William King Harvey, the two men whose careers are chronicled here. To many they were heroes, two of the fiercest warriors in the CIA's war against the KGB. To others they were villains guilty of illegal and immoral actions. For the moment it is safe to say only that their secret deeds do not always become them when spread upon the public record. They fought in the trenches of concealment and deception, across the lines of falsehood and betrayal, and what passed for virtue there sometimes appears grotesque in the clear light of day. It is the same in any war. What is heroic in combat is criminal in peace. Just as combat sanctions physical violence, so espionage grants license to moral violence.

For decades Angleton and Harvey maneuvered about this darkling plain without any expectation that they would ever be held publicly accountable for their actions. If they did not fear public censure, neither did they receive public counsel. Now, like monsters of the deep, they are suddenly hauled to the surface and thrown flopping on the deck for inspection. Before we decide whether they are aberrations or prototypes, we must first know the pressures of the depths where they swam.

I first encountered the remarkable person of James Angleton on the night of December 22, 1974. *The New York Times* had just published a major exposé identifying Angleton—somewhat unfairly, it turned out—as the mastermind of a massive and illegal spy campaign against antiwar and civil rights activists. I was working the night desk at The Associated Press in Washington, and in true wire-service fashion I called Angleton for what I was sure would be the obligatory "No comment." We talked for more than an hour, and since that night I have had scores of conversations with him, perhaps more than a hundred, both on the phone and in person. I was not the only reporter who talked regularly with Angleton, but I think I stuck with it longer than most, even though he rarely "leaked" any information that could serve as the peg upon which to hang a news story. Despite the paucity of news, talking to Angleton was a marvelous education in the ways of the CIA. Over time, he explained to me its organization, its personnel, its modus operandi, and its internal rivalries. It was from Angleton, for instance, that I first heard some of the more colorful stories about Bill Harvey.

Harvey always hung up on me when I called, although I did

manage a brief conversation with his wife some months after he died. Angleton encouraged my first thoughts of writing a book about Harvey and advised me that the best hope for persuading Mrs. Harvey to cooperate was to point out that it was because her late husband had been such a forceful figure that he was now the subject of controversy. Had he been a file clerk all his life, his actions would not be of interest to me, I argued at Angleton's suggestion. Mrs. Harvey still refused her cooperation. The argument is worth mentioning here only to recite to Angleton as an equally good reason for writing a book about him. He, too, has refused to cooperate in any way.

Angleton and I have not spoken since the spring of 1978, when he first learned that I had come across information that was intensely critical of his professional performance. Since then he has refused to respond to my inquiries. The result is that although Angleton has served as a source of information about Harvey in particular and the CIA in general, he has not provided any information about the events in this book that most directly concern him. That was his choice, not mine.

A word about my other sources. In order of importance they were: retired intelligence officers; documents released under the Freedom of Information Act; and the public record. In almost every instance the information provided by these sources was fragmentary and had to be pieced together. Intelligence officers usually know only a portion of the story, since operations are so tightly held within the CIA. The problem is further complicated by the fact that men bound by a secrecy oath tend to display a very selective memory when talking to a reporter. Classified documents released by the government invariably have key words or entire passages deleted for security reasons. Nevertheless, the Freedom of Information Act remains a useful discovery tool if for no other reason than the effect that even the partial release of official documents has on otherwise recalcitrant witnesses. The public record is, naturally, the most fragmentary of all, and in many cases is just plain wrong. The amount of misinformation that has appeared in print and then been elevated to history through constant repetition is appalling.

Since most of the people I interviewed insisted upon anonymity, it is hard to say much about them without giving their identities away. One thing can be said in general, and that is that these men (and one woman) were not critics of the CIA. They were staunch supporters. Almost without exception they spent their entire adult lives working for the CIA. They had some very specific complaints about the way certain operations were run, but they remained loyal to the institution and were saddened by the hard times upon which it has fallen. They raged against former officers who revealed secrets in violation of their oath, yet in the next breath they disclosed facts that until that moment were known only to a handful of men. Not wishing to discourage them, I never bothered to point out the inconsistency in that, although they must have realized it. Sometimes, I think, they did not appreciate that what they were saying would merge with what others had told me into an account that was much more revealing than any single person had intended. Other times, they simply fell victim to the need to justify their actions. It is trite but true to say that they did what they did for the good of their country. Unfortunately, it is also true that it frequently didn't work out that way.

WILDERNESS OF MIRRORS

Loss of Innocence

I

A maid found his body at approximately nine-thirty Monday morning, February 10, 1941. He was lying on the bed, face up, dressed in dark-blue trousers, a green sweater, and socks but no shoes. Next to him was a .38-caliber automatic revolver caked with the gore from a massive head wound inflicted by a single soft-nosed bullet that had entered at the right temple and blown a hole the size of a man's fist behind the left ear.

He had checked into the Hotel Bellevue near Washington's Union Station the night before, registering under the name of Walter Poref and paying $2.50 for the room in advance. His wallet, which contained $50.09, carried papers identifying him as Samuel Ginsberg, a forty-one-year-old native of Russia.

There were no signs of a struggle. The door had been locked from the inside. After knocking several times, the maid had used her passkey to open it. There was no fire escape, not even a ledge, by which anyone could have entered or left the room through the fifth-floor window. Police found three notes. To his wife, Tonia, he wrote in Russian: "This is very difficult, and I want very badly to live, but it is impossible. I love you, my only one. It is difficult for me to write, but think about me and then you will understand that I must go." To a friend, Suzanne LaFollette, he wrote in German: "I am dying with the hope that you will help Tonia and my poor boy." And to his attorney, Louis Waldman, he wrote in English: "My wife and boy will need your help. Please do for them what you can."

By noon the coroner had drawn up the suicide certificate, but when police notified Louis Waldman of his client's death, the attorney screamed murder. Samuel Ginsberg, Waldman said, was in reality General Walter Krivitsky, the former chief of Soviet military intelligence in Western Europe, who had defected to the United States in 1938. More than once, Waldman insisted, Krivitsky had told him, "If ever I am found dead and it looks like an accident or a suicide, don't believe it. They are after me. They have tried before."

Two years before his death, Krivitsky had informed the State Department that he had been accosted near Times Square in New York by an alleged Soviet operative named Sergei Bassoff. "The General then asked Mr. Bassoff if he intended to shoot him, and Bassoff replied in the negative," a department memo recounted. Bassoff contented himself with the ambiguous statement that "we have read all that you have written and we suppose you are writing more." Krivitsky did write more, including a series of articles in *The Saturday Evening Post,* that among other things, accurately predicted the 1939 alliance between Hitler's Germany and Stalin's Russia. He also wrote his memoirs, and shortly after their publication, Krivitsky again contacted the State Department, saying "he was afraid an attempt would be made on his life inasmuch as he . . . thought he had observed a couple of Soviet agents watching his residence."

It was hard to tell how many of these threats were real and how many were Krivitsky's imagination. As a former friend, Paul Wohl, said, "Krivitsky was afraid and accused most everyone of being an [Soviet] agent or spy." Yet Krivitsky had good reason to be afraid. A friend and fellow defector named Ignatz Reiss had been found by the side of a road near Lausanne, Switzerland, with twelve bullets in his body. Even the skeptical Wohl, who had had a falling out with Krivitsky over money, did not discount the peril. One month before Krivitsky's death, Wohl had written to their mutual acquaintance, Suzanne LaFollette: "Will you please inform your honorable friend K. that an ominous person is in New York: Hans. . . . His [Krivitsky's] devious practices hardly justify this warning. I hesitated to send it. It may be better to let the rats devour each other." Wohl later told the FBI that he had seen the ominous Hans standing at a bus stop on Fifth Avenue. He had first encountered Hans about five years before at The Hague, where Krivitsky ran his intelligence operations in the guise of an Austrian rare-book dealer. According to Wohl, Hans seemed to serve as chauffeur and handyman for Krivitsky. He also told the FBI that "Hans was the most expert locksmith he had ever come across."

In his memoirs Krivitsky described Hans as "my most trusted aide in many unusual assignments." He had even told Hans of his intention to defect and had urged him to come along. But Hans had remained loyal to Stalin, and after failing to dissuade Krivitsky, had set out to kill him. The last time Krivitsky had seen Hans was on a railroad station platform in Marseilles shortly after he had asked the French authorities for asylum. "I judge that the plan was to abduct me from the train and take me to a safe place in Marseilles . . . where I could either be kept until the arrival of a Soviet boat or disposed of more simply," Krivitsky wrote. But Hans had fled when Krivitsky's French bodyguard pulled a gun. Krivitsky was certain that Hans had been sent to the United States to try again.

Washington's chief of detectives insisted that all of the physical evidence found at the death scene and all subsequent developments "clearly and conclusively show the man took his own life." Krivitsky had spent the weekend before his death on a farm near Charlottesville, Virginia, owned by a former German Army officer named Eitel Wolf Dobert. Dobert led police to a local store where both the manager and the clerk positively identified a photograph of Krivitsky as the same "Walter Poref" who had purchased the .38 automatic and the soft-nosed ammunition found at the Hotel Bellevue. "I am more positive than ever that this was a case of suicide," said another police official. "There is no doubt in my mind that Krivitsky planned to end his life while he was in the Dobert home." The most that police were willing to acknowledge was the possibility that Krivitsky had been hounded to his death by threats from Soviet intelligence.

But Krivitsky had not bought a silencer for his .38, and it was difficult to understand how, in a hotel where guests regularly complained about the paper-thin walls, a shot could be fired in the still of the night and not be heard, especially when the rooms on either side were occupied. The police had not bothered to dust the gun for fingerprints or to check the door latch for signs of tampering by an "expert locksmith" such as Hans.

The FBI refused, officially at least, to investigate the case. "We are not in this case and are not going to be baited into it by newspaper promotion tactics," FBI Director J. Edgar Hoover scribbled at the bottom of a memo. Nevertheless, the chief of the Washington Field Office was informed that "the Bureau wants a very discreet check into the matter of Krivitsky's death. . . . This matter must be handled very discreetly so as to preclude the possibility of the Bureau's getting publicity in connection therewith. . . . The Bureau is denying to the press that an investigation is being conducted." The FBI turned up nothing, discreetly or otherwise.

Not until six years later would an alert State Department researcher poring over the captured files of the German Foreign Ministry come across a coded telegram dated September 21, 1939, from Berlin to the German ambassador in Washington. It referred to a man called Stein, who "is to be appointed and paid 500 dollars on the Washington account." The telegram went on to explain that "the Editor-in-Chief of the *Deutsche Allgemeine Zeitung* has taken over Stein for his stay in the United States and is paying him a salary. . . . Stein is to be rendered assistance if necessary." That seemingly innocuous message was given sinister import by a note attached to a second telegram, sent on the following day. "According to a communication from the Abwehr Division of the Wehrmacht High Command, Stein has only been commissioned to follow Krivitsky's traces."

The State Department dispatched a secret cable to the United States political adviser in Berlin: "It is possible Stein was implicated or may have information concerning the death of Walter Krivitsky." The Germans had had ample motive and opportunity to kill Krivitsky, the cable pointed out. Krivitsky "had predicted the Soviet-German pact" and had spent the last days of his life "on the farm of an acquaintance, Eitel Wolf Dobert, an ex-German Army officer." (The cable did not mention it, but the dates of the Foreign Office telegrams indicated that Stein had been dispatched to the United States at the same time that Krivitsky's revelations were appearing in *The Saturday Evening Post.*) Washington directed that "records of the Foreign Office and the Abwehr should be checked for more data. Secure if possible the present location of Stein, data concerning his travel in United States and his possible relations with Soviet police or military from *Deutsche Allgemeine Zeitung* and other sources. Furnish full name and photograph."

Six months went by without an answer from Berlin. "Encountering difficulty identify Stein as FONOFF [Foreign Office] employed at least five that name, none with recorded service in U.S. *Deutsche Allgemeine Zeitung* now being checked. Full report follows."

For ten days "in the heavily bombed, extremely cold and poorly lighted" remains of a library in the Russian sector of Berlin, two researchers scanned back copies of the *Deutsche Allgemeine Zeitung* for a mention of the mysterious Stein. "The name Stein appeared but once," they reported, "as one Fritz Stein, author of an article originating in Paris in 1941." Apparently the Stein sent to the United States had not produced a single article for the newspaper that paid his salary.

A further search of the Foreign Office files turned up "references to a certain Stein in Rio de Janeiro, 1941 [which] might possibly give a promising clue." An entry in the Foreign Office log for February 20, 1941, referred to "Telegram No. 222 of the Naval Attaché, Rio de Janeiro: 'Abflug Stein.' " Although "the documents to which the entries refer have . . . been destroyed," Berlin reported, "records in Rio, especially those of the airlines, may shed light on the Stein whose flight ('Abflug') is mentioned as having occurred 10 days after Krivitsky's murder."

From there the trail went cold. No records of Stein's flight to Rio could be found. Krivitsky's death remained on the books as a suicide, although his friends and a number of officers in the fledgling American intelligence community had no doubt that he had been murdered. "My personal view is that he was executed," said one intelligence officer who reviewed the case.

No one had better reason to suspect foul play than Whittaker Chambers, who had defected from the Soviet cause at approximately the same time as Krivitsky. Terrified that he was about to become a victim of Stalin's purges, KARL, as Chambers was known to his Soviet controllers, had abandoned his duties as a courier for a Washington spy ring and fled to a bungalow in Daytona Beach, where he and his wife took turns sitting up through the night with a loaded revolver. Chambers felt that he could not be too careful, considering the murder of Ignatz Reiss in Switzerland and, closer to home, the disappearance of Juliette Poyntz, an underground associate who had walked out of her New York apartment one day, leaving all her belongings behind, and was never seen again. When he learned of Krivitsky's death, Chambers immediately arranged for the Russian's widow and son to go into hiding with his own family.

Chambers and Krivitsky had first met through a free-lance journalist named Isaac Don Levine, a Ukrainian exile who had assisted Krivitsky in the preparation of his memoirs. After each had overcome his suspicion that the other had been sent to kill him, the two defectors had become close friends. Krivitsky urged Chambers to follow his example and tell the world everything he knew about the machinations of Stalin's spies. "Informing is a duty," he told Chambers. "One does not come away from Stalin easy." Chambers resisted, fearing not only a vengeful Russian intelligence service but the FBI as well. "I wonder if you really know how deep the water is," Chambers said to a friend who was pressing him to speak out. Finally, prodded by Krivitsky and incensed by the duplicity of the Nazi-Soviet pact, Chambers consented to tell his story to the government, insisting that he speak personally with President Roosevelt but settling for Assistant Secretary of State Adolf Berle. Chambers spent a long evening at Berle's home, rattling off the names of Soviet spies, underground contacts, and mere sympathizers he had known. One of the names he mentioned was that of an up-and-coming State Department officer, Alger Hiss. Months later, Levine told Chambers that Berle had relayed his information to Roosevelt but "the President had laughed." When the FBI learned of Chambers's allegations, J. Edgar Hoover dismissed them as "either history, hypothesis or deduction." On December 1, 1942, the FBI recorded that "the instant case regarding Whittaker Chambers is being closed at this time."

Krivitsky had also known of Hiss—at least a Soviet defector named Alexander Barmine would later claim that Krivitsky had once included Hiss's name in a list of Soviet agents. Unlike Chambers, who would be recalled for further questioning and ultimately would produce documentary evidence against Hiss in the form of the famous "pumpkin papers," Krivitsky was beyond recall—a tragic circumstance, for not only could he have helped clarify the evidence against Hiss, but he could also have testified about other, more important clues he had left. As the journalist Levine later testified under oath, Krivitsky "told me . . . that he had knowledge of two Soviet agents who had been introduced into the British service, one into the code room of the Imperial Council, the other into that of the Foreign Office. . . . He knew the name of one of these men. His name was King. . . . He knew something about the second man, his characteristics, but he did not know his name nor his alias. The characteristics were that of a young Scotsman who had been imbued with Communism in the early thirties, and who subsequently was induced to enter the service of the British diplomacy."

Krivitsky had imparted this information to Levine in strictest confidence, but Levine had betrayed that confidence in the fall of 1939 when the alliance between Hitler and Stalin suddenly raised the prospect that a Soviet spy in London would be serving the Nazis as well. Levine contacted the State Department, which made arrangements for him to meet with the British ambassador in Washington. "Lord Lothian listened to my story, and there was a very obvious smile on his face, a smile of incredulity. However, since I did give the name, he thought, in view of the introduction from the State Department, that the matter should be looked into. Two or three weeks later, sometime in October, 1939, I received a telephone call from the British Embassy. . . . It appeared there was no longer any smile on Lord Lothian's face. They found that King was in the code room in the Foreign Office, and apparently they had put him under surveillance. The information was confirmed. The man was arrested and now they wanted to know about the second man, the Scotsman whom I described even to the point of his clothes . . . according to Krivitsky's description of the man to me."

In January of 1940 Krivitsky had secretly boarded a British vessel in Nova Scotia and was escorted by convoy to Liverpool. Living under the name Walter Thomas, he spent more than a month in England answering questions put to him by representatives of British intelligence, but he was unable to provide any further information about the identity of the second man. He was, however, able to tell the British in equally vague terms about a third man, a young British journalist sent to Spain to spy for the Russians during the Spanish Civil War.

Krivitsky and Chambers were the right defectors at the wrong time. Had they been listened to more carefully, the careers of several well-placed Soviet agents might have been aborted at an early stage. The two defectors had offered detailed information about Soviet intelligence operations, yet no one in Western intelligence exhibited any interest until the journalist Levine practically force-fed them to the authorities. Even so, Krivitsky's pleas for protection from the assassins he feared were stalking him had been fobbed off by the State Department with evasive suggestions that he contact the local police. Chambers would not be interviewed by the FBI until four years after his defection, and it was not until 1945 that anyone began to take him seriously.

The prewar complacency about Soviet espionage was almost touching—a clinging to the belief that great nations did not resort to such seamy stratagems, that men of good family and proper education did not betray their countries. The onset of war marked the loss of innocence, but the expediency of the alliance with Russia against the Axis powers precluded any meaningful retaliation against Stalin's spies. "I was told not to take any action. I was to watch them, to take note, but do nothing," said Peer de Silva, a security officer with the Manhattan Engineering Project who worked with the FBI in the surveillance of Soviet agents. "We were convinced they had deep penetrations of the government," said Robert Collier, one of only three agents assigned to the FBI's Soviet espionage division, but "nobody was paying any attention to what was happening."

Finally, in 1945, as the world crawled out from beneath the rubble of war, events conspired to shake the West from its indifference toward Soviet espionage. With the end of the wartime alliance against Fascism came the beginning of the competition between capitalism and Communism that would dominate the second half of the century, and the gray dawn of the Cold War cast a new light upon the shadow world of espionage. Suddenly, Soviet agents were seen not as the petty malefactors of a backward colossus but as the secret army of a malevolent power bent on world domination. To counter this threat, the United States raised a secret army of its own: the Central Intelligence Agency.

In a memo to Harry Truman, presidential adviser Clark Clifford defined the new Agency's primary mission: "Our suspicion of the Soviet Union . . . must be replaced by an accurate knowledge of the motives and methods of the Soviet government." But knowledge could not keep pace with events: a Soviet-backed civil war in Greece; the installation of a Kremlin puppet in Czechoslovakia; Communist agitation and subversion in France and Italy; the detonation of Russia's first atomic weapon. The CIA was thrown into the breach not to gather intelligence as originally intended but to stem the tide whenever and wherever Communist expansion threatened American interests. Espionage—the business of stealing the enemy's secrets—was soon dwarfed by covert action—the business of manipulating foreign governments through a host of paramilitary, propaganda, and political schemes.

But always deep within the Agency there remained a hardened inner core that never took its eyes off the main target: the Soviet Union and its intelligence service, the KGB, which one way or the other had driven Krivitsky to his death. The CIA would storm about the globe, fighting behind the lines in Korea, overthrowing leftist regimes in Iran and Guatemala, suppressing a Communist insurgency in the Philippines, but always the flame burned brightest at the core. This was espionage, pure and elemental. This was combat as ruthless and unforgiving as any of the brushfire wars that peppered the landscape of the Cold War.

No one waged this secret war with greater intensity, with colder rage, than James Jesus Angleton and William King Harvey, two very different men—different from each other and from the rest of humanity—who were better known to their adversaries in the Kremlin than to their own countrymen. For the better part of three decades they confronted the KGB in a daily battle of deception, a battle fought in a maze of agents and double agents, spies and counterspies, intelligence and counterintelligence. Though neither Angleton nor Harvey knew it at the time, their battle had begun with the death of Walter Krivitsky. The death itself was a mystery that would never be satisfactorily solved, but the warnings that Krivitsky had left about the young Scotsman in the Foreign Office and the British journalist in Spain would prove all too accurate. Angleton and Harvey would play key roles in the case that Krivitsky had outlined in such vague and indistinct strokes. But that was only one of many cases in the labyrinth of espionage. Searching for solutions, Angleton and Harvey would be lured deeper and deeper into the labyrinth, pursuing the traces of Soviet plots, both real and imagined, each step taking them farther into a bewildering world of intrigue that Angleton called the "wilderness of mirrors."

The Poet and the Cop

In many ways James Jesus Angleton was as singular a man as ever worked for the United States government. He would become more singular with the passage of time, but even in 1945, at the age of twenty-eight, he was a breed apart. He was the firstborn son of Hugh Angleton, a man who had moved west to Idaho not long after the turn of the century and then set off for Mexico with "Black Jack" Pershing in pursuit of Pancho Villa. There he had taken a wife, a seventeen-year-old Mexican beauty, and brought her home to Boise, where James Jesus was born in 1917. He was a sickly child who suffered from tuberculosis and had to spend much of his youth in the hot, dry climate of Arizona, which he hated. When the boy was sixteen, Hugh Angleton moved his family to Italy to seek his fortune, which he found in Milan as the head of National Cash Register. His eldest son went off to Malvern College in England and then on to Yale University.

James Jesus was the sum of all those varied parts—and more. He was possessed of (some would say possessed by) a mind of the first rank—a mind not content to dwell on the surface but

11

always probing deeper in search of a hidden meaning; a mind fully confident of its powers and unafraid to draw the most unorthodox conclusions; a mind that attracted others by its brilliance and held them with its complexity. Two of his loves were fly-casting and poetry—coaxing forth the secret life that lurked beneath the water's surface; unraveling the enigmas of Ezra Pound's *Cantos* or E. E. Cummings's elliptic verse.

At Yale, Angleton and his roommate, Reed Whittemore, who would later become a poet of some note, founded a literary journal, *Furioso,* which during its short and irregular life published the best American poets of the day: Pound, Cummings, Archibald MacLeish, William Carlos Williams, Wallace Stevens. "Dear Angleton—in certainly printing a certain poem you and your confrère have paid me one deep compliment, and I heartily thank you for both," Cummings wrote. The idiosyncratic poet took an interest in the young undergraduate, and as Angleton approached graduation, Cummings wrote to Pound that "Jim Angleton has been seemingly got hold of by an intelligent prof & apparently begins to begin to realize that comp mil ser [compulsory military service] might give the former a respite from poisonal responsibility . . . maybe he's developing?" Instead, Angleton went on to Harvard Law. It was not until 1943 that an intelligent prof, Norman Holmes Pearson of Yale, recruited his former student into the X-2, or counterintelligence, branch of the Office of Strategic Services, an ad hoc aggregation of scholars, aristocrats, and eccentrics who made up America's wartime intelligence service. "He took to it like a dog to water," Pearson said later, and a phrase composed by Cummings in a letter to Angleton's young wife, Cicely, captured the reason why. "What a miracle of momentous complexity is The Poet," Cummings wrote.

Angleton began his OSS career with two weeks of basic training in Maryland's Catoctin Mountains. Another recruit, Dr. Bruno Uberti, a refugee from Fascist Italy, recalled that at the end of training each student was required to evaluate his classmates. Angleton guessed that Uberti must have been a very good basketball player, judging by the way he jumped. "It was true that I had been a good basketball player," Uberti said. "I had played on the

Italian national team." Afterward, Angleton confided to Uberti that he had once seen him play in Milan.

"I considered him extremely brilliant but a little strange," Uberti said of Angleton. "I met a lot of important Americans from [General William] Donovan [head of the OSS] on down, but Angleton was the personality which impressed me the most. He made a terrific great impression. A very exceptional man. He had something more. He had a strange genius I would say—full of impossible ideas, colossal ideas. I would have liked to have been one of his friends, but he never gave me a chance because he was so secretive."

In 1943 Angleton checked into the ramshackle and shell-scarred Rose Garden Hotel on London's Ryder Street, headquarters for the combined counterintelligence operations of the OSS and MI6, Britain's secret service. It was midway through the war, and the Americans knew nothing of counterintelligence. Angleton and the rest of the Americans had come to London to learn the business from the British, and one of their tutors was a young man named Harold "Kim" Philby. Philby "gave a one- to one-and-a-half-hour talk on the subject of turning agents—double agents," one of the Americans recalled. "I do remember being very impressed. He really knew what he was doing."

Philby, former correspondent for *The Times* of London, had joined MI6 in the summer of 1940, less than six months after Krivitsky had warned the British authorities about a young British journalist sent to spy for the Russians during the Spanish Civil War. A routine trace had been run on Philby's name, and the answer came back: "Nothing recorded against." Those who knew him personally must have recalled the left-wing activism of Philby's youth, but that seemed nothing more than an adolescent peccadillo, now long past.

Philby had come to Marx as a student at Trinity College, Cambridge. He had begun his journey in 1931 by joining the Cambridge University Socialist Society, and like many other students disenchanted with capitalism and alarmed at the rise of Fascism, he had moved steadily left toward the Soviet alternative. He had been to Berlin, had heard Hitler's venomous denunciations of the Jews and witnessed Nazi intimidation of the Communist Party, and by the time he came down from Cambridge in 1933, he was a fellow traveler. At the age of twenty-one he had rushed to riot-torn Vienna, where the shelling of workers' tenements by government artillery marked the downfall of social democracy in Central Europe. There his conversion had become complete with his marriage to Litzi Friedman, a young Jewish girl who was an avowed Communist.

Back in London with his new bride, Philby underwent a radical, and at the time inexplicable, change. He suddenly avoided his fellow Cambridge Marxists and began frequenting the German Embassy. By 1936 he had joined the Anglo-German Fellowship, which was a Nazi front organization. The next year, he left Litzi, his only remaining overt link to Communism, and headed for the Spanish Civil War—a young British journalist sent to spy for the Russians.

As *The Times*'s correspondent with Franco's army, Philby was decorated by the Generalissimo himself and reviled by his former comrades of the left, many of whom were dying on the other side of the lines. A narrow escape from death when a Russian artillery shell killed three occupants of the car in which Philby was riding was not close enough as far as his former comrades were concerned. They could not know that he was serving the cause with as much valor and daring as they. Their contempt must have vexed Philby deeply, but he let his guard slip only once—when Eric Gedye, a journalist Philby had known and respected in Vienna, lamented to Litzi about the bad company into which her wayward husband had fallen. "Months later, when I'd forgotten the incident, she telephoned me out of the blue with a message from Kim," Gedye recalled. "It was simply this: 'Tell Eric not to be misled by appearances. I'm exactly what I've always been.' " The cryptic message was revealing only in retrospect. For some time to come, everyone would continue to be misled by appearances.

So well had Philby changed his colors that had there been any concern over his ideological tendencies when he applied for work with British intelligence, it would have been over his Fascist, not his Communist, leanings. But there was no concern at all. Philby had gone to the right school, worked for the right newspaper, joined the right club. His father, the noted Arabist St. John Philby, was a personal acquaintance of two of the highest-ranking officers in MI6. As Colonel Valentine Vivian, deputy chief of MI6, put it, "I was asked about him, and I said I knew his people."

After a brief fling in propaganda operations, Philby joined Section Five of MI6, the counterespionage division of Britain's secret service. From the start he was regarded as a comer. Graham Greene, the novelist, worked for him during the war and said that "no one could have been a better chief than Kim Philby. . . . He worked harder than anyone and never gave the impression of labor. He was always relaxed, completely unflappable." Philby was considered so valuable that when *The Times* tried to hire him back, the Foreign Office, speaking for the officially nonexistent MI6, replied that "we should be bound to recommend most strongly against his removal from his present job. . . . His present work is so important, and he performs it with such ability that I am afraid his departure would be a real loss to us."

If "Philby was the most gifted of the British," as one intelligence officer said, "Angleton was the most gifted of the Americans." A fellow X-2 officer said that "Jim was a very respected American among our British counterparts. He was probably more on a basis of equality with his British counterparts than anybody." Specifically, Angleton was permitted access to the jealously guarded ICE traffic, the intercepted messages in the German Abwehr code, which the British had succeeded in breaking. It was entirely natural that Angleton and Philby should gravitate toward one another. Although Angleton was five years Philby's junior, they had much in common. Both had expatriate fathers—Angleton's in Italy and Philby's in Arabia—and both had been drawn toward establishment institutions—Angleton to Yale, Harvard Law, and the OSS; Philby to Cambridge, *The Times,* and MI6. In addition, they shared a fascination with counterintelligence—a fascination that in Philby arose from the necessities of his double life, and in Angleton stemmed from an intellectual predilection for the complex. According to one officer, "Philby was Angleton's prime tutor in counterintelligence," although the same might have been said about any number of Americans assigned to X-2 in London. In later years more than a little irony would attach to the fact that the Americans, and Angleton in particular, had studied the art of counterintelligence under the Soviet Union's master penetration agent.

The British enjoyed considerable success with their "double-cross" operations during World War II, capturing Nazi spies in England and turning them into double agents who both revealed the workings of German intelligence and sent back deliberately misleading information to Berlin. The intricacies of the double-cross system were described in an official report by John Masterman, who wrote that "the best agents for deception on a high-level are long-distance agents who have been carefully built up and who have served a long apprenticeship before any major deception is attempted through them." During the apprenticeship, however, a double agent "is not an asset but a liability," Masterman noted, for the buildup "process implies that he must communicate a great deal of true information." The greater the desired deception, the higher the value of accurate intelligence that had to be given away in order to establish the agent's "bona fides." The challenge was to draw the balance so that the agent did "not give to the enemy information so valuable that it would be likely to outweigh any subsequent benefits which might accrue through him."

Masterman's double-cross principles were as instructive for the detection of double agents as for their running. Although in the first instance an agent's bona fides would be judged by the accuracy of the intelligence he provided, he could not be accepted as genuine on that basis alone. The value of his intelligence had to be weighed against whatever deception the enemy might be able to achieve if the agent were really a double agent. It was a most difficult calculation, since the nature of the deception could only be guessed at by assuming that it had to be worth more than the accurate intelligence the enemy was willing to give up. The more valuable the intelligence, the greater the potential deception would have to be. Carried to its logical extreme, the calculation became an absurdity, since it was always possible to conjure up a deception that was greater than the intelligence. Everything read backward, as in a mirror. The more valuable an agent's service, the more reason to fear a deception. The greater the truth, in short, the bigger the lie. That paradoxical principle would serve as the bedrock of Angleton's own counterintelligence theories for the next thirty years.

Late in 1944 Angleton was dispatched to Italy to assume control of OSS counterintelligence operations as the Allied forces drove northward up the peninsula against the retreating German army. The Germans surrendered in May of 1945, and shortly afterward the OSS in Italy and elsewhere was disbanded. While officials in Washington bickered over the form that America's peacetime espionage establishment would take, Angleton stayed on in Rome as commanding officer of a small caretaker organization called the 2677th Regiment of the Strategic Services Unit (SSU). At the age of twenty-eight, he was the senior American intelligence officer in Italy. "He was a little bit too young for the job," an SSU officer in Trieste thought. "I felt that perhaps he didn't have the wherewithal to do the job."

The veterans of the OSS in Italy, mostly young toughs of Italian-American extraction who had spent the war in the trenches and in some cases behind enemy lines, did not know what to make of this Ivy League aesthete who had sat out the war in London. "He struck us right off the bat as weird," one of them said. "The guy was just in another world." At the SSU offices on the Via Archimede, Angleton's would always be the lone light burning in the middle of the night. "I caught him one night," an SSU officer recalled. "He had all these goddamn poetry books out." When his light was not burning, Angleton might be found in Genoa, paying a visit to the expatriate Ezra Pound, who was being held on charges of treason for his wartime broadcasts of Fascist propaganda. Angleton quickly became known behind his back as "the Poet," or, more derisively, as "the Cadaver" because of his emaciated appearance. The women in the office found this enigmatic wraith somewhat attractive. "Fatten him up and he'd look like Gregory Peck," they said. If Angleton resembled Gregory Peck physically, spiritually he was a ringer for the Romantic poet John Keats. Like Keats, Angleton had come to Rome to die of tuberculosis. "Every day he was complaining he was dying of TB," one of the SSU men said. "He had a premonition that within three years he'd be dead."

Whether that premonition was based on sound medical advice or on mere Romantic angst, there was nothing resigned or fatalistic about Angleton, who despite his failing health and poetic reveries easily dominated and intimidated those beneath him. "Whenever you went to Rome to meet with Angleton, you found him propped up behind his desk facing you through two big stacks of papers," an SSU officer from Milan recalled. "You would sit on a sofa across from the desk and he would peer at you through this valley of papers. The sofa had broken springs and as a result you were about two feet below his face. He always made you feel like this. . . . One of the qualities required to work for Angleton is detachable testicles. . . . He wants complete and absolute mastery over the minds of the people that work for him." Angleton brooked no rivals, real or imagined. Max Corvo, a veteran of the OSS in Italy, related what happened when he returned to Rome as a civilian after the war. "Jim thoroughly suspected that I had been sent there either to undermine him or take over for him. He never hesitated to show his animosity. One of my wife's friends who was stationed in Rome with SSU was fired on the spot because she associated with us. . . . He suspected everybody. . . . He would spend an hour and a half every morning going through his office to see if it had been bugged."

No matter what they thought of Angleton's quirks, both superiors and subordinates agreed that he was a first-rate spy. Colonel William Quinn, head of the SSU, recalled his impression of Angleton during a trip through Austria, Switzerland, and Italy in the spring of 1946. "I was amazed at the breadth of his understanding and knowledge," Quinn said. "I felt we really had a jewel." In May of 1946 Angleton's skills were recognized with a decoration personally bestowed by the king of Italy. "He really came up with some amazing things," one officer said. Angleton later confided to a friend that he had ferreted out the secret correspondence between Hitler and Mussolini that was used at the Nuremberg war crimes trials, as well as the exchange of letters between Stalin and Tito that foreshadowed their 1948 split. Through his close ties with the renascent Italian carabinieri—"He bribed all the police as they were being put back together," one colleague said—Angleton, by his own account, acquired the Soviet instructions to the Italian Communists for supporting the civil war in Greece. Even a war-grizzled veteran who personally disliked the young upstart with his "brand-new trench coat and bright shiny second lieutenant bars" had to concede that "the guy was really damned good."

Angleton's men fanned out through postwar Italy, recruiting agents at every level, a relatively simple task given the hold the conquering Americans had on the country's political and economic future. Men who had lost everything in the war or who faced the prospect of languishing in a prison camp could easily be persuaded to cooperate. A major on the Italian General Staff told one of Angleton's men that all he wanted from life was an assignment to Bulgaria, Rumania, or Turkey. His desires were relayed to Angleton, and "within six months this particular major became the military attaché in Istanbul," an SSU officer said. "I imagine that a guy like that worked for the rest of his life for us." A prominent banker from Milan was suddenly released from an internment camp and thereafter served as a conduit for secret payments to American agents in northern Italy. Another Italian was so indebted to the SSU that he allowed himself to be smuggled into Switzerland in the trunk of a car so that a plastic surgeon from Bern could give a more Oriental slant to his eyes before he was dispatched to the Far East as a long-range undercover agent.

The Americans were not the only ones recruiting agents, and frequently the greatest challenge Angleton faced was keeping his newfound assets away from British and French intelligence operatives. When the head of German counterintelligence for northern Italy, Georg Sessler, surrendered his entire network, including his mistress, Angleton ordered the windfall kept from the British, who he feared would simply execute the Nazi spy. When the British found out about Sessler on their own, Angleton was forced to relinquish him to a prisoner-of-war camp, but before he could be brought to trial, the SSU arranged his escape by bribing his Italian jailers. The SSU gave Sessler a new identity, reunited him with his mistress, and established the couple as proprietors of a pension in the south of France. "He's long-term," an SSU officer said of the eternally grateful Sessler.

With so many intelligence agencies shopping for agents, it was inevitable that some would sell their services to more than one bidder. The SSU had tapped a particularly rich vein by paying $100 a week to a code clerk in the Vatican for a daily synopsis of the intelligence reports sent in by the papal nuncios around the world. Each day an Italian newspaperman who served as the go-between would deliver an envelope containing the synopsis to a kiosk in the Piazza Bologna, where a second runner would pick it up and deliver it to the SSU offices. Suspicious about who else might be receiving copies of the synopsis, Angleton ordered an observation post set up in an apartment overlooking the piazza. "We watched the guy bring the envelope to the kiosk," an SSU man recalled, "only some days it would be as many as three envelopes." One of the extra envelopes was being picked up by a runner for the Russian Embassy. The SSU agents filmed the entire sequence from their observation post and delivered a tightly edited version to Myron Taylor, the American envoy to the Vatican, who arranged a private screening for Pope Pius XII. The next day "that clerk disappeared from the face of the earth," an SSU officer said. "No trace."

Of all the sources Angleton tapped in Italy, perhaps the most valuable was the Jewish underground, which was organizing the exodus of survivors of the Holocaust through Italy to Palestine. Fighting for their very existence, the Jews had of necessity developed the most tenacious and most effective underground network in Eastern Europe. Angleton won their trust, establishing a bond that would give him special standing in the new state of Israel. One of Angleton's Israeli confidants, Teddy Kollek, who many years later would become mayor of Jerusalem, explained the bond in an almost mystical way. "I believe Jim saw in Israel a true ally at a time when belief in a mission had become a rare concept," Kollek wrote. "He found comparatively more faith in Israel, and more determination to act on that faith, than anywhere else in the world." An American who worked closely with Angleton on Israeli affairs gave a more pragmatic explanation, saying that Angleton saw Jewish emigration from the Soviet Union to Israel as a pipeline through which the KGB could send its spies into the Middle East and even to the United States. The KGB was in a perfect position to blackmail Soviet Jews, agreeing to let them out but threatening reprisals against the family members left behind if the émigrés did not carry out their espionage missions. United in the common purpose of weeding out Soviet espionage agents, "the Israelis gave him their sources behind the Iron Curtain," another officer said. "He got some sensational documents from these sources."

Angleton's sources were of no use to him, however, when it came to spotting one Russian spy who in September of 1945 stood, quite literally, before his eyes. In later years Angleton would disclose to only a very few people that Kim Philby had stopped off to see him in Rome on his way back to London from Istanbul, where, it turned out, he had just completed one of the more ticklish missions of his double life.

The mission had begun about a month before, when Sir Stewart Menzies, head of MI6, called Philby into his office to evaluate a report that Konstantin Volkov, nominally a minor consular official but in reality the senior Soviet intelligence officer in Istanbul, wanted to defect. In return for money and asylum, Volkov was prepared to reveal the true names of two British spies inside the Foreign Office and a third who was a counterintelligence officer. Philby probably had some idea of who the two spies in the Foreign Office might be, and he certainly had no doubt about the identity of the counterintelligence officer. If Volkov were permitted to tell his story, Philby would surely be undone. "I stared at the papers rather longer than necessary to compose my thoughts," he related years later in his memoirs. "I told the chief that I thought we were on to something of the greatest importance." Philby said he needed "a little time to dig into the background" and would report to the chief with recommendations for action first thing the following morning.

Ten days had already elapsed since Volkov first made contact with the British Embassy in Istanbul, insisting that all communications be by diplomatic pouch because the Russians were able to decipher some of the British cable traffic. Playing for time, Philby alerted his Soviet handler to the impending disaster, then advised Menzies that Volkov's warning against use of telegraphic communications required "that somebody fully briefed should be sent out from London to take charge on the spot." Three days after word of Volkov's approach had reached London, Philby was on a plane for Istanbul via Cairo. His arrival was delayed two days by an electrical storm that forced his plane to set down in Tunis, and another two days were wasted in Istanbul while he awaited the British ambassador's personal approval to proceed.

The plan for recontacting Volkov was a simple one. A British diplomat was to invite him to his office for a piece of routine consular business. Philby watched as the diplomat, whom he called Page, dialed the Soviet consulate. "Page's face was a study in puzzlement, telling me that a hitch had developed. When he put the receiver down he shook his head at me. . . . 'I asked for Volkov, and a man came on, saying he was Volkov. But it wasn't Volkov. I know Volkov's voice perfectly well. I've spoken to him dozens of times.' Page tried again, but this time got no further than the telephone operator. 'She said he was out,' said Page indignantly. 'A minute ago she put me on to him.' " The next day Philby and Page tried again. "I heard the faint echo of a woman's voice, then a sharp click," Philby related. "Page looked foolishly at the silent receiver in his hand. 'What do you make of that? I asked for Volkov, and the girl said "Volkov's in Moscow." Then there was a sort of scuffle and slam, and the line went dead.' " Page made one more try, this time in person at the Soviet consulate. "Nobody's ever heard of Volkov," he fumed to Philby upon his return. The case was dead—and probably Volkov as well.

An official inquiry was launched into the loss of so potentially lucrative a source. Philby maintained that Volkov's own insistence on using the diplomatic pouch had caused the fatal delay. "Nearly three weeks had elapsed since his first approach to Page before we first tried to contact him," he pointed out. "During that time, the Russians had ample chances of getting on to him. Doubtless both his office and his living quarters were bugged. . . . Perhaps his manner had given him away; perhaps he had got drunk and talked too much; perhaps even he had changed his mind and confessed." Or perhaps someone had tipped off the Russians to Volkov's intention to defect. Philby found that theory "not worth mentioning in my report." In any case, the inquiry located the most likely cause of Volkov's undoing. A British official in Istanbul admitted that he had indiscreetly mentioned Volkov's name in a telephone conversation with the embassy in Ankara. The telephone line was assumed to be monitored by the Russians.

Philby was safe, at least for the moment. "The Volkov business proved to be a very narrow squeak indeed," he said, looking back on the affair. If Angleton suspected anything untoward when he saw Philby in Rome shortly afterward, he did not report it. Philby might have gotten away with it entirely had it not been for William King Harvey.

At about the same time that Angleton was exchanging thoughts with Philby in Rome, Bill Harvey was sitting in a small room in New York City, listening intently as a plump, dowdy, brown-haired woman named Elizabeth Bentley confessed that she had been a courier for a Soviet spy ring. Harvey had left his desk at FBI head-quarters in Washington to come to New York for a firsthand look at this woman who, if she was telling the truth, represented the Bureau's first big break in combating Soviet espionage. Harvey left the interrogation of Bentley to other FBI agents while he sat quietly and simply tried to get a feel for this woman who would consume the next two years of his life. During fourteen days of questioning, Bentley reeled off the names of more than a hundred people linked to the Soviet underground in the United States and Canada. "Fifty-one of these persons were deemed of sufficient importance to warrant investigative attention by the Bureau," an FBI memo stated. "Of those 51 individuals, 27 were employed in agencies of the U.S. government." One of those twenty-seven was named Hiss.

Bentley was the third defector to have warned the FBI about Hiss, or a man fitting his description. Whittaker Chambers had been the first, but his unsubstantiated allegation carried little weight in the face of Hiss's powerful friends and brilliant career at the State Department. Graduate of Harvard Law, clerk to Oliver Wendell Holmes, protégé and confidant of Secretary of State Edward Stettinius, personal friend of Under Secretary Dean Acheson, Hiss was beyond the reach of so unsavory a character as Chambers. In the fall of 1945, however, independent though hardly ironclad confirmation of Chambers's charge suddenly came from an unexpected quarter. A Soviet code clerk named Igor Gouzenko defected in Ottawa, bringing with him hundreds of documents detailing the workings of an extensive Russian spy ring. According to an FBI account of Gouzenko's interrogation, "the Soviets had an agent in the United States in May, 1945, who was an assistant to the then Secretary of State, Edward R. Stettinius." A short time later Bentley defected and identified Hiss by name, although she incorrectly gave his first name as Eugene.

In a few years the name Hiss would be on every tongue, but to Bill Harvey in 1945 Hiss was only one of several senior government officials suspected of treason. Bentley had mentioned Hiss almost as an afterthought at the end of her 107-page statement. Such other names as those of Harry Dexter White, Assistant Secretary of the Treasury, and Lauchlin Currie, administrative assistant to the President, played a more prominent role in her tale of espionage. Harvey, just turned thirty and with barely five years' experience in the FBI, suddenly found himself in the middle of what loomed as the greatest spy scandal in the nation's history. For the first but not the last time, he was the keeper of secrets that when finally revealed would cause a public sensation. His special knowledge set him apart. The everyday world in which most people lived, in which Hiss, White, and Currie were trusted government servants, was unreal to him. His reality was a world in which the most commonplace events, such as a cab ride shared by White and Hiss, took on special and sinister meaning. He was as far removed from the normal commerce of human lives as if he were locked in a prison. To Harvey, it was not a prison but an inner sanctum.

Harvey had begun his career with an unsuccessful campaign for public office and thereafter withdrew behind walls of silence, as if he found sanctuary in secrecy. His father was the most prominent attorney in Danville, Indiana, a small town twenty miles west of Indianapolis, and his grandfather was the founder of the local newspaper. In 1936, on the strength of his father's name and the endorsement of his grandfather's newspaper, Harvey had run for prosecuting attorney in Hendricks County while still a student at Indiana University Law School. Despite the Danville *Gazette*'s promise that "Billy is a keen student and his election would be a great benefit to the people of Hendricks County," Harvey was a Democrat in a staunchly Republican county, and he lost by 880 votes out of 12,000 cast.

Staying in Indiana only long enough to collect his law degree, Harvey and his young wife, the former Elizabeth McIntire, moved to the small Ohio River town of Maysville, Kentucky, where he opened a one-man practice. Libby, as everyone called her, had grown up in nearby Flemingsburg, across the street from a cousin of Harvey's. Her father was the leading attorney in Flemingsburg and only too pleased to help his son-in-law set up practice down the road in Maysville. Harvey went through the motions, joining the Rotary Club and working with the Boy Scouts, but he never really made a go of it in Maysville. "He didn't have the personality to succeed in a small town," said a local insurance broker who counted himself Harvey's best friend in Maysville. "In a small town you have to be nice to people and smile. He didn't meet people well. . . . He didn't indulge in small talk. He could walk down the street and not speak to anybody." Harvey did little more than "sit around in the office and fiddle with his collection of guns and knives," a local attorney said.

No one was very surprised in December of 1940 when Harvey left Maysville and joined the FBI, starting in the Pittsburgh Field Office at an annual salary of $3,200. By 1945 he had made his way to FBI headquarters in Washington as part of a small vanguard of three agents—himself, Robert Collier, and Lish Whitsun—targeted against America's ostensible ally, the Soviet Union. "We were the first ones to be fighting the Soviet side of it," Collier recalled. And now the defection of Elizabeth Bentley finally gave them something to fight with. "Bentley made a lot of things we suspected into reality," Collier said.

Like so many of her generation, Bentley had turned to Communism in the 1930s out of disillusionment with the inability of democracy to combat the evils of Fascism and the Depression. As Bentley told it, she had begun her career as a spy by collecting blueprints of commercial vat designs from an engineer named Abraham Brothman. Her Soviet handler, Jacob Golos, had more grandiose schemes in mind, however. He taught Bentley the rudiments of espionage—

to throw off automobile surveillance by walking the wrong way on a one-way street, to remove all identification marks from her clothing—and in the summer of 1941 dispatched her to Washington to make contact with Nathan Silvermaster, a Russian-born employee of the Department of Agriculture. As Bentley told it, Silvermaster collected documents from an underground network of Communists throughout the government, and she hauled them back to Golos in New York in her knitting bag.

She would later claim that she had been driven to confess by her "good old New England conscience." However, an FBI memo suggested that she feared the Bureau was already onto her and was simply trying to save her skin. Whatever her motive, Bentley had chosen her moment well, arriving at the FBI's doorstep on the heels of Gouzenko's defection in Canada and amid the increasing postwar distrust between the United States and Russia. The vigor of the FBI's reaction to her stood in sharp contrast to the indifference with which Krivitsky and Chambers had been greeted seven years before.

Within twenty-four hours of Bentley's appearance and before he had verified any of her information, J. Edgar Hoover sent a top-secret message to the White House. "As a result of the Bureau's investigative operations," he puffed, "information has been recently developed from a highly confidential source indicating that a number of persons employed by the Government of the United States have been furnishing data and information to persons outside the Federal Government, who are in turn transmitting this information to espionage agents of the Soviet Union." Hoover named twelve officials as being either witting or unwitting "participants in this operation," no doubt taking private satisfaction in the fact that five of them had served with his arch-rival, the Office of Strategic Services. Within a matter of days, Hoover had assigned a total of 227 agents to conduct "technical surveillances, mail covers and physical surveillances" of the government officials suspected of espionage. The surveillance confirmed that Bentley, or GREGORY as she was code-named within the Bureau, was telling the truth. "In no instance has GREGORY reported information which could not either directly or circumstantially be verified," an FBI memo stated. Bentley said that a laboratory for reproducing government documents had been set up in the basement of the Silvermaster home. A break-in by FBI agents "determined that such a photographic laboratory does now exist sufficiently well equipped for the copying of documents." Bentley identified a photograph of Anatoli Gromov, first secretary of the Soviet Embassy in Washington, as that of the man she knew as "Al," one of her Soviet contacts. At four o'clock on the afternoon of November 21, 1945, a team of FBI agents watched Gromov arrive for a scheduled meeting with Bentley on the corner of Eighth Avenue and Twenty-third Street in Manhattan.

By themselves, neither a basement darkroom nor a street-corner rendezvous constituted proof of espionage, but other information provided by Bentley left no doubt in Hoover's mind that espionage had been committed. "GREGORY has reported with a high degree of accuracy situations . . . which were only known within the government itself as examples of material which was passed through GREGORY . . . for use by the Soviet Government," a Bureau report said. Bentley claimed that Major Duncan Lee of the OSS had passed information about "peace maneuverings going on between the satellite Axis nations through the medium of OSS representatives in Sweden and Switzerland," a vague but accurate description of Operation SUNRISE, the secret surrender of one million Axis troops in northern Italy brokered by Allen Dulles. Bentley also alleged that Lee had told her of an OSS plan to open an official liaison channel with Soviet intelligence, a plan that Hoover had derided in government councils as typical of the harebrained schemes emanating from General William "Wild Bill" Donovan and his "Oh-So-Social" set of Ivy League bluebloods. Hoover was so impressed with Bentley's inside knowledge that he was willing to stake his reputation on her credibility. He assured the Secretary of State that GREGORY's "statements and reliability have been established beyond any doubt."

There was one problem, however. Despite intensive surveillance of the suspects identified by Bentley, the FBI could uncover no evidence of an ongoing espionage operation. One year after the surveillance had begun, Hoover was forced to report that his agents had turned up nothing but "repeated inconsequential contacts" among suspected members of the spy ring. The Bureau intercepted a letter from one suspect, Michael Greenberg, to Hiss, asking for help in getting a job with the United Nations Organization. The Bureau monitored a phone call from another suspect, Henry Collins, inviting Hiss to dinner. The Bureau monitored a three-hour meeting in Hiss's office with still another suspect, Robert Miller. The Bureau followed Harry Dexter White to Hiss's home in Georgetown. Was this a sinister pattern or the random socializing of fellow bureaucrats? "It was like a bowl of Jell-O," the FBI's Robert Collier said. "You couldn't grab hold of anything."

Harvey drafted a memo to the Attorney General reporting that "a highly confidential and reliable source"—an FBI euphemism for a wiretap—had discovered that one suspect, Charles Kramer, had helped Senator Claude Pepper write a speech advocating the dismantling of all American facilities capable of producing atomic weapons. In another memo, Harvey reported that one of Bentley's suspects had suggested that Czech nationals be used to assist the Army's censorship operations in Europe. "In view of the extent of Soviet penetration and domination in Czechoslovakia, the utilization of large numbers of Czechs in connection with military censorship in the European theater would necessarily place a number of undoubted Soviet agents in positions where they would have access to considerable information of value," Harvey warned. "Most significant," Hoover jotted at the bottom. Perhaps, but it would never stand up in a court of law. As Harvey noted in a memo drafted for Hoover's signature, "It does not appear that sufficient probative evidence exists at the present time in connection with this case upon which to base a successful substantive prosecution."

Without more substantial evidence the case was dead, but the Bureau's best source was no longer in a position to provide that evidence. "A substantial portion of GREGORY's activities as a courier . . . ceased in December, 1944, and she has not been actively used since that time," Harvey wrote. According to Bentley, Anatoli Gromov had ordered her "to turn over all of my Washington contacts. I was told by Al to tell these people that I was anticipating going to the hospital for an appendectomy and that . . . they would be contacted by another individual." Bentley made her last courier run a few days later. Thereafter she maintained desultory contact with her Soviet controllers, but only to straighten out her tangled finances and occasionally to advise on the care and feeding of her former Washington stable.

It was as if the Soviets had anticipated Bentley's defection and deliberately set out to minimize the damage she could do. Bentley said that one of her Soviet contacts, "Jack," had explained to her "that the present policy of the Russians was to split up the larger groups that were obtaining information into smaller groups and implied that I personally was taking care of too many groups." As "Jack" told it, the idea "was that in the event anything happened to any one member of this whole group, the identities and activities of the other members would not be known to this individual and therefore they could operate with extreme security."

The FBI's task was clear—in Harvey's words, "reactivating the Informant GREGORY as an operating Soviet agent and utilizing her . . . as a double agent." With Bentley once again shuttling secrets between her government contacts in Washington and her Soviet handlers in New York, the Bureau would be able to catch the suspected spies in the act of espionage. Harvey pondered the best "procedure of having Informant GREGORY attempt to discreetly renew her contacts." It was "a very difficult problem."

Although she had taken her first Soviet contact, Jacob Golos, as a lover, Bentley had not gotten along so famously with his successors. At one of her final meetings with "Al," she had arrived in an ornery mood fortified by several dry martinis. "I told him in plain words what I thought of him and the rest of the Russians and, further, told him that I was an American and could not be kicked around," Bentley related. Harvey suggested that Bentley could finesse that bit of ugliness by explaining that because of her "nerve wracking, long and faithful service to the Soviet cause, she was then overwrought and inclined to say things she of course did not fundamentally believe."

The real problem was not Bentley's lack of rapport with "Al" but the fact that the defection of the code clerk Gouzenko in Ottawa had forced the Russians to pull in their horns not only in Canada but also in the United States. "Al" suddenly left the country aboard a Soviet ship bound for Argentina, and Harvey noted "considerable alarm on the part of known and suspected Soviet agents." There were, according to Harvey, "numerous indications of connections" between the CORBY, as Gouzenko was code-named, and GREGORY cases. Both had referred to a Soviet agent who fit the description of Hiss, and both had identified a number of Canadians who ran messages back and forth between Soviet intelligence officers in New York and Ottawa. Just how interlinked the two spy rings were would not become apparent until a few years later, when the FBI discovered the trail that led from Gouzenko to the British physicist Klaus Fuchs and from there in the direction pointed by Bentley to Julius and Ethel Rosenberg.

Prospects for reactivating Bentley all but vanished when "Al" failed to appear for his next scheduled meeting. The one remaining hope was to recruit another, still active member of the alleged spy ring as a double agent. At Harvey's direction, Bentley telephoned Helen Tenney, an OSS employee who, Bentley said, had once turned over to her "a considerable quantity of written data reflecting the activities of OSS personnel in virtually all sections and all countries of the world." While two FBI agents eavesdropped from a nearby table, Bentley and Tenney renewed acquaintance over cocktails at a Washington restaurant and made plans to meet again a few weeks later in New York.

On the basis of the first meeting, Harvey assessed the prospects for turning Tenney into a double agent. "Tenney was extremely cooperative and apparently very happy to see the informant," Harvey wrote, but there was no indication that her "fundamental ideological orientation with regard to the Soviet Union and the Communist Party, USA, had changed one iota." He cabled New York that it was "not desired Informant GREGORY make any effort to double Tenney at this time."

Having abandoned its last hope of penetrating the Bentley network, the FBI seemed no closer to piercing the veil of Soviet espionage than when Krivitsky and Chambers had defected in 1938. The distance traveled could be measured only indirectly. Krivitsky and Chambers had been ignored; Bentley had been fawned over, even though none of her allegations could be proved. She "has been extremely cooperative and the information furnished by her has been of the greatest possible value," Harvey gushed as he recommended that the FBI take the unprecedented step of helping Bentley get hotel reservations for a three-week vacation in Puerto Rico— provided "that Bentley will not appear connected with Bureau in any way."

At one point Harvey slipped and revealed his bias by referring in writing to Bentley's suspects as "Soviet espionage agents." Clyde Tolson, Hoover's alter ego, quickly called him to account for his "loose phraseology," since "the only proof that we have that they are Soviet espionage agents is the statement of the GREGORY woman." Hoover was more adept at straddling the gap between his convictions and the evidence. "It is not, of course, the province of the FBI to make prosecutive recommendations," he waffled in a memo to Justice Department officials who were pressing him for a resolution of the matter.

Without further proof, the harshest action the government could take against the suspected spies in its midst was to ease them out. Hoover balked at outright dismissal, since that would require a Civil Service hearing in which the Bureau might be forced to reveal its sources. Hiss lingered on at the State Department until the end of 1946, when, aware that he was under suspicion and that his prospects for further promotion were nil, he voluntarily resigned for a better-paying job with the Carnegie Endowment. Other Bentley suspects also left government as their wartime agencies were gradually disbanded. Harvey found particularly galling the fact that two suspects had taken all of their accrued sick leave before resigning. "Careful consideration will be given to the possibility of developing Fraud Against the Government cases against them in regard to their apparently fraudulent use of their sick leave," he vowed, but no such charges were ever brought.

An unbroken string of eighteen- and twenty-hour days spent tracking down Bentley's leads had not produced a single prosecutable case of espionage. The FBI—and Harvey—could proceed no further. Eventually a very crude and uneven sort of retribution would be exacted. Harry Dexter White would die of a heart attack in 1948 after Bentley publicly named him as a member of her network, and Hiss would be convicted of perjury in 1950. But Harvey could foresee none of that, and in the summer of 1947 his exhaustion and frustration boiled over in an incident that resulted in his being dealt with more harshly than any of Bentley's suspects.

Thundershowers, heavy at times, had fallen throughout the evening of July 11. It was past midnight, and another downpour washed over the city as Harvey headed his car across the Potomac River into Washington. A second car splashed along in Harvey's wake, following him home from a stag party in the Virginia suburbs. Once across the Potomac, the two cars went their separate ways. Harvey drove west, passing the Washington Monument, the Jefferson Memorial, and the World War II temporary buildings that lay scattered across the Mall like so much litter. At the Lincoln Memorial he turned north and headed into Rock Creek Park, his taillights disappearing into the dark and rain.

When he had not reached home by nine o'clock the next morning, Libby Harvey could wait no longer. She phoned FBI headquarters to report her husband missing. Bill "had recently been despondent and discouraged about his work at the Bureau and had been moody," she told Mickey Ladd, head of the Bureau's Security Division. Ladd, who had been at the party the night before, recalled that "Harvey had been very quiet while some of the other men had been quite exuberant."

Pat Coyne, the agent who had followed Harvey back to town, was dispatched to cover the route from the Potomac to Harvey's home in Georgetown. Other agents began a discreet check of accident and amnesia reports with the local police. The search ended after less than an hour when Harvey called in to report that he was home.

According to a summary of the incident prepared for Hoover, "Mr. Harvey indicated that after he left Mr. Coyne, he . . . was proceeding towards his residence in a heavy downpour of rain. He drove his car through a large puddle of water just as another car going in the opposite direction hit the puddle, and the engine in his car stopped. He coasted to the curb, but was unable to get his car started and accordingly he went to sleep in his car and slept until approximately 10 A.M. when he awakened and proceeded to his home." Harvey insisted that his drowsiness was not alcohol-induced, and his colleagues backed him up. "Mr. Harvey stated that he had about two cans of beer, and from the recollection of others at the party there was no indication that Harvey was drinking any more or less than anyone else," the summary said.

Nevertheless, FBI regulations required an agent to be on two-hour call at all times, either leaving a number where he could be reached or phoning in every two hours. Harvey had violated regulations. He was described as "very much upset about the matter," but Hoover was not so easily appeased.

"Pursuant to your instructions," an aide reported, "I talked to Mr. Harvey this morning about this situation, pointing out to him that we were particularly concerned about the potential embarrassment to the Bureau in a situation of this kind since a squad car might very logically have stopped and questioned Harvey, asleep in his car, and that if he had been taken to a police station and publicity ensued, it would have caused embarrassment to the Bureau. I pointed out that while we had no question as to his sobriety on this occasion, we were concerned about the possibility of his being completely exhausted from overwork or worry . . . and that I was particularly anxious to talk to him about the situation to determine whether it would be better for him if he were transferred to another assignment, particularly in the light of his wife's statement that he had been despondent and discouraged about his work."

Harvey acknowledged "that he did periodically become discouraged about the ineffectiveness of the overall Government program in dealing with Communists and Communist espionage," but he insisted that "there was no question of his morale or attitude towards his work in this situation. . . . His worry was the natural worry that would come to anyone who dealt as intimately with the Communist problem as he had been doing for several years." Harvey rejected the idea of a transfer to a less taxing job and "stated that he preferred his present desk to any assignment that could be given to him in the Bureau."

A review of Harvey's file showed that his "record during his assignment at the Seat of Government had been a very good one.

. . . He has been consistently rated Excellent on the basis of his work in the Security Division." Hoover's aide vouched that "I personally have seen Harvey at his desk late at night on many occasions" and concluded, "I do not believe in the light of all the circumstances in this case that there is any administrative action which should be taken."

The Draconian Hoover thought otherwise and directed that a second memo be written. "It is recommended that Special Agent William K. Harvey of the Security Division be transferred to Indianapolis on general assignment." Hoover scribbled "O.K." at the bottom. Rather than accept the transfer, Harvey submitted his resignation "with the deepest regret," citing "personal and family consideration" and speaking of the "pride and personal satisfaction" of having been an FBI agent—remarkably restrained considering the circumstances, but wisely circumspect given Hoover's appetite for revenge.

Cast out from the inner sanctum of espionage, Harvey found himself in a world that had not yet heard of Whittaker Chambers and Elizabeth Bentley, that did not yet doubt the loyalty of Alger Hiss, that did not yet realize that, while the shooting war against Germany had ended, the secret war against Russia was just beginning. As if blinded by the bright light of this naive and unsuspecting world, Harvey quickly ducked into the shadows of the Office of Special Operations, a small and highly secret cadre within the newly formed Central Intelligence Agency.

There, in the command bunker for the secret war, Harvey first met Angleton, the boy wonder of the SSU, who had transferred to the CIA with the disbanding of his unit in Rome. Inevitably they clashed. "Angleton and Harvey were direct competitors—I mean direct competitors—from the word go," one CIA officer said. "We had a real fight going between Angleton and Harvey." The two were a study in contrasts—physically, culturally, intellectually, and professionally. Harvey was a stocky man whose spreading girth would earn him the nickname of "the Pear." Angleton, "the Cadaver," remained consumptively thin. Harvey walked with a stiff-backed military gait. Angleton shambled along in a slumped and contemplative fashion. Harvey had grown up in the same small

Midwestern town as his father and his father's father. Angleton was an expatriate's son. Harvey was Big Ten. Angleton was Ivy League. Harvey read Rudyard Kipling, the storyteller who glorified the "Great Game" of espionage and beat the drum of duty, honor, and empire. Angleton read Ezra Pound, the mad poet who stood accused of betraying his country. Harvey had learned the game of espionage in the regimented FBI; Angleton in the free-wheeling OSS. Harvey collected firearms. Angleton crafted fishing lures. Harvey was a cop; Angleton a spy. Each was a prototype of the two strains—FBI refugees and OSS veterans—coming together to form the postwar espionage establishment at the CIA. The OSS veterans—Allen Dulles, Richard Helms, Angleton, and others—would dominate the CIA for the next quarter century, but it took Harvey, the FBI reject, to spot the Soviet spy in their midst.

Philby Undone

An element of farce had attended the CIA's birth. Admiral William Leahy, chief of staff to President Harry S. Truman, recorded the occasion in his diary. "At lunch today in the White House . . . Rear Admiral Souers and I were presented with black cloaks, black hats and wooden daggers."

"To My Brethren and Fellow Dog House Denizens," the President proclaimed. "By virtue of the authority vested in me as Top Dog, I require and charge that Front Admiral William D. Leahy and Rear Admiral Sidney W. Souers receive and accept the vestments and appurtenances of their respective positions, namely as Personal Snooper and as Director of Centralized Snooping."

Hoover did not think the creation of a rival intelligence operation so amusing. He had grudgingly suffered the OSS in time of war but was inclined to be less accommodating in time of peace. His plan for a postwar intelligence organization was simple enough: expand the Bureau's South American operations to cover the globe. When Truman opted instead for "Wild Bill" Donovan's proposal to create a "central intelligence service" that would report directly to the President, Hoover resorted to sabotage, ordering his agents in South America to burn their files rather than turn them over to the CIA.

Hoover was not motivated solely by spite, as Angleton pointed out. "There was a very grave problem of the security standards of the Agency coming from World War II," he said. Bentley had identified no fewer than five employees of the OSS as members of her spy ring. What other Soviet agents had escaped detection and made the transition from the OSS to the CIA?

If Hoover needed any further reason to distrust the CIA, there was the fact that it harbored Bureau fugitives such as Bill Harvey. Unemployed and with a paycheck for ninety-seven days of unused leave as his sole means of support, Harvey had leaped at the chance to join the CIA. Utterly ignorant of Soviet espionage operations, the CIA had needed Harvey as badly as he needed it. Harvey, who possessed near-photographic recall, was the next best thing to Bureau files. Hoover could order the files burned, but he could not erase Harvey's memory banks. Yet memory, or even experience, was not all that mattered at the CIA. The Agency was a tonier set than Harvey had known at the FBI. He was stepping from the world of ex-cops and small-town lawyers into an organization of academics and Wall Street attorneys. Many of the men he met were heirs to considerable family fortunes. Harvey was crossing the tracks, joining the establishment. It was not an altogether harmonious union.

"I felt Harvey had a love-hate relationship to the establishment," said Carlton Swift, a relative of the meat-packing tycoon and one of Harvey's new colleagues. "He had an emotional distrust of the establishment, yet he had a desire to be part of it." When Swift met Harvey's wife, Libby, a small-town girl and college dropout, "she reinforced my idea that he was envious of the establishment, socially self-conscious at not being a part of the elite that ran the Agency. . . . She was proof that he wasn't part of it. . . . He solved his ego problem by saying, 'They're no good.' . . . I became a fair friend of his and used to listen to him recount his cases—Bentley, Hiss and the rest. He would give me a long lecture on the prevalence of treason in the upper classes. . . . Those brought up in the 30s and given a good education with money and a social conscience felt the burden of producing more for their society. [They] liked to see in Communism [their] great contribution to society. . . . [They] weren't consciously committing treason. They rationalized . . . that they were being far-sighted patriots by supporting international Communism. . . . I remember [Harvey's words] perhaps because I was young and impressionable. . . . Harvey really had deep emotional feelings about it."

Feelings aside, Harvey had a fund of knowledge about Soviet espionage that was unmatched anywhere in the United States government, and he was soon placed in charge of a tiny counterintelligence unit known as Staff C. "We'd all just gotten into the business," a member of Staff C said. "Harvey had experience in the Bureau and had seen more than we had." Harvey "exuded missionary zeal," said a CIA officer named Peter Sichel. The impression was heightened by a lifelong thyroid condition that made his eyes bulge from his head—"stand out on stems, practically," one member of Staff C said—as if he were a man possessed. Harvey's briefings, punctuated by the ritualistic clicking of his cigarette lighter, would last for hours as he disgorged almost verbatim the files of cases he had worked on. "He had an incredible memory for things in which he was involved," a senior officer in the Agency said. "He had everybody sitting on the edge of their chairs," a female staff member recalled, not because he was a spellbinding speaker but because "he spoke in a froglike voice that was at times so low that it was very difficult to hear."

As the CIA's leading expert on Soviet espionage, Harvey should have been in close contact with the Bureau, but FBI agents dealt with him at their own peril. "We liked Bill and he was one of us," said Robert Lamphere, a member of the Bureau's Security Division, "but as far as Hoover was concerned, he was the enemy." Harvey responded in kind. "I would be in Harvey's office," one agent recounted, "and he would get a phone call and say, 'I can't talk much now because there's an FBI man here.'"

Such bureaucratic jealousies seemed particularly petty in the context of the rapid and alarming succession of world events. In July of 1949 the State Department issued a White Paper conceding that China had fallen to the Communists, and in August Russia exploded her first atomic device, ending the American monopoly. Meanwhile, the United States had come upon new and startling evidence of Soviet espionage. Through a combination of good luck, hard work, and Russian carelessness, the Armed Forces Security Agency had succeeded in breaking the theoretically unbreakable Soviet cipher. Among other things, the break disclosed the existence of a Soviet spy who was so well placed that he could obtain the verbatim text of a private telegram from Winston Churchill to Harry Truman.

Midway through World War II a gifted team of American cryptanalysts had mounted an attack against the Russian cipher system, using as their basic weapon the charred remnants of a Soviet code book that had been salvaged from a battlefield in Finland. The book contained a list of 999 five-digit code groups, each one representing a different letter, word, or phrase. A large portion of the list had been destroyed by fire, and what remained seemed of little value, since the Soviets employed a system of super-encipherment in which random numerical values were added to the original five-digit code groups. The code book might reveal, for instance, that the five-digit group for the word *agent* was 17056, but it would not reveal that the "additive," as it was called, was 05555. With the additive the word *agent* would appear in the enciphered message as 22611 (17056 plus 05555), which the code book would list as the five-digit group for a word or phrase with an entirely different meaning. Only someone in possession of both the code book and the additive would know to subtract 05555 from 22611 and arrive at 17056 and the word *agent.* Since each code group used a different additive, the effect was an infinity of codes.

To the American cryptanalysts, who had already mastered the intricacies of Japan's top diplomatic code, mere super-encipherment did not pose an insurmountable obstacle. Through collateral intelligence—the exact date and time of the message, the particular unit to which it was sent, the movement of the unit upon receipt—they could sometimes hazard an educated guess about the subject matter. Testing five-letter code groups representing words that the Russians might logically have used to refer to that subject would occasionally yield a solution. But without a key to the constantly changing additive, the overall system was still unbreakable—and would have remained so had not the Russians committed a colossal blunder.

Amid the confusion of war, Moscow had sent out duplicate sets of additives to various Soviet installations around the world. When the cryptanalysts discovered that the same series of additives had been used more than once, they had all the leverage they needed to break the Soviet cipher system. Having used guesswork to deduce the additives for a Soviet message intercepted in one part of the world, they could test those same additives against the massive backlog of messages intercepted in other parts of the world. Sooner or later the same additives would appear and another message could be deciphered. It was an excruciatingly tedious task with less than perfect results. Since only a portion of the code book had been salvaged, many of the 999 five-digit groups used by the Soviets were missing. Knowing the additive might yield the proper five-digit group, but if that group could not be found in the code book, the word remained indecipherable. Whole passages were blanks, and the meaning of other phrases could be only vaguely grasped.

Because of the laborious nature of the task, years would elapse between the actual transmission of a Soviet message and its decoding by the Armed Forces Security Agency. The first big break did not come until 1949, when the cryptanalysts found a duplicate additive in the New York–to–Moscow channel and were able to decipher enough of a Soviet message to identify it as the text of a 1945 telegram from Churchill to Truman. Checking the message against a complete copy of the telegram provided by the British Embassy, the cryptanalysts confirmed beyond doubt that a Soviet spy had somehow been able to obtain the verbatim text—cable number and all—of a private communication between two heads of state.

The implications were appalling, but the security officer's nightmare was the cryptanalyst's dream. The Armed Forces Security Agency requested copies of all transmissions handled by the British Embassy and began matching them against the encoded messages in the New York–to–Moscow channel, working backward through the code book and arriving at the additive. Besides determining which messages had fallen into Soviet hands, the cryptanalysts were coming up with solutions to new additives that could be checked against messages intercepted in other parts of the world. The results remained fragmentary, but by the fall of 1949 enough shards had been pieced together to demonstrate with disconcerting clarity that during the war years there had been a massive hemorrhaging of secrets from both the British Embassy in Washington and the atomic bomb project at Los Alamos, New Mexico.

One of the first Soviet spies to be undone by the code break was the German-born physicist Klaus Fuchs. A reference in one of the deciphered messages indicated that a Soviet agent had a sister at an American university. When matched against the backgrounds of the scientists working on the atomic bomb, that otherwise unremarkable detail aroused the first vague suspicions against Fuchs, whose sister, Kristel, had briefly attended Swarthmore College. According to an FBI memo, Fuchs became the "prime suspect . . . when we were able to obtain a document at the Atomic Energy Commission which had been written by him." That same document had shown up in the New York–to–Moscow link. On February 1, 1950, Hoover informed the White House that "we [have] just gotten word from England that we have gotten a full confession from one of the top scientists, who worked over here, that he gave the complete know-how of the atom bomb to the Russians." In a subsequent letter, Hoover reported that "Fuchs said he would estimate that the information furnished by him speeded up by several years the production of an atom bomb by Russia."

Once the code break had identified Fuchs as the prime suspect, a number of other incriminating traces leaped from the files. Among those arrested as a result of the Gouzenko defection in Ottawa in 1945 had been a suspected Communist agent named Israel Halperin, who, according to an FBI memo, "had in his possession an address book in which appeared, among others, the name Klaus Fuchs." Another memo stated that the Bureau had received a translation of a captured German document written in 1941 that listed Fuchs as "apparently a Communist worthy of consideration for apprehension by the German army." Why had that captured document taken so long to surface? Hoover demanded to know. An inquiry revealed that the document had been in the possession of "Supervisor W. K. Harvey up to the time of his resignation in the late summer of 1947. This material became delinquent in that it was not being handled on a current basis due to the shortage of personnel. After the resignation of Mr. Harvey, this material was reassigned, the delinquent handling of the material was corrected, and in early 1948, it was handled on a current basis."

Harvey was fortunate to be beyond Hoover's reach in 1950, for he had been the unwitting custodian of one other piece of the Fuchs puzzle. In his confession Fuchs said his American contact had been a chemist named "Raymond." Asked to pick out "Raymond" from a series of mug shots, Fuchs pointed to a picture of Harry Gold, a naturalized American citizen of Russian parentage. As an FBI memo noted, "Gold first came to the attention of this Bureau in connection with the activities of Abraham Brothman, concerning whom Elizabeth T. Bentley furnished information."

Gold at first proclaimed his innocence, insisting that he had never been west of the Mississippi, much less to Los Alamos, where Fuchs had worked on the atomic bomb. But when FBI agents searched his home in Philadelphia and found a Chamber of Commerce brochure for Santa Fe, Gold cracked and gave a complete confession that led ultimately to the arrest, conviction, and execution of Julius and Ethel Rosenberg.

The trial of the Rosenbergs would become one of the most disputed court cases of the century, in part because the government, hoping to protect its most secret source, never introduced one of the most damaging pieces of evidence against them: the decoded traffic from the New York–to–Moscow channel. The Rosenbergs were identified in the traffic only by cryptonyms, but the picture that emerged of a husband-and-wife team of agents matched them precisely, even down to the fact that the woman's brother was a part of the plot. At the trial Ethel's brother, David Greenglass, who had worked on the bomb at Los Alamos, was the chief prosecution witness, having admitted his role in return for leniency.

If made public, the evidence contained in the intercepts would have stilled much of the controversy surrounding not only the Rosenberg trial but several other espionage cases as well. Sometimes the evidence fell short of convincing. In the case of Hiss, a message intercepted in the Washington-to-Moscow channel revealed that a Soviet agent had actually been aboard Ambassador Averell Harriman's plane as it returned to Moscow following the 1945 conference at Yalta. Hiss had been aboard that plane, but so had others, including, of course, Harriman. Other times, however, the evidence was convincing beyond doubt, as when Moscow changed its agents' cryptonyms by transmitting a message listing both their true identities and their new cryptonyms.

"Crypt ops," as they were called, were the most reliable sensory organs in the espionage body. A code break eliminated the problem of relying on agents of questionable reliability and uncertain loyalty. An agent might deliberately be passing on false and misleading information, but a message transmitted in a supposedly unbreakable cipher was unquestionably the real thing. A code break shattered all the mirrors and permitted a straight line of sight across the wilderness. The breaking of the Soviet cipher could have tipped the scales of the secret war in favor of the West as surely as had the cracking of the German Enigma code in World War II. In 1948, however, the Soviets suddenly modified their cipher system in a way that made it once again unbreakable. Two years later, investigators discovered that the Soviets had been alerted to the code break by William Weisband, a disloyal employee of the Armed Forces Security Agency. The man who betrayed America's ultrasecret was never prosecuted for his crime, since a public trial would have required revelation of the code break. Instead, Weisband spent one year in jail for failing to answer a summons to appear before a grand jury. Despite Weisband's leak to the Soviets, the code break would remain a closely guarded secret for more than thirty years while cryptanalysts continued to cross-check the backlog of intercepted messages, eventually reconstructing most of the old Russian code book. Whatever marginal value the continued secrecy of the project might have had seemed more than outweighed by the public suspicion and distrust of the government's actions in the Hiss and Rosenberg cases.

Astoundingly, the British officer assigned to work with the FBI in tracking down the Soviet spies whose cryptonyms appeared in the traffic was Kim Philby. In 1949 Philby was sent to Washington as the MI6 representative "for the specific purpose of liaising with the Bureau on the cases arising from these intercepts," a CIA officer said. Philby's assignment was a logical one, since he had once been in charge of British counterintelligence operations against the Soviet Union. In retrospect it seemed possible that Philby's Soviet handlers had instructed him to engineer his assignment to Washington after they learned about the code break from Weisband. Whether by accident or by design, Russian intelligence was able to monitor the FBI's efforts to unravel the Soviet spy nets.

Philby was in "as perfect a spot for the Soviets as they could possibly get a man," said Robert Lamphere of the Bureau's Security Division. The damage Philby could do was limited only by the risks he and his Soviet controllers were willing to run. With Philby in Washington at the plexus of free-world intelligence, the Soviets frequently suffered the exquisite agony of knowing too much, of not being able to act on his information for fear they would compromise their best source. An FBI memo pointed out that "Philby . . . was aware of the results of the Anglo–United States investigation leading to the identification of Klaus Fuchs," yet the Soviets had not warned Fuchs of his peril. Philby "also knew of the interrogation of Fuchs as well as the full cooperation given by him . . . yet no action was taken by the Soviets to save any American members of the espionage ring which ultimately was uncovered as a result of the Fuchs revelations." According to another memo, "Philby and his Russian spy chiefs in Moscow even knew that the FBI planned to arrest the Rosenbergs and Morton Sobell, yet they chose to sacrifice them, most probably to keep Philby's identity a secret." The Soviet source inside the British Embassy who had obtained the text of the Churchill-to-Truman telegram was a different case. For reasons known only to Moscow, he was worth saving, even at the risk of exposing Philby.

The FBI's search for the source had dragged on for the better part of two years with no break in sight. "We had received some dozen reports referring to the source, who appeared in the documents as HOMER, but little progress had been made in identifying him," Philby later wrote in his memoirs. "The FBI was still sending us reams about the Embassy charladies and the inquiry into our menial personnel was spinning itself out endlessly." Philby knew who HOMER was and could gauge exactly how close the investigators were coming. As long as they concentrated on workers who might have filched a copy of the Churchill telegram from the burn bag, HOMER was safe. Sooner or later, however, the focus would shift to the diplomats who had actually handled the telegram, and the real HOMER would inevitably fall under suspicion. All the while, cryptanalysts continued to pore over the intercepts, searching for some clue that might give HOMER's identity away. Philby received drop copies of the messages as they were decoded by the Armed Forces Security Agency, and it must have been chilling to know that it was only a matter of time before his own Soviet cryptonym would also appear in the decoded material. Once that happened, how long would it be until some reference in the traffic gave his own identity away?

Philby's ability to monitor the investigation for the Russians was due to end in the autumn of 1951, when his two-year tour in Washington would be over. Having decided that the situation must be resolved before then, he put the investigation on the right track by reminding London of Krivitsky's warning about "the young Scotsman who had been imbued with Communism in the early 30s and who subsequently was induced to enter the service of the British diplomacy." As Philby told it, "I suggested that these data, such as they were, should be matched against the records of diplomats stationed in Washington between the relevant dates in 1944–45 of the known leakages." That was a very close calculation on Philby's part, since there was, in his words, "the nasty little sentence in Krivitsky's evidence that the Soviet secret service had sent a young English journalist to Spain during the Civil War." Philby figured that the lead was too vague to pose a threat to him. "There were no further identifying particulars, and many young men from Fleet Street had gone to Spain." Besides, the fact that he had pointed the investigation in the right direction with his reminder about the "young Scotsman" would discourage any suspicions occasioned by the flimsy coincidence between Krivitsky's "nasty little sentence" and Philby's past. Philby was right. Krivitsky's evidence never weighed very heavily against him. As it turned out, he did far greater damage to himself with a dinner party he gave in the spring of 1951.

Libby Harvey, as was increasingly her habit, had had too much to drink. "This is god-awful," she proclaimed in a loud voice, jabbing at the roast beef on her plate. Her dinner partner, Robert Lamphere of the FBI, tried without success to shush her. She was right about the roast beef, though. It was cold. Philby had let the cocktail hour go too long, and that had done neither the roast beef nor Libby any good.

Libby was poised at the top of a long slide into alcoholism. Her sister back in Kentucky blamed it on the "highfalutin' society in Washington." One of Harvey's CIA colleagues said the same thing from a different perspective. "Libby was an awfully nice girl who came from humble origins. He started to move up in the world. He moved too fast for Libby. She couldn't keep up." That statement had an unintended double entendre, for Harvey had acquired a considerable reputation as a skirt-chaser. As far as Libby was concerned, it was a deserved reputation. He was "out about three nights a week and sometimes it would be five o'clock in the morning when he'd get in and sometimes it would be seven o'clock," she said later during the divorce proceedings. "He was always supposed to be at work," she added with unmistakable sarcasm. Libby probably had her own ideas about where her husband was that night in the summer of 1947 when he did not return home from the FBI stag party. Perhaps her call to the Bureau to report him missing was made more out of anger than concern for his well-being. If she wanted to pay him back for his infidelity, she certainly succeeded.

One of Libby's friends in Kentucky claimed that Harvey plied his wife with liquor in order to keep her submissive while he went about his extramarital activities. "He fed it to her," Libby's friend said with undisguised venom. Another friend said that Libby drank only to keep pace with her husband, who had his own drinking problem. According to Philby, "The first time [Harvey] dined at my house . . . he fell asleep over the coffee and sat snoring gently until midnight when his wife took him away, saying, 'Come now,

Daddy, it's time you were in bed.' " The second time the Harveys dined at Philby's it would have been a merciful blessing had Libby fallen asleep over her roast beef.

It was the largest party Philby had given since coming to Washington as MI6 liaison officer. All of the CIA and FBI officers he knew and dealt with on a regular basis—Harvey, Angleton, Lamphere, and others—were there with their wives. Philby was a good man to get to know. Any British officer awarded the plum of the Washington liaison job was clearly on the way up. Some people were already beginning to think of him as one day becoming the head of MI6.

Dinner over, Philby and his guests adjourned to the living room for more drinking. Sensing that the evening was getting out of hand, Lamphere said his good-byes as soon as decency permitted, departing before the arrival of Philby's houseguest, the outrageous Guy Burgess.

According to a memo later written by Angleton, Burgess was "a close and old friend of Philby. He was his classmate at Cambridge and they continued to maintain a close relationship up to the present. For example, during the period that Philby was the chief [MI6] representative in Istanbul, he was visited by [Burgess] who stayed at his home." To hear Philby tell it, Burgess had helped him get his start with MI6. Burgess, a flagrant drunkard and an unabashed homosexual, was the epitome of indiscretion and had not lasted long at MI6. He had drifted off to a job with the BBC before catching on in the Foreign Office as the confidential secretary to the minister of state. In 1950 Burgess had been assigned to the British Embassy in Washington as a second secretary, and Philby had taken him into his house. Now after barely a year in Washington, Burgess was on the verge of being recalled to London for abusing his diplomatic privileges. He had been stopped for speeding three times in one afternoon, each time berating the police for interfering with his diplomatic immunity. He had been so offensive that the governor of Virginia had reported the incident to the Department of State.

Outrageous though he was, Burgess was too irrepressible and too witty to be ignored. He had a reputation as a caricaturist and was fond of telling how he had drawn a sketch of a wartime meeting of the British Admiralty that had to be classified top secret. The besotted Libby fulfilled Lamphere's premonition of disaster by begging Burgess to sketch her. He obliged with an obscene cartoon of Libby, legs spread, dress hiked above her waist, and crotch bared. Harvey swung at Burgess and missed. The party was about to degenerate into a drunken brawl. Angleton quickly steered Harvey to the door and walked him around the block to cool off while Libby regained her composure. Burgess continued on as though nothing had happened. The evening ended without further violence, and the guests staggered off into the night. The entire incident might have been blessedly forgotten had it not crossed paths with the search for source HOMER.

The review of the Krivitsky file that had been prompted by Philby's reminder turned up a small circle of a half-dozen diplomats who vaguely conformed to the description of a young Scotsman imbued with Communism in the early 1930s. One of them was Donald Maclean, another graduate of Cambridge, who had served in Washington from 1944 to 1948. Maclean was the son of a prominent British family from the island of Tiree off the Scottish coast. At Cambridge he had been an avowed Communist who told his mother that he was going to Russia to join the Revolution and who published articles predicting that the "whole crack-brained criminal mess" of capitalism was "doomed to disappear." After graduation he had not gone to Russia, although his good friend Guy Burgess had. Maclean had abruptly abandoned his revolutionary fervor and joined the Foreign Office, where he became at once the model bureaucrat. By 1944 he had risen to the post of second secretary in Washington, where, among other things, he was in charge of the embassy code room, and in particular of the ambassador's private cipher in which Churchill's cables to Truman had been sent.

Maclean fit all the known facts about the identity of source HOMER, but not enough facts were known to support a case against him. Finally the cryptanalysts succeeded in breaking out an additional piece of information from the intercepts: HOMER had met with his Soviet contact twice a week in New York on the pretext of visiting his pregnant wife, a pattern of activity that corresponded precisely with Maclean's twice-a-week trips to see his pregnant wife, Melinda, who was staying in New York City with her American mother.

It would take years to sort out the damage Maclean had done, but it was clear at once that his access to state secrets went far beyond the private communications between Churchill and Truman. According to a State Department document, Maclean had sat on a committee that "was an adjunct of the wartime British-American Combined Chiefs of Staff" and that dealt with "political and economic problems growing out of the joint conduct of the war." Another document revealed that "Maclean had a thorough knowledge of one aspect of secret Anglo-American exchanges on the North Atlantic Pact." Specifically, in the spring of 1948 Maclean had participated in a series of secret British-Canadian-American meetings to discuss "joining with France, the Benelux and perhaps other governments in negotiating mutual security arrangements to meet the danger of Soviet expansion." The talks led ultimately to the creation of NATO. "If Maclean was then a Soviet agent," the document continued, "the information he possessed concerning these talks would have been of considerable interest and some importance to the Soviet Government at that time."

There was more. Maclean had sat on another trilateral panel, which dealt with such fundamental atomic energy concerns as projected uranium needs and the availability of ore supplies. "Some of the information available to Maclean in 1947–48 was classified Top Secret and would then have been of interest to the Soviet Union," a damage report conceded. He had also been issued a "nonescort" pass to the headquarters of the Atomic Energy Commission, a privilege not accorded even to the highest-ranking officers of the United States armed forces. When Hoover found out about that, he noted indignantly: "I was always required to have an escort."

As for purely British secrets Maclean had betrayed, that was a matter best left to his own government. However, one American document noted that Maclean's supervision of the embassy code room had given him "access to all U.K. diplomatic codes and ciphers as well as the opportunity to scan all incoming and outgoing communications." No wonder the luckless Volkov had warned the British Embassy in Istanbul that the Soviets were able to decipher cables sent to London.

When he first fell under suspicion in the spring of 1951, Maclean was head of the Foreign Office's American Department in London. He was placed under surveillance and denied further access to sensitive documents. Meanwhile, Burgess had arrived in London to face a disciplinary board for his indiscretions in the United States. The two were seen lunching together on several occasions.

On Friday morning, May 25, 1951, the Foreign Office authorized MI5, the British equivalent of the FBI, to interrogate Maclean the following Monday. At almost precisely the same moment, Burgess was telling a young companion he had picked up during his transatlantic crossing that they might have to scrap their plans for a weekend in France. "A young friend of mine in the Foreign Office is in serious trouble," he said. "I am the only one who can help him." That afternoon, Burgess rented an Austin and drove to Maclean's home in the outlying suburb of Tatsfield. MI5 sleuths tailed Maclean as he left his offices in Whitehall and walked to the Charing Cross station to catch the five-nineteen train, but they dropped their surveillance there for fear he would spot them. At eleven-forty-five that night, Burgess and Maclean pulled up to the slip at Southampton and boarded the cross-Channel night boat for Saint-Malo. A sailor shouted after them, asking what they planned to do about the Austin left on the pier. "Back on Monday," they called. Later, a taxicab driver testified that he had driven two men resembling Burgess and Maclean from Saint-Malo to Rennes, where he thought they had caught a train for Paris. They were not seen again until 1956, when they appeared at a press conference in Moscow.

Philby and Geoffrey Paterson, the MI5 representative in Washington, broke the news to the FBI's Bob Lamphere, who had directed the American end of the search for HOMER. "They were both in a very embarrassing situation," Lamphere recalled. "Paterson had been lying to me about where they were on the Maclean investigation," giving no indication that it had progressed so far. As for Philby, Lamphere said, "he was wondering—as I later learned—whether we would put two and two together." Philby apparently had not expected Burgess to accompany Maclean in his flight to Moscow. The dual disappearance had linked Philby to the case as one of only a handful of people who both knew Burgess and was aware of the suspicions against Maclean.

Within hours of learning of Burgess's disappearance, Philby buried his camera and the rest of his spy paraphernalia in the woods along the Potomac. Should he follow Burgess and Maclean into exile or remain in place and hope that no one would put the pieces together? "The problem resolved itself into assessment of my chances of survival, and I judged them to be considerably better than even," Philby wrote later. "I enjoyed an enormous advantage over people like Fuchs who had little or no knowledge of intelligence work. For my part, I had worked for 11 years in the secret service. . . . For nearly two years I had been intimately linked to the American services. . . . I felt that I knew the enemy well enough to foresee in general terms the moves he was likely to make. I knew his files—his basic armament—and, above all, the limitations imposed on his procedures by law and convention."

The CIA's dilemma was only slightly less perplexing than Philby's. The Agency could not comfortably share its secrets with someone so indiscreet as to open his house to the egregious Burgess. Yet the mere fact that Philby had befriended Burgess hardly seemed sufficient grounds upon which to repudiate the official representative of MI6, embittering relations with the British and, in the bargain, damaging a man's career—a brilliant one, at that. The situation was ready-made for equivocation and procrastination. Philby's tour in Washington was due to end in a few months in any event. But the new Director of the CIA confronted the problem head-on.

General Walter Bedell Smith, Dwight D. Eisenhower's former chief of staff, whom Churchill had nicknamed "the American Bulldog," had not asked to be CIA Director. In fact, he had twice turned down the job. Truman, disturbed by the onslaught of McCarthyism at home and angered by the CIA's failure to provide a warning of the Communist attack in Korea, had persisted. "As you know, I wanted to avoid the Intelligence job if possible," Smith wrote to Eisenhower, "but in view of the general situation, and particularly the Korean affair, I did not feel I could refuse for a third time." Smith's reluctance was based not on a yearning for retirement after five years of war and three years as the American ambassador to Moscow but on prior acquaintance with the organization he was inheriting. Writing his friend George Allen, the American ambassador to Yugoslavia, Smith had but one favor to ask. "I assume you have in Belgrade, as we did in Moscow, some of the personnel in whom I will shortly have a direct interest. I would be grateful for your personal and secret estimate of their capabilities and qualifications. My experience in Moscow was not particularly reassuring." To another friend he wrote simply, "I expect the worst and know I won't be disappointed.

As apprehensive as he was, Smith could not have anticipated the ferocity of the CIA's running feud with the FBI. Shortly after Smith took over, Hoover learned that CIA officers had called on Bureau representatives in Mexico, Spain, and Italy to protest FBI usurpation of CIA jurisdiction abroad. Sensing a plot, the ever-suspicious Hoover immediately dispatched one of his agents to inform Smith that the FBI would not stand for such a brazen bureaucratic power play. "Smith became angry because the lowly FBI was telling him to go fuck himself," the agent recalled. "He was so mad that when he tried to lift his coffee cup it was shaking so badly he had to put it down. He said, 'I've got a good mind to throw you out of my office.' I said, 'General, neither you nor any man in your Agency is man enough to throw me out.' Twenty minutes after I got back to the Bureau a handwritten message arrived from Smith inviting Hoover to lunch. Hoover told me to accept." Lyman Kirkpatrick, then Smith's executive assistant, was present for the lunch and recalled Smith saying, "Edgar, suppose you tell us what's wrong. Why can't we seem to get along?" "Well, General," Hoover replied, "the first thing wrong is all these ex-Bureau people over here sniping and proselytizing, and in particular Bill Harvey."

Harvey was sternly counseled not to do or say anything in the future that might offend the prickly FBI Director, but the incident seemed only to enhance his stature within the CIA, for Smith would rely upon him heavily in dealing with the Philby dilemma. He began by directing Harvey, Angleton, and everyone else who had known Burgess to write down everything they knew about the missing diplomat.

On June 18 Angleton handed in a four-page top-secret memo describing a number of Burgess's more eccentric moments, including the night at Philby's when he "drew an insulting caricature of one of the female guests and precipitated a social disaster." Angleton also related an encounter with Burgess in a Georgetown restaurant. "Subject appeared unexpectedly and asked the undersigned for the loan of a few dollars," he reported in his best bureaucratese. "He wore a peculiar garb, namely a white British naval jacket which was dirty and stained. He was intoxicated, unshaven and had, from the appearance of his eyes, not washed since he last slept. He stated that he had taken two or three days' leave and had 'an interesting binge' the night before at Joe Alsop's house. . . . [Burgess] ordered a drink of the cheapest Bourbon available" and babbled on about a scheme to import several thousand British naval jackets of the kind he was wearing and "sell them for fantastic profits to exclusive shops in New York." Burgess was an automotive buff, Angleton continued, and "he pressed [me] for a date when [we] might meet in order that he might test the overdrive on the Oldsmobile."

As for Burgess's relationship with Philby, Angleton noted that "Philby had consistently 'sold' subject as a most gifted individual. In this respect, he has served as subject's apologist on several occasions when subject's behavior has been a source of extreme embarrassment in the Philby household. Philby has explained away these idiosyncrasies on grounds that subject suffered a severe brain concussion in an accident which had continued to affect him periodically."

Angleton went on to point out that Philby's secretary "had enjoyed a special relationship" with Burgess, but the memo stopped well short of drawing any sinister conclusions from the facts which it reported. Angleton's memo did "not suggest any suspicion of Philby," said a CIA officer who studied it closely. "It related two or three incidents, the bottom line of which was that you couldn't blame Philby for what this nut Burgess had done."

By that point, however, Angleton's memo was irrelevant. Five days earlier, Harvey had submitted a top-secret memo of his own, pointing out that not only was Philby close to Burgess and aware of Maclean's peril, but he was also the officer who had presided over the abortive defection of Volkov in Istanbul. Kim Philby was a Soviet agent, the very counterintelligence officer Volkov had tried to tell the British about, Harvey concluded. Philby had sent Burgess to warn Maclean that he had been found out.

Harvey would later tell friends that it had come to him as he sat stalled in traffic one morning on his way to work. That moment in which the anomalies in Philby's career resolved into a pattern of betrayal where others could see only untoward coincidence had been hard earned. It had come from years of working with the files so that an isolated incident like the Volkov affair could lodge somewhere in the back of his mind to be recalled when new developments suddenly gave it meaning. It had come from the Bentley and Hiss cases, which had convinced him that good breeding was not a bar to treason—and in fact was a positive incentive. It had come from the social snubs, real or imagined, that fed his distrust of the establishment. And finally it had come from the obscene insult to his wife, which had fixed the relationship of Philby and Burgess with outraged clarity in his mind.

Smith forwarded Harvey's and Angleton's memos to MI6 in London with a cover letter stating that Philby was no longer welcome as the British liaison officer in Washington. Working from Harvey's premise, MI5 compiled a dossier against Philby, listing his left-wing youth, his marriage to Litzi Friedman, his sudden conversion to Fascism, Krivitsky's warning about the British journalist in Spain, Volkov's abortive defection, and the flight of Burgess and Maclean. "I have toted up the ledger and the debits outnumber the assets," the head of MI5 informed the CIA.

Philby played his part with customary élan, readily conceding that his association with Burgess had forever destroyed his usefulness to Her Majesty's secret service, but steadfastly denying that he was guilty of anything more than bad judgment. He understood that no matter how persuasive the circumstantial evidence, the case against him could not be proved so long as he did not break down and confess. Even the knowledge that by now the United States had succeeded in decoding Russian cables containing his Soviet cryptonym did not shake Philby, for he correctly judged that neither the CIA nor MI6 would ever reveal such sensitive intelligence information.

Without a confession the official verdict against Philby could go no further than "guilt unproven but suspicion remaining." Nevertheless, the career of the man Allen Dulles called "the best spy the Russians ever had" was effectively ended, and pop-eyed Bill Harvey, the "odd man out" in the world of CIA sophisticates, deserved a major share of the credit. Cut loose from the service, Philby would drift for several years in a limbo of failed business ventures and hack writing jobs, consuming greater amounts of alcohol and earning lesser sums of money. Finally he would catch on as a low-level British agent operating under journalistic cover in the Middle East, but never again would he be in a position to betray the West's most closely held secrets.

He had done enough as it was, although the CIA's operations against the Soviet Union had been so uniformly unsuccessful that it was difficult to determine precisely which failures to blame on Philby. He had been privy to the details of a disastrous Anglo-American attempt to foment an uprising against the puppet Soviet regime in Albania, but Mike Burke, the CIA officer who had directed the operation from Italy, flatly asserted that "the operation would not have succeeded regardless of Philby." Harry Rositzke, the CIA officer in charge of dropping agents behind the Iron Curtain, said that Philby "learned a great deal about our air operations," but he quickly added that the obstacles to inserting an agent successfully into the police-state confines of the Soviet Union were overwhelming, with or without Philby. The operations Philby had been briefed on were a matter of record, but there was no telling what his many friends in the CIA and the FBI had let slip in the course of conversation. "Philby turned out to be very embarrassing to [a number of] senior officers who had told him a lot of stuff they never should have told him," a CIA man said.

No one had known Philby better or spent more time with him than Angleton. By the time Philby arrived in Washington in 1949 as the MI6 liaison officer, Angleton had become what Philby called "the driving force of OSO"—the CIA's Office of Special Operations. Angleton seemed to be everywhere at once—orchestrating covert action against the Communists in Italy, cementing CIA ties with the Jewish leaders in Palestine, tracking down counterintelligence leads left over from the Bentley case—and such a broad mandate inevitably entailed frequent contacts with MI6. In addition, Philby said, "a genuine friendliness" existed between himself and Angleton. Philby claimed that he manipulated this rapport to "string him along . . . provoke Angleton into defending, with chapter and verse, the past record and current activities" of CIA assets. Even as he was being recalled to London for interrogation, Philby said, he was able to pass "a pleasant hour in a bar" with Angleton, who "did not seem to appreciate the gravity of my personal situation." If that was true, it was the second time that Angleton had met with Philby in the midst of a major crisis in the spy's career. The first time had been in Rome in 1945, following the abortive Volkov defection. Neither time had he given the slightest indication that he suspected anything untoward.

After Philby had been unmasked, Angleton would claim to have had his doubts about him all along. Two of Angleton's closest friends would support that contention, but three CIA officers who reviewed the Philby file in depth insisted that Harvey was the first to point the accusing finger. Angleton explained the absence of documentary evidence to support his claim by saying that one did not put in writing something so sensitive as suspicions about the loyalty of a trusted member of a friendly intelligence service. An officer who had examined the record insisted that "Philby was the greatest blow Angleton ever suffered."

Angleton was not the only intelligence officer to have been duped by Philby. Until the disappearance of Burgess and Maclean, everybody had been taken in. Even then, Harvey was the only American to put the pieces together, and he had been assisted by a special source of intelligence: the decoded Soviet messages. Harvey had learned about the intercepts while still at the FBI and had somehow contrived through his Bureau friends to continue reading the traffic even though the CIA had not yet been told about the code break.

The decoded passages were too fragmentary to provide any hard evidence against Philby, but there was enough there to reinforce the suspicions aroused by the Volkov affair and the disappearance of Burgess and Maclean. Since he was not supposed to have access to the intercepts, Harvey could make no mention of them in his memo.

Angleton, too, had a special source of intelligence on Philby. Like so many other things in Angleton's career, this special source stemmed from his Israeli connection. Teddy Kollek had first met Philby in Vienna during the traumatic months in which he switched his allegiance to the Soviet camp. Kollek had a keen awareness of Philby's left-wing ties. According to one account, he had actually been present at Philby's marriage to the Communist Litzi Friedman. When Kollek arrived in the United States in 1949 as a member of a purchasing mission for the new State of Israel, he renewed his acquaintance with Philby and struck up a friendship with Angleton, the CIA man handling the Israeli account. Like everyone else meeting Angleton for the first time, Kollek was fascinated. "Jim is by no means an ordinary person," he recalled. "He is an original thinker. . . . He liked to sit up talking until four or five in the morning and often spoke in riddles that you had to interpret or feel, rather than analyze with cold logic." It was from Kollek, Angleton later said, that he first learned of Philby's left-wing youth and his short-lived marriage to Litzi Friedman.

Special sources aside, the fact remained that Harvey, not Angleton, had made the case against Philby, a fact that only increased the rivalry between the two men. When Harvey saw Angleton's four-page memo describing the relationship between Philby and Burgess, he wrote at the bottom: "What is the rest of this story?" According to one senior officer, the feud between them became so intense that Harvey at one point accused Angleton himself of being a Soviet agent. A lie-detector test supported Angleton's innocence, but his ego remained in shock. "He could not take credit for suggesting Philby was a penetration no matter how much he wanted to believe it," one officer said. "Harvey could take credit, and I think Angleton held a grudge against Harvey because of it."

Whatever his personal feelings, Angleton would spend the rest of his professional life in counterintelligence as if he were trying to atone for his failure to detect Philby. In many respects, that would be the single most lasting effect of the Philby affair on American intelligence.

Fair Play Reconsidered

Like all counterintelligence cases, the Philby affair was a maze of contradictions that invited alternative solutions. An FBI memo raised some of the more troubling questions about the case: "If Philby did use Burgess as a courier, it was the most unprofessional way to alert Maclean that he was under investigation. In a normal Soviet espionage operation, Soviet agents have both means of regular access to their Soviet handlers as well as emergency methods of contact. In normal operations, it would have been sufficient for Philby to alert his Soviet handler who could have taken over and relayed the information to appropriate officials. By using Burgess, Philby unnecessarily compromised all three of these valuable agents. In addition, he knew that Burgess was a drunkard and a homosexual and would not be considered a reliable courier since he could well have revealed his operation while in a drunken stupor on his way back to England."

This otherwise inexplicable lapse in Soviet spycraft suggested that the Russians had deliberately blown Philby in order to protect an even more valuable penetration agent. The Soviets had once protected Philby by doing nothing to prevent the FBI from rolling up the Fuchs and Rosenberg networks. It was not inconceivable that they could have given Philby up in favor of some other source, particularly since they knew that the Armed Forces Security Agency had succeeded in breaking his cryptonym out of the cable traffic. It was even possible that Philby, despite his later claims and despite Harvey's analysis, had not sent Burgess to warn Maclean. There were other British intelligence officers—some senior members of MI5 in particular—who were close to Burgess and knew that Maclean was under suspicion. Perhaps one of them was the third man. No one could say with any certainty what the real situation was— except that it was probably worse than anyone realized.

In 1951 Soviet spies were so thick in Washington that in the case of Philby and Burgess they actually lived in the same house. Even though that network had been neutralized, there remained the possibility of other, as yet unknown, penetrations. For its part, the CIA had failed utterly in its own attempts to penetrate the Soviet Union. Peer de Silva, the former security officer for the Manhattan Engineering Project, who in 1951 became the chief of operations for the CIA's Soviet Bloc Division, said that "a close review of our operational files led me to [conclude] that practically every one of our parachuted agents was under Soviet control and was reporting back to us under duress. The KGB was writing their messages and feeding back information they wanted us to have, which was either false, misleading or confusing. We therefore had almost no assets, in terms of agents, within the borders of the USSR or the Baltic states."

There was nothing for it but to press ahead, to hope that the worst was over and that time would heal the wounds left by Soviet penetration agents. But events soon reopened those wounds and spread the infection of panic throughout the government. Publicly, Senator Joseph McCarthy was in full cry. Secretly, new developments in the Burgess and Maclean affair demanded attention.

In 1951 only a handful of men appreciated the full significance of the disappearance of Burgess and Maclean. Harvey's allegation against Philby remained a tightly held secret, and although the disappearance of the two diplomats was a public sensation, only those officers privy to the code break and the search for source HOMER realized how long and how well Maclean had served the Soviet cause. The facts available to everyone else, both in and out of government, suggested only that Burgess and Maclean were a pair of dissolutes who had destroyed their careers by their indiscretions and hoped to make a new start in life on the other side. The few who knew the full story did nothing to discourage that naive perception, but in 1954 the facade was finally stripped away by the defection in Sydney, Australia, of a Russian intelligence officer named Vladimir Petrov. During his debriefing, Petrov said that his assistant, Filipp Kislitsyn, had formerly been in charge of a special section in Moscow that served as the depository for all of the material turned over by Burgess and Maclean. They were "long-term agents who had each been independently recruited to work for Soviet intelligence in their student days at Cambridge University," Petrov quoted Kislitsyn as saying. "Their flight was planned and directed from Moscow, and Kislitsyn was present during the planning of the escape operation," Petrov continued. "The reason for their flight was that they had discovered that they were under investigation by the British Security Service."

Petrov's information added nothing to Harvey's understanding of the Burgess and Maclean affair, but it came as a revelation to those intelligence officers and government officials who had not been told about the communications intercepts or the suspicions about Philby. The senior intelligence officer for the Joint Chiefs of Staff sounded thunderstruck. "It would appear that very nearly all U.S./U.K. high-level planning information prior to 25 May 1951 [the date Burgess and Maclean fled] must be considered compromised," he wrote. "Rather than attempt an estimate of how much damage has been done, it might be more profitable to quietly inquire into just who may be taking the place of these two men in the apparatus at this time. It is inconceivable that the pipeline dried up and operations stopped on 25 May 1951."

In July of 1954, just three months after Petrov's defection, President Eisenhower directed Lieutenant General James Doolittle to "undertake a comprehensive study of the covert activities of the Central Intelligence Agency" and to "make any recommendations calculated to improve the conduct of these operations." Two months later, Doolittle handed Eisenhower a sixty-nine-page top-secret report that confirmed what everybody now realized: the CIA was losing the secret war against the KGB. "Because the United States is relatively new at this game, and because we are opposed by a police-state enemy whose social discipline and whose security measures have been built up and maintained at a high level for many years, the usable information we are obtaining is still far short of our needs." Doolittle recommended a number of specific remedies, including the exploration of "every possible scientific and technical avenue of approach to the intelligence problem," and the "intensification of CIA's counterintelligence efforts to prevent or detect and eliminate penetrations of CIA." More fundamentally, he urged the CIA to become "more ruthless" than the KGB. "If the United States is to survive, long-standing American concepts of 'fair play' must be reconsidered," Doolittle said. "We must develop effective espionage and counterespionage services and must learn to subvert, sabotage and destroy our enemies by more clever, more sophisticated and more effective methods than those used against us."

The Doolittle report foreshadowed much of what the CIA, and Angleton and Harvey in particular, would undertake in the ensuing years. Within weeks of the report's submission, the new CIA Director, Allen Dulles, placed Angleton in charge of an expanded Counterintelligence Division that would intensify to the point of fanaticism "efforts to prevent or detect and eliminate penetrations of CIA." Harvey had already been named chief of the CIA's base in Berlin and was hard at work on a "technical avenue of approach to the intelligence problem" that would mark the CIA's most daring foray in the secret war.

For Harvey to go abroad while Angleton remained behind in counterintelligence seemed a curious reversal of roles. Harvey had spent virtually his entire career in Washington, both at the FBI and the CIA, working exclusively, and in the case of Philby, brilliantly, on counterintelligence. Angleton had performed with equal brilliance overseas in postwar Italy, but he had fallen down on the Philby case. The assignment of Harvey to Berlin and Angleton to counterintelligence, however, was neither reward nor punishment for the Philby affair. A bottom line had not yet been drawn on that case. There was enough suspicion to warrant Philby's severance from the British service but not enough evidence to bring charges against him. CIA officers were instructed to avoid him, but in 1955, when he was publicly accused for the first time of being the "third man" in the Burgess and Maclean affair, the British Foreign Minister had no choice but to assure the House of Commons that there was "no reason to conclude that Mr. Philby has at any time betrayed the interests of his country."

Harvey went to Berlin and Angleton stayed in Washington out of personal preference. Harvey was heeding the call to glory. Angleton was following the path to power. Harvey was heading for the front, leaving the tedious and thankless tasks of headquarters behind. Germany was where the line between East and West had been drawn, and Berlin, located a hundred miles behind the Iron Curtain, was the symbol of Allied determination to stand fast in the face of Soviet encroachment. "Germany was the biggest show we had, and Berlin was probably the most important base the Agency had," one CIA officer said. After the Director of Central Intelligence, the base chief in Berlin was probably the most visible CIA officer in the world. In the secret corridors of espionage, however, visibility did not bring power. That ineffable commodity was the reward of those who labored from within. It was no accident that of the young men present at the CIA's creation, the two who would in the long run exert the most influence over the Agency's operations were Angleton and Richard Helms, both of whom held headquarters assignments throughout their careers. Helms would rise to the Director's office, while Angleton remained in counterintelligence, never climbing a step higher than where he stood in 1954 but ever broadening his base until his was the most powerful and impregnable fiefdom in the secret realm.

Harvey's first overseas assignment marked a merciful end to his increasingly unhappy life with Libby. Their marriage was breaking under the strain of his infidelity and her drinking, and on more than one occasion had degenerated into physical violence. He would fly into a rage, "throw glasses, card table, anything he could pick up," Libby testified during the divorce proceedings. "He hit me several times . . . on the nose and kicked me a couple of times. . . . I had to go to the doctor and have an X-ray and had to have applications of heat put on it." Libby went home to Kentucky, and Harvey escaped with their five-year-old adopted son to Berlin.

Soon after the divorce became final, Harvey married a WAC major named Clara Grace Follich, whom he had met at the CIA station in Frankfurt. C.G., as everyone called her, left her job as administrative assistant to General Lucien Truscott, the CIA commander for all of Germany, and after a honeymoon in Majorca, the couple moved into a fortresslike white-stucco villa in Berlin. C.G. continued to work for the CIA in Berlin, managing the Agency's safe houses. (To guard against the possibility the houses might be used as secret trysting places, C.G. decreed that the cleaning ladies hired to look after them must be past the age of desire.) The newlyweds adopted a daughter, an infant who had been left on the doorstep of another CIA officer's home by an East German woman who wanted her child to grow up free. Harvey's friends kidded him that his daughter was the ultimate Soviet penetration agent. "Is this kid wired?" they cracked. "Knock it off," he grumbled.

Harvey had first seen Germany in 1950 when the CIA base at Pullach on the outskirts of Munich picked up an aging and down-at-the-heels Austrian count claiming to be in contact with a Soviet cipher officer in Vienna who was prepared to tell all in return for $25,000 in cash and resettlement in the West. The Pullach base was skeptical, even though the CIA station in Vienna observed the count entering Soviet headquarters at the Imperial Hotel and was able to confirm that the Russian officer he claimed to be in contact with actually existed. Pullach cabled headquarters recommending that they break contact with the count, but Harvey wanted to see for himself. The Soviets had changed their entire cipher system in 1948 after learning of the code break, and any chance, however slim, to crack the new system could not be overlooked. Harvey arrived at Pullach along with a "Pelican Team" of interrogators equipped with sodium pentothal. The "truth serum" only succeeded in making the count violently ill, but a simple polygraph convinced Harvey that he was a fraud who had worked for the Russians as a low-level informant but had no knowledge of Soviet ciphers or contact with anyone who did. Pullach sent out a "burn notice," notifying all CIA stations and Allied intelligence services that the count should be ignored if he ever tried to peddle his shoddy goods again. Harvey's mission to Pullach had proved fruitless, but it was a memorable one nonetheless. On his way to a dinner party one evening, he stopped off for cocktails at the base chief's house, where he lingered on and on, downing one martini after another and ignoring repeated hints about the late hour until his expectant host finally tracked him down by phone with news that the food was growing cold. When at last Harvey sat down to dinner, he promptly fell asleep—in his salad, according to Peer de Silva's account.

If Harvey's reputation preceded him to Berlin, he did not disappoint. At a cocktail party given to introduce him to the State Department types, he again fell asleep, this time in an easy chair with a drink in his hand, cocked at a precarious angle. The assembled diplomats hovered nearby, absorbed in the fate of the tipping drink.

Harvey's drinking would become legend during his years in Berlin. His capacity, like his growing bulk, was enormous. On a trip to Copenhagen, Harvey checked in at the Hotel d'Angleterre in midafternoon and waited at the bar to meet the local station chief for dinner. The station chief arrived to find the bartender staring in wonder as Harvey downed his seventh double martini. They adjourned to the dining room, where Harvey ordered another round and wine with dinner. At home, Harvey served his guests martinis in water goblets. Relations with his MI6 counterpart were never better than the night he put an olive in his colleague's glass and filled it with water while two senior officers from London grew glassy-eyed over the real thing.

Harvey did not speak a word of German on the day he arrived in Berlin and scarcely more on the day he left, a fact that he was loath to admit. "I can remember sitting next to Harvey on a plane, and he was pretending to read a German newspaper," said an officer in the CIA station at Frankfurt. "He didn't read a word of German. I knew it, and he knew I knew it." Harvey's lack of German may have been a source of embarrassment to him, but it did not hamper his effectiveness. Berlin was an occupied city, and the Germans quickly learned to speak the language of the occupying powers.

In theory, Harvey was subordinate to the American military commanders in Berlin. In practice, he answered to no one—as Brigadier General Kermit Davis, chief of staff for the American Military Command, found out. During the winter, Davis walked home for lunch each day along a path plowed through the snow just wide enough for two men to pass. For two days in a row, Davis had encountered a pair of men dressed in trench coats and berets, conversing together in German. Each time, they bore down on him two abreast, forcing him off the plowed path into the snow. On the third day, Davis stepped aside with resignation as the two men strode toward him, but as they passed, he threw a body block, knocking them both into the snow. Calling them "Kraut sons of bitches," Davis was surprised to hear their muttered oaths coming back at him in English. He realized they were Americans and followed them far enough to see them enter the CIA compound. Storming into Harvey's office, Davis demanded that some action be taken against the two men, who had been so disrespectful to the second-highest-ranking American officer in Berlin. Harvey laughed and said the two men should be commended for the effectiveness of their cover as "Kraut sons of bitches."

The action in Berlin was wide open and rough. The walls of Harvey's office were lined with racks of firearms, and a thermite bomb perched atop each safe, ready for the emergency destruction of files in the event of a Russian invasion. Shortly before Harvey arrived in the city, Dr. Walter Linse, director of a CIA-financed organization that collected intelligence from an underground network of laborers in East Germany, was wrestled into a taxicab one morning as he emerged from his apartment. Police gave chase as the taxi sped toward the Soviet sector, guns blazing. Linse was never seen again—the victim of one of the two-score kidnappings that occurred in Berlin over a two-year period.

When Harvey arrived in this Wild West of espionage, he ordered all CIA officers to carry sidearms when conducting operations. Harvey himself "kept three or four in his desk and never less than two on him." At a square-dancing party one warm summer evening in Berlin, Harvey was perspiring profusely under a heavy tweed sports jacket but rejected all suggestions that he take it off. "Can't," he growled, flipping open the jacket to reveal a pearl-handled revolver strapped under each sweaty armpit. Why not check the guns at the door? one of the gaping onlookers asked. "Can't," Harvey growled again. "When you need 'em, you need 'em in a hurry."

He was the only CIA officer in Berlin or anywhere else who carried a gun at all times. "If you ever know as many secrets as I do," he liked to say, "then you'll know why I carry a gun." He would thoroughly unnerve a visitor by taking a loaded revolver from his desk and toying with it as they spoke, spinning the chamber and sighting down the barrel. If he was a houseguest, he would warn his host to make sure that no small children wandered into his room in the middle of the night, because he slept with a gun under his pillow and was likely to wake up shooting.

Harvey's fixation on guns was not wholly irrational. By unwritten code, the CIA and the KGB did not kill each other's officers, but if ever the KGB were to make an exception, the man who had ended the career of Kim Philby would be a good place to begin. To most of his colleagues, however, Harvey's guns seemed like so much "braggadocio" or "window dressing," a melodramatic exaggeration of the dangers he faced. "It was a very boring thing," one officer said, "especially to people who had jumped out of airplanes and who had been involved in combat." Others saw it as a hangover from his FBI days, like the key chain he wore on his left hip, which did not belong in the subtler and more sophisticated world of espionage—as opposed to drinking, which somehow came with the territory. "He had FBI written all over him," said Mike Burke, chief of covert action in Frankfurt. "That fellow Harvey is a conspiratorial cop," Allen Dulles remarked. "The only trouble is I can't tell if he's more conspiratorial or cop."

Shortly after he arrived in Berlin, Harvey was visited by Frank Wisner, head of the CIA's Operations Directorate, who asked to be taken to meet the mayor of Berlin. Wisner, Burke, and Tracy Barnes of the Frankfurt station squeezed into the back seat of Harvey's car. Harvey got behind the wheel with a gun jammed in his belt, turned to an aide sitting next to him in the front seat, and barked, "Finger the turns"—FBI lingo meaning point the way. "It was like a Grade C movie," Burke related. Later, when Wisner was preparing to return to Washington aboard an ocean liner, he received a bon voyage telegram from Barnes saying: "Don't forget to finger the terns"—meaning gulls.

The same men who enjoyed their *bons mots* at Harvey's expense had also put him where he was, and Berlin during the 1950s was the front line of the secret war between the CIA and the KGB. It was an assignment for which he was as perfectly suited as General George S. Patton was for combat. Bill Harvey was the secret war made flesh.

If Harvey was the point man for the secret war, Angleton was the paper man, building his counterintelligence staff and its file-keeping capabilities into a more menacing force than Harvey's entire armory of guns. Although the Doolittle report had recommended a 10 percent cut in CIA personnel in order to eliminate the "large number of people some of whom were of doubtful competence" who had joined the Agency during the Korean War, Angleton's counterintelligence cadre was vastly expanded in size. What had begun as a tiny staff of two or three researchers under Harvey in 1947 had grown to 125 under Angleton. "Prior to Angleton the counterintelligence staff was nothing," a CIA officer who had worked for both Angleton and Harvey said. Flexing his added muscle, Angleton set out to fulfill the mandate of the Doolittle report by developing a new source of intelligence known as HT/LINGUAL, a project that violated not only "long-standing American concepts of 'fair play'." but the law as well.

On November 21, 1955, Angleton recommended to Richard Helms, the number two man in the Operations Directorate, that "we gain access to all mail traffic to and from the USSR which enters, departs or transits the United States through the Port of New York." The CIA, with the approval of the Post Office, had been photographing the outsides of envelopes for three years, but the number of letters actually opened was very small. "Presently letters are opened without the knowledge of the Post Office Department on a completely surreptitious basis, namely, swiping a letter, processing it at night and returning it the next day," Angleton explained to Helms, adding the complaint that the "material is not being exploited nearly to the extent it could be." With HT/LINGUAL, "more letters will be opened," he promised. "It is estimated that it will be possible to make discreet interior examination and photograph the contents of approximately two per cent of all incoming communications from the USSR, or approximately 400 per month."

Opening the mail on such a scale would provide "an entirely new avenue of information in the field of counter-espionage," Angleton argued. Precisely because opening letters was patently illegal, he reasoned, the Soviets would regard mail as a secure means of communication. "It must be assumed that foreign espionage agents have relied on this policy of the United States Government and this has resulted in the extensive use of the mails for intelligence purposes to our detriment," he counseled. Philby had boasted that he knew the limitations imposed on his adversary's procedures "by law and convention." But if he had assured the Soviets that the CIA would never tamper with the United States mail, he had badly misled them.

Each morning three CIA officers reported to a special room at New York's LaGuardia Airport, where a postal clerk delivered from two to six sacks of mail. For his trouble—and his continued silence—the postal clerk received an annual bonus of $500 from the CIA. Working with a Diebold camera, the three officers photographed the exteriors of about 1,800 letters each day. Each evening they stashed about 60 of the letters in an attaché case or simply stuffed them in their pockets and took them to the CIA's Manhattan Field Office for opening. Some of the letters were selected on the basis of a "watch list" of names compiled by Angleton's staff, but most were picked at random. In Manhattan, the CIA officers, all graduates of a one-week "flaps-and-seals" course, used a steam kettle to soften the glue on an envelope and a narrow stick to pry open the flap. A proficient flaps-and-seals man could do the job in five seconds. In an effort to increase the take, the CIA developed a steam oven that could handle a hundred letters at a time, but the flaps-and-seals men found it unreliable and went back to the steam kettle. Once photographed, the letter was put back in its envelope and returned to the mail stream the next day. The film was sent by registered mail or courier to CIA headquarters in Washington. There, a small "Projects Branch" within the Counterintelligence Division processed the film, analyzed the content of the letters, and indexed the names.

HT/LINGUAL began slowly but rapidly picked up speed. Only 832 letters were opened during the first year of operation, but two years later 8,000 letters were being opened annually. Angleton recommended the establishment of a laboratory in the Manhattan Field Office that could "increase our production about 20 per cent" and at the same time inspect the letters for "secret writing and/ or microdots." With the laboratory in operation, more than 14,000 letters were being opened each year. Gradually the watch list grew from a small core of 10 to 20 names to some 600, including such organizations as the American Friends Service Committee and the Federation of American Scientists, as well as authors like Edward Albee and John Steinbeck, and even a member of the Rockefeller family. Correspondents whose letters were opened at random included congressmen, senators, and a presidential candidate, Richard M. Nixon. A total of 215,820 letters would actually be opened, producing a computerized index of 2 million names. "From the counterintelligence point of view, we believed that it was extremely important to know everything possible regarding contacts of American citizens with Communist countries," Angleton explained.

From the beginning, he recognized that the operation was illegal and that exposure would cause "serious public reaction in the United States," perhaps leading to a congressional inquiry. But an aide to Angleton was confident that if the operation were blown, "it should be relatively easy to 'hush up' the entire affair." At worst, "it might become necessary . . . to find a scapegoat to blame for unauthorized tampering with the mail." In any case, "the effort was worth the risk."

Virtually every other CIA officer who reviewed HT/LINGUAL came to exactly the opposite conclusion. The Agency's Inspector General found very little counterintelligence potential in the operation, since it must "be assumed that Russian tradecraft is as good as our own and that Russian agents communicating with their headquarters would have more secure channels than open mail." Passing references in the letters to crop conditions, prices, or the weather might be of some incidental intelligence value but hardly enough to justify either the risk or the cost of opening the mail. After a preliminary sampling of letters, the most that Angleton could claim for HT/LINGUAL was the "interesting" fact that eight letters from the heartland of Godless Communism had contained "some religious reference." Beyond that, the first batch of mail was no help at all. "An examination of the contents of 35 communications from the Georgian Republic prior to the 9 March 1956 uprising showed no indication of discontent in any manner," he acknowledged. The mail was later to prove useful in helping the FBI and Angleton's counterintelligence staff keep track of members of the Rosenberg network who had fled to Russia yet still corresponded with friends and relatives in the United States, but almost by definition the operation was not likely to yield anything more valuable than that. Since Soviet citizens assumed that their letters were routinely opened and read by the local authorities, the Inspector General pointed out, "it is improbable that anyone inside Russia would wittingly send or receive mail containing anything of obvious intelligence or political significance." Summing up his evaluation of HT/LINGUAL, the Inspector General said that "most of the offices we spoke to find it occasionally helpful, but there is no recent evidence of it having provided significant leads or information which have had positive operational results. The Office of Security has found the material to be of little value. The positive intelligence derived from this source is meager."

HT/LINGUAL played to the enemy's strength. The CIA could not hope to match the KGB in police-state tactics. The law forbade it. Of course, the law could be broken, as with HT/LINGUAL, but it had to be done in such restrictive secrecy, hidden not only from the public but from the rest of the government, that the operation was a pale shadow of what the Soviets could mount. To succeed somehow in duplicating Soviet tactics despite the law would be a *de facto* admission of defeat, since the CIA would be corrupting the very political system it was fighting to preserve from Russian subversion. Angleton was not the only CIA officer whose attempts at becoming "more ruthless" than the KGB would lead him into a self-defeating imitation of Soviet tactics, although the danger was naturally greatest in the field of counterintelligence, which concentrated exclusively on thwarting those tactics. In later years, Harvey would resort to practices far more ruthless than opening mail.

It was easy enough to say of such excesses, as Angleton did of HT/LINGUAL, that "I reconciled it in terms of the knowledge I had, and my colleagues had, regarding the nature of the threat." But the simple fact was that they didn't work. Almost without exception, the CIA's real achievements relied not on police-state tactics but on the weapon of which the KGB had a critically short supply—technology. The Doolittle report, despite its call to "subvert, sabotage and destroy our enemies," recognized the potential of the "technical avenue of approach." It was a potential that would be realized in striking fashion during Harvey's stay in Berlin.

Carl Nelson of the CIA's Office of Communications stood at his hotel-room window and looked out on Vienna's Ringstrasse, a circumferential boulevard laid down where ramparts once guarded the seat of the Hapsburg empire. Across the street stood the Imperial Hotel, headquarters for the Soviet occupation forces, which shared uneasy dominion over the city with British, French, and American troops. The object of Nelson's interest—a pair of cables connecting the Imperial Hotel with the Soviet command in Moscow—was so close he felt he could reach out his hand and touch it. Later, he strolled through the streets, following the path of the cables overhead to the outskirts of the city, where they snaked underground to connect with the long-distance lines leading to Moscow. Nelson traced their subterranean route on a blueprint as they ran parallel to the main highway that connected the airport with the city center.

It was the fall of 1951 and Nelson was searching for the best location to install a wiretap. But before he could find it he was taken aside by British officials and informed that MI6 was already monitoring the Soviet lines. A full two years before, MI6 had purchased a private house set back a short distance from the highway in the suburb of Schwechat. Engineers had resurfaced the driveway with a sturdy expanse of reinforced concrete and beneath it had dug a seventy-foot tunnel from the basement out to the cables.

Nelson's scratching about was only one of several, slightly comical complications that had bedeviled the British operation since its inception.

Casting about for a cover, MI6 had first set up a Harris tweed import shop in one of the buildings next to the highway, confident that such quintessentially British goods would not attract enough customers in Vienna to interfere with the real business of installing the tap. To its dismay, MI6 found Harris tweed to be immensely popular with the local population. The first shipment from England was an instant sellout, and British operatives were soon buried beneath an avalanche of import license applications as they struggled to keep pace with the demand. Withdrawing from its unwanted bonanza, MI6 moved into the private home and finally managed to install the tap. According to the plan, a British officer was to pick up the first set of tapes recorded by the monitoring station from a schoolgirl who would be carrying them in her bookbag while strolling in Schoenbrun Park. When the MI6 man approached his pubescent contact, however, a Viennese policeman collared him on suspicion of child molestation. British officials hurriedly explained the situation to the Viennese authorities, and Operation SILVER, as it was called, proceeded without further incident until Nelson stumbled upon it, forcing the British to share their hard-earned communications intelligence with the Americans.

Nelson could not have struck SILVER—the first successful attack on a major Soviet landline—at a more opportune time. The advent of ultra-high-frequency line-of-sight radio communications had sharply reduced the amount of intelligence that could be gleaned from the airwaves. Lower frequencies, with their longer waves, would bend around the curve of the earth and could be monitored at great remove from the source. The higher frequencies, with their shorter waves, did not follow the curve of the earth. Traveling in straight lines, they could be intercepted only at points directly in line with the transmitter and receiver. "You could no longer sit back in your own territory and listen to Russian radio communications," a CIA officer explained. The result, a CIA document noted, was the creation of "gaps in our intelligence coverage which were particularly unfortunate during the period of Cold War escalation."

At the same time that technology was working against the interception of Soviet radio signals, however, Carl Nelson had scored a major breakthrough in the interception of messages carried over landlines. Twenty years later, Nelson's breakthrough would remain such a closely held secret that it would be referred to only in the most guarded terms, even within the CIA. "[T]he Office of Communications, in the course of its continuing efforts to provide secure communications for the Agency, became aware of a principle which, when applied to target communications, offered certain possibilities," one document noted cryptically.

Nelson had discovered that SIGTOT, a cipher machine manufactured by the Bell System for use by the United States in its worldwide communications, was vulnerable to intercept. He had invented a way to tap into any cable carrying SIGTOT's enciphered message and monitor that message, not in its encoded form but in plain text. No code-breaking was required. Once he had hooked up the proper combination of capacitors, amplifiers, and assorted gadgets, Nelson could sit back and watch the clear text clatter forth at sixty words per minute onto an ordinary teletype machine. The only limitation was that the tap had to be installed within twenty miles of the point from which the signal originated. Very simply, Nelson had discovered that as SIGTOT electrically encrypted a message from the clear text to a meaningless jumble of letters, it gave off faint echoes of the clear text, which traveled along the wire with the enciphered message.

Immediately and at great expense, the United States abandoned SIGTOT for a more secure cipher system, while Nelson set out to determine whether the other side's communications system was equally vulnerable. Operation SILVER proved that it was. Just as with SIGTOT, echoes—Nelson called them "transients" or "artifacts"—of the clear-text messages being enciphered by the Russians at the Imperial Hotel on Vienna's Ringstrasse could be sorted out from the encoded signals monitored at the listening post in the suburb of Schwechat. American intelligence had scored its biggest coup since the wartime code break that had uncovered source HOMER. This time, however, the British were not let in on the secret, even though MI6 had dug the tunnel and installed the tap.

Once Nelson's technique was proved in operation, five more taps were installed on Soviet landlines in and around Vienna, but the original tap at Schwechat proved the most valuable, for it revealed that the Soviet Union would not commit itself to a military advance through the Balkans, a piece of intelligence holding enormous significance for the disposition of American troops during the fighting in Korea.

The CIA moved rapidly to exploit Nelson's invention before the Russians found out about the "artifacts." "Exploratory discussions were held in Washington to plan the mounting of an attack on Soviet landlines in East Germany with special emphasis to be placed on the Berlin area," an Agency document recorded. Second only to Moscow, Berlin was the hub of the Soviet communications system. "As a result of the 19th century imperial control of the great European nations, all cables ran from the provinces into the capitals and back out again," a CIA officer explained. "In French colonial Africa, for instance, you couldn't call directly between two provinces. The call would go back to Paris and out again." In Eastern Europe, "everything came to Berlin. When the Soviet commandant in Bucharest or Warsaw called Moscow the call went through Berlin."

In Berlin, Nelson found that the blueprint of the city's telephone and telegraph system resembled nothing so much as a giant pinwheel. The lines were laid out in two concentric loops, encompassing the entire city, both East and West. At various points along the circumference of each loop, there were switching stations from which lines shot out to bring service to each district of the city. Nelson traced the cables as they arced across East Berlin from Altglienecke in the south, through Karlshorst, headquarters of the Soviet command, and on to Lichtenberg farther north. The cables continued into West Berlin, but the system had been severed with the division of the city into Soviet and Western sectors. Although the lines linking the two halves of the city remained in place, they were no longer connected to their terminals. Looking at the blueprint, Nelson could see that all that was required to tap into the East Berlin system was to reconnect the lines.

Harvey, as CIA base chief in Berlin, arranged for an agent inside the Lichtenberg switching station to be given precise instructions for connecting the cables to a line that had its other end in West Berlin's central post office. The reconnected lines were there for all to see, and it would only be a matter of time before East German phone men came across them. But the hookup would have to do until enough samples of the traffic could be collected to determine whether a permanent tap would be worth the effort.

With West German assistance, a CIA technician set up banks of monitoring equipment inside the post office. For three weeks, the technician stayed locked in a stifling, closetlike room, maintaining watch over the equipment while it recorded reel upon reel of tape. The test was a success. As in Vienna, the equipment was able to pick up the clear-text echoes of enciphered messages. "At this point we knew it could be done," a CIA paper said, "The next step was the problem of installing a permanent tap on the target lines."

Building a tunnel would not be as easy as it had been in Vienna. This would be no short dig from house to street. A tunnel in Berlin would have to originate in the Western sector and burrow hundreds of yards across a heavily patrolled border into the eastern half of the city. No one had ever attempted anything like it. The closest thing the CIA had to a tunnel expert was a young engineer in the Office of Communications with a degree in soil mechanics. British intelligence, at least, had some experience in the highly specialized art of vertical tunneling, and had developed a method for digging upward through soft soil without having the roof collapse. The Americans and British would have to pool their resources.

A CIA document set forth the division of labor. The CIA would "(1) procure a site . . . and drive a tunnel to a point beneath the target cables . . . (2) be responsible for the recording of all signals produced . . . (3) process in Washington all of the telegraphic material received from the project." MI6 would "(1) drive a vertical shaft from the tunnel's end to the targets; (2) effect the cable taps and deliver a usable signal to the head of the tunnel for recording; and (3) provide for a . . . center . . . to process the voice recordings from the site." The project was code-named GOLD, and Harvey was placed in overall command.

Selection of the tunnel site was crucial. It had first of all to be within striking distance of the cables. Every foot in length meant another load of dirt that had to be excavated and disposed of under the noses of the Vopos, the East German border guards. Every foot in length increased the problem of ventilating the tunnel. Without proper ventilation, the electronic equipment needed for the tap would overheat. Under normal conditions, ventilation shafts could be sunk at regular intervals along the tunnel's length to provide a source of cooling air. In a clandestine operation, fresh air had to be pumped from a hidden source at the mouth of the tunnel, and there were limits to how far the air could be pumped.

The cables made their closest approach to Western territory at the city's extreme southern edge, a sparsely settled expanse of farmland and refugee shacks known as Altglienecke. Still a thousand feet away from the border, they lay just eighteen inches beneath a drainage ditch on the far side of Schoenefelder Chaussee, a heavily traveled highway linking the main Soviet air base in Germany with East Berlin. Geological maps showed the terrain to be uniformly flat and composed of a soft, almost sandy soil that would yield easily to pick and shovel, but aerial reconnaissance revealed disparities in the drainage of the soil. Wet, poorly drained areas showed up as dark, while dry, well-drained areas appeared light. Water had to be avoided. It would complicate the digging and damage the electronic equipment. One area, its most prominent landmark a graveyard on the eastern side of the border, showed up white in the aerial photos. There, said the CIA's soil mechanic, would be the best place to dig a tunnel. Digging directly under the graveyard was "ruled out for aesthetic reasons," he recalled. "We didn't want the Russians accusing us of desecrating German graves." So the line of attack was laid slightly to the north of the graveyard.

Harvey flew back to Washington to brief Allen Dulles, Frank Wisner, Richard Helms, and other senior Agency officials on the plan. "There were those who manifested reservations," a CIA document noted dryly, but those reservations paled in the face of Harvey's fervor. "Without Harvey there would have been no tunnel," the soil mechanic said. "The easy thing was to say 'No' and be on the safe side and not take a chance, but Harvey would keep badgering the chiefs, stripping away their objections." A senior officer who listened to Harvey's briefing agreed. "I don't think the Director or Frank Wisner or Dick Helms would have gone ahead with it if they hadn't had a guy like Harvey in West Berlin." Dulles approved the operation, directing that "in the interest of security, as little as possible concerning the project would be reduced to writing." A CIA officer reviewing the project years later commented that "it is probable that few orders have been so conscientiously obeyed."

Early in 1954 two teams of Army engineers began work on the tunnel at sites six thousand miles apart. In Berlin a Corps of Engineers unit started construction of a warehouse directly over the spot chosen for the mouth of the tunnel. In New Mexico, at the White Sands Missile Proving Ground, sixteen handpicked Army sergeants working under the direction of Lieutenant Colonel Leslie Gross, a combat engineer recently returned from Korea, sank a test tunnel beneath the desert.

The commander of the engineers in Berlin could not understand why a warehouse had to have a basement with a 12-foot ceiling. That was not the way the Army built warehouses. For one thing, it meant that an enormous amount of earth had to excavated and hauled away in dump trucks. The commander refused to proceed until a direct order from Washington changed his mind. In the strictest of confidence, Washington explained that he was not really building a warehouse but a radar intercept station designed to look like a warehouse. Washington did not explain that no sooner would the basement be finished than another crew of engineers would start to fill it in again with the 3,100 tons of dirt that would be produced by a tunnel 1,476 feet long and 6½ feet in diameter.

In New Mexico, the crew of sixteen sergeants successfully completed a 450-foot test tunnel through soil of approximately the same composition as in Berlin. The major concern had been that the tunneling would cause the soft earth to settle, leaving a telltale furrow aboveground. The deeper the tunnel, the less chance that settling, or "slump," would occur. But the deeper the tunnel, the more dirt would have to be excavated from the vertical shafts at either end, and the more weight would press down from above.

The engineers chose 20 feet as the optimum depth of the tunnel floor, leaving 13½ feet of undisturbed earth between its roof and the surface.

The crew of sixteen abandoned the New Mexico tunnel and flew to Richmond, Virginia, where the material needed for Operation GOLD was being assembled in a real Army warehouse. One hundred and twenty-five tons of steel liner plates that would be bolted together to form the tunnel walls were sprayed with a rubberized coating to prevent them from clanging during construction. All the equipment was packed in crates labeled "spare parts" and "office supplies," shipped by sea to the German port of Bremerhaven, placed aboard the regularly scheduled supply train for Berlin, and finally trucked to the new warehouse near Altglienecke.

The Vopos, watching through their binoculars less than a hundred yards away, were not easily fooled. They could see that the Americans had come to spy. Warehouses were not surrounded by double rings of barbed wire, powered by expensive diesel generators, and manned by troops wearing the insignia of the Army Signal Corps. What really gave the game away was the parabolic antenna, an AN/APR9, the most sophisticated electronic receiver in the United States inventory, which was perched atop the warehouse roof. Clearly, the warehouse was to be used as a radar intercept station that would scour the airwaves for pulses emitted by the nearby Soviet air base at Schoenefeld. The Vopos would have been dumbstruck to learn that the AN/APR9 had been selected not by an electronics wizard but by the CIA's soil mechanic because "I thought the antenna cluster looked real sexy."

By August of 1954 the warehouse was ready. The ground floor was stocked to capacity with crates of "spare parts" and "office supplies." Below, the cavernous basement stood empty, waiting to be filled again with dirt. All that remained before the sixteen sergeants could start digging was—a softball game.

The closest calculation of the entire operation would be to determine the precise point at which to stop burrowing eastward and start digging upward toward the cables. The engineers needed an object of known size in the Soviet sector upon which to base their measurements. None existed, so they tried to infiltrate one in the form of a softball. But each time a long fly ball sailed across the border, the Vopos picked it up and good-naturedly heaved it back before a technician stationed at a peephole in the warehouse could take his readings.

Abandoning their bat and ball, the engineers dispatched two CIA agents to have a flat tire on Schoenefelder Chaussee. While changing the tire, one of the agents placed a tiny reflector next to the road. An electronic surveyor's transit hidden behind the peephole sent out a beam that struck the reflector and bounced back, giving the precise distance between the two points. The engineers were confident they could hit the target within 6 inches either way.

Starting from a point in the easternmost corner of the warehouse basement, they sank a vertical shaft 18 feet in diameter to a depth of 20 feet, then drove pilings halfway into the floor of the shaft. Next, a steel ring 6½ feet in diameter and fitted with hydraulic jacks around its circumference was lowered into place. Braced against the exposed section of the pilings, the ring, or "shield," was fitted flush against the tunnel's face. Everything was now ready for the long subterranean journey eastward toward Schoenefelder Chaussee.

Three men attacked the tunnel face with pick and shovel. After excavating the face to a depth of 2 inches, they shoved the shield forward by jacking it against the pilings. Over and over again, the process was repeated: excavate, jack forward, excavate, jack forward. After advancing a foot, the diggers were able to bolt the first ring of steel liner plate into place. After another foot of progress, a second ring of liner plate. Plugs in the face of each plate were uncapped and mortar pumped under pressure to fill any voids between the tunnel walls and the surrounding earth, leaving no room for "slump." One thousand cubic yards of mortar would be consumed before the tunnel was completed. When the tunnel reached 6 feet in length, the shield's hydraulic jacks no longer needed to be braced against the pilings. The crush of the "overburden" held the completed portion of the tunnel so firmly in place that it could now serve as the brace against which the shield was jacked forward.

Divided into eight-hour shifts, the sergeants worked round the clock—three men at the face with pick and shovel, two loading the "spoil" into a box that was picked up by a forklift and hauled back to the mouth of the tunnel, where a winch raised it to the basement for dumping. Not all the spoil had to be brought up to the basement. Some was packed in sandbags and stacked along the sides of the tunnel. Ventilation ducts were placed on top of the sandbags, bringing a stream of chilled air to the sweating men at the tunnel face. As steel liner plates were needed, they were brought by forklift from the ground floor of the warehouse, down a ramp to the basement, and over to the shaft to be lowered to the waiting forklift below. The engineers took constant sightings from a peephole directly above the shaft to make sure that the tunnel did not wander off course. Minute changes in direction were made by jacking one side of the shield farther forward than the other.

About 50 feet out, the diggers struck water. At first the soil mechanic thought he had encountered a perched water table—a pocket of water prevented from percolating downward by an impervious stratum of soil. The smell suggested a different answer. In steering clear of the graveyard, the engineers had struck a course straight through the drainage field of the warehouse's own septic tank. The aesthetic drawbacks of the graveyard were nothing by comparison. There was no choice but to forge ahead.

The demands of security forced delays at every step. Ordinarily, a sharp blow with a sledgehammer could be counted on to free the hydraulic jacks, which frequently jammed, but that made too much noise, so each time the jacks had to be disassembled and reassembled. Aboveground, a twenty-four-hour watch was kept with a Questar astronomic telescope from an observation post in the warehouse attic. The lookout was linked to the tunnel face by field telephone, and he ordered digging stopped each time the East German guards passed over the tunnel on patrol. The boredom of lookout duty "was relieved once in a while when the Vopos would entice one of the farm girls behind a haystack," a CIA officer said.

As the most visible CIA officer in Berlin, Harvey could safely visit the site only at night, taking a circuitous route that involved at least one change of cars. Major General Ben Harrell, chief of staff for the Army command in Berlin, recalled a nighttime tour of the tunnel with Harvey. "Harvey and I drove way across Berlin and went into a parking area and changed cars. It was real cloak and dagger as far as I was concerned. . . . Coming back, Bill asked me to come up and have a drink. He poured me a full glass of scotch without anything else in it. When I finally got home, my wife asked me where I'd been." Covered with mud and reeking of alcohol, Harrell could only offer the lame response, "I've been out with Bill Harvey on business."

On another nocturnal visit to the tunnel, Harvey sat quietly in the backseat of his car and listened to the driver and another G.I. carry on the soldier's eternal dialogue. "I'm getting horny as hell," one said. "Me, too," the other replied. "George is the only one who's had a piece of ass lately." When Harvey arrived at the tunnel, he ordered the duty officer to find out who George was and "get him the hell out of here." George's pillow talk could blow the entire operation. Investigation revealed that George was a dog, the warehouse mascot.

The tunnel was completed on February 25, 1955, a long, thin catheter ready to draw off the secrets of the Soviet military command in Berlin. Harvey walked along its length until he stood directly beneath the Schoenefelder Chaussee. The final 50 feet were separated from the rest of the tunnel by a heavy door of steel and concrete designed against the inevitable day the operation would be blown and the Vopos would come storming through. At Harvey's instruction, the door bore a neatly lettered inscription that warned in both German and Russian: "Entry is forbidden by order of the Commanding General."

Now it was up to the British to install the taps. A second shield was brought in to dig the vertical shaft up to the cables. The technique was the same as before except that the face of the shield was fitted with slats to keep the ceiling of the shaft from crashing down on the workmen. A single slat was removed to expose a small portion of the earth above, the earth was scraped out, the slat replaced, another slat removed, and another section of ceiling scraped out. When the earth behind each slat had been excavated, the entire shield was jacked upward and the process repeated, inching slowly, slowly toward the cables. Finally, three black rubber-sheathed cables, each one as thick as a man's arm, emerged from the ceiling. With the help of a hydraulic jack, they were pulled downward into the tap chamber so that the technicians could have some headroom in which to work. A reinforced-concrete roof was erected to support the weight of the traffic overhead, but the rumble of each approaching lorry was an unnerving experience. Even though the chamber was insulated so as not to reverberate like a huge drum, "it was a weird sensation to be in the chamber when an iron-shod horse trotted across it," one CIA officer reported.

Even the air pressed heavier in this claustrophobic chamber. A double steel door at the entrance kept the space pressurized in order to prevent nitrogen gas sealed within the cables from escaping when the wires were laid bare. The nitrogen was a standard technique used to ward off moisture and to monitor the integrity of the cables. A leak anywhere along the line would cause the pressure of the nitrogen to drop and set off an alarm. The back pressure in the chamber prevented any leaks, but the breathing and perspiration of the technicians working in the dense atmosphere created such a moisture problem that they were frequently forced to evacuate the chamber so that the air-conditioning equipment could dehumidify it.

The tap was the riskiest moment of the entire venture. The East Germans regularly monitored the integrity of the circuits with a "fault finder," a device that transmitted a pulse along the line that would come bouncing back the moment it discovered a break. The trick was to draw off such an infinitesimal portion of the signal that the loss would go undetected. With the rubber sheath removed and the back pressure keeping the nitrogen from escaping, the British technicians painstakingly clipped wires to the rainbow of color-coded circuits at their fingertips. The wires carried the signal down to banks of amplifiers in the tunnel and back up to rejoin the circuit. The amplifiers boosted the captured mites of sound and shot them through the tunnel along lead-sheathed cables that rested atop the sandbags to rows of sound-activated Ampex tape recorders in the warehouse. Visitors to the warehouse were struck by the eerie sound of 150 recorders hissing and whirring as they started and stopped in response to the stolen signals.

Processing the take was a task of staggering proportions. The three cables contained a total of 172 circuits carrying a minimum of 18 channels each. The CIA was in danger of becoming a victim of its own success. Having plugged into the Soviet command network, the Agency had to devise a method of sifting through the miles and miles of tape before the intelligence died of old age. What if the tapes recorded Soviet preparations for an attack on West Berlin but were not processed in time to sound the alarm?

A few circuits could be monitored at the site and items of particular interest immediately cabled to Washington or London. The most closely monitored circuits were not those of the Soviet high command but the East German engineering and police circuits. By listening to these, the CIA could tell where East German repair crews were at work and what plans the Vopos had for patrolling the area. The first hint that the tunnel had been discovered was likely to come over these circuits. Everything else was shipped home under armed guard aboard military aircraft. Recordings of the telegraph circuits were flown to Washington, where Carl Nelson's invention could sort out the plain-text artifacts from the encoded signals. Tapes of phone conversations went to London, where a team of White Russian émigrés waited to translate them. In Washington the tapes were delivered to building T-32, one of the World War II "Tempos" that disfigured the Mall between the Washington Monument and the Lincoln Memorial. The floors of T-32, known as "the Hosiery Mill" because of the many strands of communications intelligence that came together there, sagged under the weight of the machinery assembled to process the tapes. The entire building was sheathed in steel in order to prevent the electronic pulses that ricocheted about the premises from escaping into the atmosphere, possibly to alert the other side.

The heart of the system was "the bumblebee," so called because, like the real bumblebee, all the laws of physics decreed that it would never get off the ground. "The bumblebee" played the tapes at 60 inches per second, four times the speed at which the captured signals had originally been transmitted, breaking down the 18 channels of each circuit into separate recordings—"demuxing," in the communicators' jargon. The 18 separate recordings were then placed on slow-speed recorders linked to teletype machines that printed out the message in clear text at 100 words per minute. The printed messages, still in their original Russian or German, were ripped from the teletypes and hand-carried to teams of translators and analysts on the floors above. To keep pace with "the bumblebee," the translators and analysts worked a schedule of two weeks on and one day off.

Inevitably, some of the circuits produced unintelligible signals, and a special five-man team of communications experts stationed at Nuremberg was called on to tackle the problem. On one occasion, the Russians were found to be using a two-channel teletype in which letters were transmitted alternately, to be divided into separate messages at the receiving end. If, for instance, one channel transmitted the word *m-i-s-s-i-l-e* and the other the word *r-o-c-k-e-t*, the tape would record *m-r-i-o-s-c-s-k-i-e-l-t-e.* No sooner had the two-channel mystery been solved than the Soviets switched to a three-channel teletype.

Sometimes circuits disappeared from the landlines for no apparent reason. The call signs of the missing circuits were cabled to Nuremberg, where the CIA team searched the airwaves for them, more often than not finding that the Russians had simply switched from landline to radio. When a circuit disappeared from the air, a check with T-32 in Washington frequently determined that the circuit had been moved underground.

Processing the tapes increased the chances of a leak by geometric proportions. Trying to remain as inconspicuous as possible, the fifty Russian- and German-speaking officers assigned to the Hosiery Mill were crammed into a windowless room with only 45 square feet of working space per person. The deputy chief of the processing section briefed them on the need for security. "It is greatly in your interest not to know where any of the material you are processing is coming from," he began. Even so, "for the opposition to stop the flow, all they would have to know is that we have this many Russian and German speakers together."

"From the beginning, it was realized that the duration of this operation was finite," a CIA report on GOLD said. Sooner or later a mistake would give the operation away, or the East Germans would come across it in the course of routine maintenance. The British had made one mistake early on, but it had been caught in time. They had miscalculated the amount of heat given off by the amplifiers that lined the final fifty feet of the tunnel between the antipersonnel door and the tap chamber. Despite the best efforts of the air conditioning, the space was growing noticeably warmer. In the summer of 1955 a CIA officer flew to Berlin to study the problem. Uncapping the plugs in the steel liner plates through which the mortar had earlier been pumped, he drilled ten holes of varying depth into the surrounding earth. Into the holes he inserted thermometers connected by wire to a chart in the recording room. The thermometers confirmed that the earth was becoming warmer. On the first cold day of fall, the heat radiating from the equipment room, which was located directly under the Schoenefelder Chaussee, would melt the glaze of frost on the highway, leaving a dark, wet rectangle that would surely arouse suspicion. A chilled water-circulating system was hastily installed in the tunnel, using up Sears, Roebuck's entire East Coast inventory of plastic pipe, and the temperature of the earth began to fall.

There were other, more transitory scares. One morning a microphone positioned in the tap chamber picked up a series of alarming thuds. The lookout in the peak of the warehouse couldn't see what was happening. A dense fog obscured his view. "After the sun burned away the fog, visual observation showed that the East German police had set up a temporary automobile checkpoint directly over the chamber," a CIA report said. "The 'thuds' the microphone picked up were caused by the police officer in charge stomping his feet on the road surface to keep warm."

On April 21, 1956, eleven months and eleven days after the first Ampex tape recorder had whirred to the sound of the Soviet military command, the microphone in the tap chamber picked up a sound even more alarming than the thuds—voices exclaiming at what they had found. There had been no patch of melted frost on the highway nor, as far as anyone could tell, any other clue to alert the Soviets to the tunnel. "Analysis of all available evidence—traffic passing on the target cables, conversations recorded from a microphone installed in the tap chamber, and visual observations from the site—indicates that the Soviet discovery . . . was purely fortuitous," a CIA postmortem concluded. Another document attributed the discovery to "unfortunate circumstances beyond our control—a combination of the fact that one of the cables was in very poor physical condition . . . and a long period of unusually heavy rainfall. It appeared that water entered the cable in sufficient quantity to make it inoperative, thus necessitating digging up sections of the cable and causing discovery of the tap."

If discovery was inevitable, the Soviet reaction was not. "Among those most actively concerned with the project's management, a consensus developed that the Soviets would probably suppress knowledge of the tunnel's existence," a CIA analysis said. "It was felt that for the Soviets to admit that the U.S. had been reading their high-level communications circuits would cause the Soviets to lose face." But "fate intervened," the analysis continued. "The Commandant of the Soviet Berlin Garrison, who would normally have controlled the handling of the situation when the tunnel was discovered, was absent from Berlin, and the acting Commandant, Colonel Ivan A. Kotsyuba, was in charge. . . . His reaction was unexpected in that he invited the entire Berlin press corps to a briefing and tour of the tunnel and its facilities. As a result, the tunnel was undoubtedly the most highly publicized peacetime espionage enterprise in modern times prior to the U-2 incident." The Soviet end of the tunnel quickly became the major tourist attraction in Berlin, complete with snack bar. Although the United States remained silent, there was no doubt who was behind the tunnel. As a Western correspondent who took the tour reported, "It is clear that if the visitor could continue westward . . . he would emerge soon at a low but prominent American building with radar equipment on the roof."

Kotsyuba's aim was to expose, for all the world to see, the treachery of American imperialists, but he misjudged his audience. His exhibition of American perfidy was soon proclaimed a monument to Yankee ingenuity. "A venture of extraordinary audacity— the stuff of which thriller films are made," the New York *Herald Tribune* said. "If it was dug by American intelligence forces—and that is the general assumption—it is a striking example of their capacity for daring undertakings. Seldom has an intelligence organization executed a more skillful and difficult operation than that accomplished by the tunnel's diggers." *Time* magazine called it the "Wonderful Tunnel," and a Washington *Post* editorial was headlined THE TUNNEL OF LOVE. "People would come up to you just because you were American and say, 'Great op,' " an officer in the Berlin base recalled. "You'd have to say you didn't know anything about it, but they'd wink and say, 'Aw, come on.' "

The tunnel produced much more than rave reviews. It produced mountains upon mountains of intelligence, so much in fact that the processing of backlogged material was not completed until September of 1958, more than two years after the flow had stopped. What was the intelligence worth? "The tunnel was a terribly good hard source of OB [Order of Battle]," the deputy chief of the processing section said, "and OB—which Russian troops were where—was important in those days. It also made it possible to confirm the performance of all other agent assets and to identify those that were diddling you. . . . It enhanced the confidence of every position we had." Among other things, the tunnel revealed that East German railroad tracks and rolling stock were in a chaotic state of disrepair. Since the Russians would have to rely on the trains for any large-scale troop movements, the United States and Britain could take a considerably more relaxed view of the prospect of a sudden blitzkrieg against West Berlin.

Some officers were less enthusiastic about the tunnel. "It made the OB boys happy, but other than that the take was extremely marginal. The psychological impact when it was blown was far, far greater than the take." Much of the intelligence did indeed seem of marginal utility. The monitors learned, for instance, that the Russians planned to detain Major General Charles Dasher, the American commander in Berlin, during a scheduled visit to a trade fair in Leipzig. Should Dasher walk into the trap or should he stay away and risk alerting the Russians to a communications leak? The dilemma solved itself when Dasher came down with pneumonia. The tunnel also revealed that the wife of the commander in chief of the Soviet land forces in East Germany was dealing in rugs on the black market. She could be heard on the tapes complaining to her husband about the laggard Berlin taxi driver who would not tote the rugs up to her apartment. When the Russians set up a roadblock on the autobahn leading to Berlin, the tunnel confounded all the laborious exegeses of the Kremlinologists in Washington and London who attempted to analyze precisely which Western action had triggered the Soviet provocation. It turned out that a Russian sergeant had just learned that his commanding officer was cuckolding him, and he was venting his rage by harassing the Americans. The tunnel's $25- to $30-million price tag seemed a bit steep for intelligence like that.

Nevertheless, for eleven months and eleven days, the tunnel had kept a finger on the Soviet pulse. The Russian Army could not have made a military move anywhere in Europe without tipping its hand via the tunnel. When the CIA was set up in 1947, Secretary of State George Marshall was reported to have said, "I don't care what the CIA does. All I want from them is twenty-four hours' notice of a Soviet attack." "Harvey's Hole," as the tunnel became known, had put the CIA in a position to do just that, and had done it at a time when the Agency had virtually no other assets behind the Iron Curtain.

The CIA was eager to try again, this time with a tunnel—code name BRONZE—beneath an East Berlin telephone exchange, but the proposal was rejected by the White House. Although he had approved GOLD in general terms, President Eisenhower seemed taken aback by the realization that it had entailed a physical invasion of East German soil. Until the tunnel's discovery, he understood that the CIA had succeeded in intercepting Soviet military communications, but he remained deliberately ignorant of the means employed. "The essence of the information was made available to the President," Dillon Anderson, Eisenhower's National Security adviser, said, "but I don't think he wanted particularly to know that an elaborate tunneling device had been constructed."

In the future the CIA would have to content itself with less spectacular, though no less imaginative, means of monitoring communications in East Berlin. Agents were outfitted with hidden recorders to stand beneath overhead telephone lines and pick up the signals radiated by the wires. A section of plastic telephone pole was developed that an agent disguised as a lineman could place atop a real telephone pole. Inside the plastic section was a recorder to pick up the radiated signals and a transmitter to flash them back to a listening post in West Berlin.

None of these gadgets could ever match the magnitude of the communications break provided by the tunnel which Allen Dulles called "one of the most valuable and daring projects ever undertaken." At a secret ceremony, Dulles singled out Harvey for special praise and awarded him the Distinguished Intelligence Medal. It was a moment to savor as Dulles heartily slapped him on the back for a job well done. In the ten years since Harvey had been cashiered from the FBI, he had earned a reputation as America's top spy, the man who had both uncovered Kim Philby, the KGB's most valued penetration of the West, and overseen Operation GOLD, the CIA's most valued penetration of the Iron Curtain.

If Harvey had any rival for clandestine supremacy, it was Angleton, who had pulled off a considerable coup of his own by obtaining through his Israeli sources a copy of Nikita Khrushchev's secret 1956 denunciation of Stalin at the Soviet Twentieth Party Congress. By Angleton's own account, however, his coup resulted in a major human tragedy when over his objections Dulles released a copy of the precious document to *The New York Times.* Angleton contended that the uproar touched off by publication of the speech led directly to the Hungarian revolt that was so ruthlessly crushed by Soviet tanks. According to Angleton, the CIA had been training Hungarian exiles at a secret base in Germany for just such an uprising, but the appearance of the Khrushchev speech in the *Times* prematurely ignited the revolution before the Agency-trained forces were ready to enter the fray.

Angleton's analysis made a number of questionable assumptions about cause and effect, but it aptly captured the tendency of even the most clear-cut intelligence successes to backfire—as Harvey was soon to find out about Operation GOLD.

A Surfeit of Spies

"Oh shit, oh damn," Harvey exclaimed to George Kisvalter, a man who looked more like his nickname "Teddy Bear" than the handler of the CIA's prize agents. What he had just told Harvey could mean the end for Colonel Popov of the GRU, the Agency's lone penetration agent inside the Soviet military intelligence apparatus. Kisvalter had been meeting secretly with Popov for the past six years, ever since 1953, when the Russian had first volunteered his services to the CIA in Vienna by dropping a note on the front seat of an American diplomat's car.

Popov had been a stroke of incredible good fortune. By one measure, that of return on investment, he was an intelligence source of even greater worth than the tunnel. "Harvey's Hole" had cost between $25 and $30 million, while Popov was being paid $100 a month. Even that paltry sum remained in CIA hands in an escrow account to be signed over to Popov or his heirs should they ever escape to the West. Despite years of planning and labor, the tunnel had been in operation for less than one year. Popov had recruited himself and was still in service six years later. During those six years, his most unreasonable demand had been for a collapsible rowboat that he could take on outings with his mistress. The CIA had denied the request on the grounds that he would never be able to explain where he had got it.

For his $100 fee, Popov delivered such items as a list of cryptonyms for 370 Soviet "illegals" who had been infiltrated into the West. The CIA thought for a moment that it would be able to crack the true identities of all 370 when an officer recognized one of the cryptonyms from an earlier case. The cryptonym was composed of the agent's real name spelled backward. Unfortunately, the formula did not hold true for the other 369. Popov was, however, able to reveal the true identities of the agents he was handling, and it was one of these who now threatened his safety and prompted Harvey's exclamation.

Popov had arrived for his regular meeting with Kisvalter carrying a suitcase. Inside was a standard assortment of women's clothing and cosmetics, all of American make. There was a vanity mirror and behind the mirror was $20,000 in assorted Western currencies, operating funds for Popov's newest agent, a "hairdresser" named Tairova, who was to take up residence in New York City as the "wife" of another Soviet illegal. Kisvalter noted that the denominations were too large for a woman who bought her underwear at Macy's. From his pocket, Popov took an American passport, which he said had once belonged to a young woman living in Chicago. She had "lost" it while visiting her native Poland and would not be returning to the United States, he explained ominously. Her picture had been replaced with that of Tairova.

This was the first agent Popov had ever dispatched to the United States, and Kisvalter wished he had never been told about it. The FBI would have to be brought in on this one, and Hoover would probably want to arrest her. The GRU would want to know what had gone wrong, and Popov would inevitably fall under suspicion. Together, Kisvalter and Harvey composed a cable to Washington, tearing up three drafts before arriving at a version that sufficiently conveyed the delicacy of the situation without being insulting. In Washington, John Maury, head of the Soviet Bloc Division, took the cable to Dulles with a plea that the Bureau be kept at arm's length. Dulles was sympathetic but said the FBI had to be informed. "We later got bootlegged copies of the surveillance reports which showed that a dozen FBI agents had followed her from the moment she got off the plane," a CIA officer said.

Special teams of agents brought in from Chicago watched as Tairova stepped off her Air France flight at New York's Idlewild Airport, exchanged her francs for dollars, took a bus to the East Side of Manhattan, hailed a cab to Grand Central Station, and rode a subway to a hotel in the Bronx. The next day, while she was out, agents broke into her room and searched her suitcase, finding, just as Popov had said, the $20,000. The break-in was conducted with great care, but, said Kisvalter, "a trained intelligence agent is going to know when somebody goes through her suitcase no matter how carefully it is done." Tairova knew it, and the FBI agents knew she knew it. Why else would she take the escalator to the third floor of a midtown department store, walk down to the second, and ride the elevator up to the fourth floor? But the surveillance continued. FBI agents sat in a movie theater in Yonkers as she waited for her "husband," and followed the couple to his Manhattan apartment. The apartment was bugged, the phone was tapped, and an observation post was set up across the street. Tairova and her mate abruptly vanished. On the same day, a barber aboard the S.S. *United States* who was to serve as their courier between dead drops in New York and Paris jumped ship in Le Havre.

As predicted, a GRU inspector called on Popov in Berlin. The Tairova woman was claiming she had been blown from the start, the inspector said, and Popov was one of only three persons in a position to have done that. Popov was furious. The least the FBI could have done was arrest Tairova, he fumed to Kisvalter, but the Bureau had let her get away and now there was a witness against him in Moscow. Popov's only recourse was to blame Tairova. She had probably gotten cold feet and was trying to cover her cowardice, he told the inspector. The man from the GRU appeared placated, but not so the KGB. Popov was informed that the KGB had conducted countersurveillance of the entire episode and was able to confirm Tairova's story. Popov prayed that the KGB was bluffing.

He was recalled to Moscow for further questioning. Should he go back and try to brazen it through, or defect to the West? Popov remained confident that he could pull it off. The KGB seemed more upset over the discovery that he kept a mistress than over the Tairova case. "He considered that to be the prime reason for his recall to Moscow," a CIA officer said, "and we, of course, hoped that the girl friend was the real reason he was being recalled."

In Moscow the CIA maintained contact with Popov through Russell Langelle, an intelligence officer serving under diplomatic cover in the American Embassy. Meetings in Moscow were not the convivial affairs they had been in Berlin, where Kisvalter and Popov could sit securely in a safe house and talk for hours over food and drink. In Moscow there were no safe houses, no sanctuaries from KGB surveillance. Between twenty and thirty KGB observations posts ringed the American Embassy. A CIA officer could be certain that KGB footpads would pick him up each time he ventured forth. To remain unobserved, meetings could last only a few seconds, long enough to exchange a message, a roll of film, or a word of encouragement.

Langelle continued to exchange messages with Popov throughout the summer of 1959, but the quality of his intelligence had fallen off—an almost certain sign that he had come under KGB control. The CIA could only hope that Popov's access to vital information was more limited in Moscow than it had been in Berlin, or that Langelle had not been able to develop the same rapport with him as Kisvalter had. That faint hope vanished on the morning of October 16, 1959, when Popov and Langelle were caught in the act of passing notes on a crowded Moscow bus. Langelle was seized by five men, wrestled into a waiting car, and driven to a nearby building, where he was accused of spying against the Soviet Union and threatened with imprisonment or worse if he did not cooperate. After nearly two hours of KGB threats and blandishments, all of which he greeted with stony silence, Langelle was released.

The United States immediately protested the treatment of one of its "diplomats" and denied the Soviet allegation that Langelle was a spy. One week later at a news conference in Washington,

Langelle was asked, "Why do you think they seized you?" "There is no one single answer to that question," he replied artfully. Reporters pressed. "Was it part of your job to collect any kind of intelligence on the Soviet Union?" "None whatsoever," Langelle said.

As for Popov, an article in *Izvestia* described the treachery of a "Lieut. Col. P." and quoted a repentant "P." as saying, "I am ready for any punishment . . . for the supreme penalty. I deserve it." Indeed, said *Izvestia,* "there are crimes after which it is impossible to live. A bullet at the end of a contemptible life is not only a punishment but also an act of mercy."

The CIA was naturally disappointed by the loss of its penetration agent and more than a little upset with the FBI for blowing the case by its heavy-handed surveillance of Tairova in New York. If there was any consolation, it was that a new, bizarre, and even more lucrative source had recently made contact with the CIA.

The first letter, postmarked Zurich, arrived in Bern in March of 1959, addressed to Henry J. Taylor, the United States ambassador in Switzerland, who immediately turned it over to the CIA station chief. Inside, a second envelope addressed to J. Edgar Hoover contained a single-spaced typewritten letter offering to provide valuable information about Communist espionage operations in the West. The letter was in German and signed "Sniper."

"I was asked to examine the letter to see if we could determine what nationality the author was," said Howard Roman, a German-speaking CIA officer. "I could tell by the syntax that this was not a native German. Since the writing was entirely about Poland, we concluded that we were talking to a Pole." For his part, Sniper assumed that he was talking to Hoover, since that was whom he had addressed the letter to. "Hoover was mad as hell when he found out we had been opening his mail," Roman said, "but Hoover agreed to let us handle it as long as we showed the Bureau everything we got from Sniper."

No one knew what to make of Sniper. Was he a mental case, a Communist trick, or the real thing? "We analyzed the typewriter in order to determine whether it was of East European make," Roman said. "We also analyzed the watermarks on the paper. None of this yielded anything that made anybody suspicious." Angleton was certain that Sniper was some sort of Communist provocation agent, but whatever he was, he could not be ignored. Even if Sniper was a provocation, he would surely give up something of value in order to establish his credibility. "It was the old question," Roman said. "How much truth is the enemy willing to tell you in order to set you up for the big deception?"

Following Sniper's instructions, the CIA placed a small notice in the "personals" column of a Frankfurt newspaper, acknowledging receipt of his letter and commencing a correspondence that was to last for nearly two years. "At the beginning, it was rather a long time between drinks," Roman said, but as Sniper grew bolder the frequency of his letters increased. In all, there were fourteen. Through notices in the Frankfurt newspaper, the CIA gave Sniper the number of a post office box in West Berlin where he could send his letters and pick up return mail containing requests for additional information hidden in secret writing beneath the text of otherwise innocuous correspondence. A second letter drop was set up in a public bathroom in Berlin's Tiergarten. Sniper was also given a phone number to call in case of emergency.

Sniper's letters were opened by Harvey's men at the Berlin base, photographed, and forwarded to Washington for analysis and reply. "The letters were very confusing," Roman said. "Everybody analyzed them differently." When an advertisement for a hoola hoop showed up by accident one day in Sniper's post office box, some of the CIA's best minds spent weeks trying to catch his drift. According to Roman, "about four percent of the information in Sniper's letters turned out to be useful." The rest was indecipherable or of marginal interest. He wrote at great length about a notorious black marketeer who smuggled watches to Soviet military officers in Warsaw and undertook occasional spy missions for both the Russians and the Poles. "I remember one letter which Sniper said he had sent us at great personal risk, warning us that this black marketeer was making a trip to Vienna wearing a wig," Roman said. Sniper urged the CIA to take an adjoining room at his hotel, drill a hole through the wall, pump an anesthetizing gas into his room, and spirit the scoundrel away. "That was the kind of stuff that took up a lot of room in his letters," Roman said. "Then suddenly you would get two lines. . . ."

Two lines reporting that the KGB had muscled in on a Polish operation and taken over a spy inside the British Admiralty. "He never got anybody's name straight," Roman related, and this one "came out sounding like a seven-syllable Dutch name." Sniper's phonetic rendering of the spy's name resembled nothing on the Admiralty lists, but he knew that the last name began with the letter *H* and that "H" had originally been recruited while assigned to the office of the British naval attaché in Warsaw. There was only one "H" assigned to the Admiralty who had also served in Warsaw, and that was Harry Houghton, a clerk at the Portland Naval Base. In June of 1960, agents from Scotland Yard watched as Houghton and his girl friend, Ethel Gee, handed a package to a jukebox salesman named Gordon Lonsdale in front of the Old Vic theater on London's Waterloo Road. Scotland Yard staked out four more meetings over the next six months, all of them taking place on the first Saturday of the month. After each meeting, agents trailed Lonsdale to the London suburb of Ruislip, where he called at the home of Peter and Helen Kroger.

Most of Sniper's leads were not so easy to follow. His tip that the Russians had obtained an MI6 document listing British opera- tional assets in Poland proved particularly difficult. The document could be traced to a finite number of offices in London and Europe, but there were no clues to suggest who in those offices might have given it to the KGB. Unwilling to contemplate the possibility of another Philby, MI6 concluded that the KGB had simply broken into one of the offices and pilfered the document.

Then, as the year 1960 came to an end, Sniper suddenly dialed the emergency phone number given him by the CIA. "Are you ready to give me and my wife protection?" he asked. Sniper was coming out—if there was a Sniper. No one had as yet laid eyes on this mysterious source. "He spilled so much and we never met the guy," one officer marveled. Howard Roman and one other officer were dispatched from Washington to greet Sniper when he emerged, but "when Helms sent us off . . . he made it plain he thought this was a bunch of crap." Angleton thought so, too. He sent a cable to Berlin telling the base not to waste too much time waiting for Sniper.

Sniper crossed into West Berlin as advertised—bringing his mistress instead of his wife—and identified himself for the first time as Michal Goleniewski, a high-ranking officer in Polish intelligence who had done double duty as a Soviet agent reporting to the KGB on anything his fellow Poles might try to hide from their Russian mentors. That explained why Sniper had been able to reveal so much about Soviet operations.

Goleniewski had planned his defection well. In the months before his flight from Warsaw, he had stashed hundreds of pages of photographed documents in a hollow tree trunk that he passed each evening on his way home from work. By defecting at the start of the long Christmas holiday, he had given himself and the CIA a few extra days before his absence would be noticed and the alarm sounded—time enough to signal the lone CIA man in Warsaw to empty the hollow tree. "He must have stashed three hundred pages of Minox film in the hollow tree—lists of names, tables of organization," Roman said. "There were several hundred names of Polish agents in the documents."

With Goleniewski safely in hand, Scotland Yard could move in on the Admiralty spy ring without fear of blowing a source. On the first Saturday in January, a detective fell in behind Lonsdale, Houghton, and Gee as they took their monthly walk up Waterloo Road. When Lonsdale politely offered to carry the lady's straw shopping basket, Scotland Yard placed the three under arrest. In the suburb of Ruislip, security agents began a search of the Kroger home, finding a hollow-based cigarette lighter containing a one-time code pad with transmission times and frequencies, a 74-foot radio antenna laced through the rafters, and, beneath a trapdoor in the kitchen floor, a 150-watt high-frequency transmitter. The Krogers were arrested, booked, and fingerprinted. A search of the Yard's Criminal Record Office turned up matching prints belonging to Morris and Lona Cohen of New York City. The FBI had circulated their prints in 1957 after their snapshots had been found among the belongings of Colonel Rudolf Abel, head of a Soviet espionage network in the United States. In fact, the FBI had been looking for the Cohens ever since 1951 as suspected accomplices of the Rosenbergs.

According to his passport, Gordon Lonsdale had been born at Kirkland Lake, Ontario, Canada, on August 17, 1924—a ruse that held up only as long as it took the Royal Canadian Mounted Police to locate the medical records of the real Gordon Lonsdale. The child born in Canada had been circumcised; the man in custody had not. Lonsdale was a native Russian, Conon Molody, who had spent years training to pass himself off as an amiable Canadian.

While the British rolled up the Lonsdale network, Goleniewski and his CIA guardians left Germany for Washington. Twenty hours later, after a refueling stop in the Azores, where Goleniewski tasted the pleasures of capitalism by playing the slot machines at the local officers' club, the plane landed at Andrews Air Force Base on the outskirts of Washington. Goleniewski was driven to a safe house in the Virginia countryside, and his debriefing was begun in earnest.

A team of British interrogators arrived to find out more about how the Russians had obtained that list of MI6 assets in Poland. Goleniewski insisted that the list had not been stolen as MI6 believed but had been given to the Russians by an agent in Berlin. That described a much smaller universe. The number of MI6 men in Berlin at any one time was no more than ten. Their names could be traced through central registry and every reference followed through the paper maze until somewhere amid the trivia and errata of the files a suspicious pattern emerged—like the career of George Blake.

Born in Holland, the son of an Egyptian Jew, Blake was the "odd man out" in the cliquish world of British intelligence. He had earned his entrance into the club not through ancestry and education, like Philby, but by dint of heroic deeds. As a member of the Dutch underground in World War II, Blake had made his way through Occupied France to neutral Portugal and finally to England with a warning that the Germans, in a classic double-cross operation, were controlling almost every team of British agents dropped into Holland. Several years later, as MI6 station chief in Seoul, Blake had been captured by advancing North Korean troops and had suffered stoically for three years in a Communist prison before returning, once more a hero, to London. A closer look revealed some disquieting anomalies. For one thing, Blake's cousin, Henri Curiel, was a founder of the Egyptian Communist Party. For another, Blake had spent time in Moscow on his way back to London at the end of the Korean War. When interviewed by security agents, Blake's secretary recalled that he had occasionally asked her to type an extra copy—for the files, he said.

Over Easter of 1961, Blake was recalled to London for questioning by Ferguson Smith of MI5. Possessing something less than an ironclad case, Smith piled files high on his desk in an effort to intimidate Blake with the weight of the evidence against him. It worked, but just barely. "Blake broke at a time when there was hardly another question left to ask him," one CIA officer said. "If Blake had held out, they would not have had a case."

Once he had broken, Blake bragged freely about his treachery. "The amount of damage he was able to do was almost on a monumental scale," said a CIA officer with intimate knowledge of the case. "This was a guy who had an incredible dedication to getting his hands on whatever he possibly could. Blake was lashing back at British society and British life for injuries, real or imagined. He was determined to wreak maximum vengeance. The Soviets gave him a camera, and he worked to beat hell with the bloody thing," although "he couldn't always make it work," which was probably why he asked his secretary to type an extra copy.

After a brief trial, conducted almost entirely in secret, Blake was sentenced to forty-two years in prison, the longest sentence ever handed down by a British court. The information that Blake had passed on to the Russians "has rendered much of this country's efforts completely useless," the judge said in pronouncing sentence.

Bill Harvey didn't need a British judge to tell him that. In December of 1953 he had sat at a conference table in London and discussed plans for the Berlin tunnel with his British counterparts while Blake kept the official minutes of the meeting. "He knew every detail of what we were doing," said Carl Nelson, the technical mastermind of the tunnel. Nelson could remember arguing with

Blake over whether British or American tape recorders should be purchased. "I couldn't understand why he was giving me such a hard time on the choice of recorders," Nelson recalled. Now he understood. "He didn't want to use the good-quality stuff." Fortunately, at Harvey's insistence, Nelson had never disclosed to Blake or any British officer his technique for picking out the plain-text artifacts from the coded messages.

It was clear that Blake had blown Operation SILVER in Vienna as well as GOLD in Berlin. Despite its problems with Harris tweed and child molestation, the Schwechat tunnel had gone undetected for more than three years until Blake returned from captivity in Korea and was assigned to the unit in charge of the listening operation. Shortly after that assignment, the Russians complained to the Austrian authorities about a fault in the line, and the British quietly removed the tap. In retrospect, the promptness of the Russian complaint following Blake's return to duty was seen as the first sign that something had happened to him in Korea. When Blake reported the existence of a second tunnel in Berlin, the KGB apparently decided to tread a little more lightly and observe a decent interval in order to protect him.

It seemed a reasonable trade-off. The KGB would keep its penetration of MI6 and let the CIA and MI6 sink their money and manpower into processing the reams of trivia that came over the wires. After all, one high-ranking CIA officer observed, "the Soviets knew that the tunnel's chief value was early warning, and they also knew they weren't going to attack." In October of 1956, when the Soviet Army moved in to crush the Hungarian revolution, the tunnel might have provided some advance warning, but by then it had been discovered.

The realization that the Soviets had known about the tunnel carried implications that were distressing in the extreme. What if they had used the tunnel to mount a massive disinformation campaign that gorged the files of the CIA and MI6 with bogus intelligence? That would have strained the capacity of even the KGB, but it certainly seemed possible that on one or two crucial points— the deployment of nuclear weapons, for instance—the Russians could have inserted disinformation into the intelligence stream.

Such counterintelligence analysis was purely academic—art for art's sake. As one expert put it, "In practice, any significant leak such as the compromise of the tunnel became almost impossible to handle for simple reasons of manpower." It was simply not possible to track back over the miles and miles of tape from the tunnel, searching for some piece of Soviet deception. "In the end, you could only speculate anyway," the expert said. "The people who had handled the tunnel never thought twice about the implications of the tunnel's being blown from the start. To think seriously about it is not to invest the effort, since it is totally beyond your capabilities. The only thing to do is to take immediate corrective measures and shove the rest of it under the rug."

The tunnel was not the only conundrum that the unmasking of George Blake posed for Western intelligence. During his confession Blake boasted that he had told his Soviet handlers all about "Dave Murphy's big operation in Berlin." Dave Murphy was head of Soviet operations under Harvey in Berlin, and his big operation had been George Kisvalter's running of Colonel Popov. That cast a decidedly different light on the Popov affair. The FBI's surveillance of Popov's agent Tairova in New York City "was not the cause of Popov's discovery," a CIA officer said. "That was just the end play." The question then became: "At what point was he compromised?" Had Popov, like the tunnel, been blown from the start?

Further analysis of the case revealed that Blake could have betrayed Popov as early as 1955, when the CIA's prize agent was transferred by the GRU from Vienna to East Germany. Popov had left Vienna with instructions to recontact Kisvalter as soon as he got to Berlin. However, after six weeks of home leave in Moscow, Popov was assigned not to Berlin but to a GRU unit stationed elsewhere in East Germany. Stranded in the boondocks, he had devised his own plan for recontacting Kisvalter by passing a letter to a member of a British military mission touring East Germany. The British officer dutifully forwarded the letter to MI6 in Berlin, where it landed in a safe used by George Blake.

Kisvalter refused to believe that Popov had been blown at such an early stage. "Judging from the quality of information we got from Popov long after Blake left Berlin, it couldn't have been Blake who blew Popov," he insisted. But the argument over whether the FBI or Blake had been responsible for Popov's demise obscured a much more fundamental question. Angleton still maintained that Goleniewski was a Soviet provocation agent. If that was the case, then the Soviets had deliberately blown Blake as part of some larger operation. At first blush, Angleton's scenario was almost too callous and byzantine to contemplate. It meant that the Soviets had given up not only Blake but also Lonsdale and his entire network as well. And that was not all. A third Soviet spy, Heinz Felfe of West Germany's Federal Intelligence Agency (BND), had also been captured through leads supplied by Goleniewski.

The CIA had long suspected the existence of a leak somewhere in the BND. As early as 1954 a Soviet defector named Peter Deriabin had warned of two KGB agents, code-named PETER and PAUL, inside the BND, and in 1957 the CIA had performed a security analysis of the BND that identified Felfe, chief of counterintelligence operations against the Soviet Union, as a possible penetration agent. The case against Felfe had been too circumstantial to permit any action, and the suspicion had simply festered for two years until Goleniewski started writing his letters. In one of his earliest letters, Goleniewski warned that the Soviets were passing summaries of West German intelligence reports to the Poles, a tip that heightened the CIA's suspicions about Felfe but again was far too vague to support an outright accusation. One of Goleniewski's final letters, however, provided some very specific information. He reported that he had heard the KGB's chief of counterintelligence boast that of six BND officers who had visited the United States in 1956 at CIA expense, two were Soviet agents. A check of the files quickly produced a list of the six BND officers who had been the CIA's guests in 1956. One of them was Heinz Felfe. That was the break the CIA had been waiting for. Operation DROWZY, as the investigation of Felfe was known, sprang fully awake.

A tap installed on Felfe's phone picked up an unusual number of conversations with Hans Clemens, chief of a BND surveillance team in Bonn. Physical surveillance of Clemens suggested that he might be the communicator for a Soviet spy ring. When his move-

ments were plotted against the schedule of clandestine Soviet broadcasts, the coincidences were striking. Then, one Friday in November
of 1961, Clemens called Felfe to complain that he had been unable
to decipher a message. Felfe told him to send the message to him
in a registered letter. German security agents intercepted the letter
and found a single sheet of paper bearing coded instructions from
Felfe's Soviet case officer. The envelope was resealed and delivered
to Felfe on Monday morning. He had the paper in his pocket later
that day when he was arrested. Felfe thrust the paper into his mouth,
but police wrestled him to the floor and pried it from his jaws
before he could swallow.

Blake, Lonsdale, and Felfe—all had been blown by Goleniewski.
"The best defector the U.S. ever had," one CIA officer called him.
Yet Angleton maintained that Goleniewski was a Soviet provocation, a KGB trick designed to lead the CIA into some devilish
trap. What could possibly be worth the loss of three such well-
placed spies? "It's hard for me to answer that without knowing
the value of what they were trying to protect," a counterintelligence
officer responded.

The temptation was to dismiss Angleton's thesis, but a subsequent analysis concluded that Goleniewski had unwittingly allowed
himself to be used by the Russians as a conduit for passing selected
intelligence to the West. "The key to the Goleniewski case," a counterintelligence officer explained, "is that the Soviets became aware
that somebody was writing these letters. There was a feedback in
Goleniewski's later letters of things he'd learned from the Soviets
which reflected things he'd already told us. . . . . The Soviets began
inserting corrections into his previous information." The early letter
warning that the Soviets were receiving copies of West German
intelligence reports was a lead that heightened the CIA's existing
suspicions of Felfe but was too vague to be of any investigative
use. The later letter providing the tip that two Soviet agents had
been among a group of six BND officers visiting the United States
was a lead that "was so specific and such a sock that it was suspect."
An analysis done by Howard Roman of Goleniewski's fourteen
letters pointed out that their general content had at first concerned
Polish cases but that the focus had gradually shifted to intelligence

picked up from the Soviets. "He had been dropped as an agent by the Soviets and this was one thing that was eating at him when he turned to us," a counterintelligence officer said of Goleniewski. "He was out of favor, but in fairly short order after he began writing to us, they picked him up again, and the content turned around to things the Soviets were telling him, particularly about the British."

Viewed from that perspective, Angleton's conviction that, witting or unwitting, Goleniewski was a Soviet provocation agent appeared much more plausible than it had at first. Not all the information Goleniewski included in his letters was necessarily fed to him by the KGB for CIA consumption. Some of his most important leads might well have reflected information he learned before he came under Soviet control. Only the Felfe lead looked like a deliberate plant, and the loss of Felfe had by no means been an unmitigated disaster for the KGB. The Felfe case touched off such a scandal in Germany that serious consideration was given to dissolution of the BND, and all that the KGB gave up was a spy who had already fallen under deep suspicion through the defector Deriabin's warning about PETER and PAUL and the CIA's security analysis of the BND. There were elements of the case that suggested that once Goleniewski had delivered the Felfe lead, the KGB decided the game was no longer worth all the damage he was doing on his own. In what looked like a deliberate attempt to get him out of its hair, the KGB ordered his travel restricted and enlisted his aid in searching for a penetration agent who he knew could only be himself. Terrified that the KGB was on to him, Goleniewski fled.

This analysis of the case could not be proved, but one thing was certain. Goleniewski, with or without the knowledge of the KGB, had planted a germ within the body of the CIA that would become a debilitating disease, all but paralyzing the Agency's clandestine operations against the Soviet Union. The germ was the suspicion that the CIA itself had been penetrated by the KGB, that a Soviet mole had burrowed to the Agency's core. "Goleniewski was the first and primary source on a mole," a CIA officer said. According to Roman, "Goleniewski claimed that the Russians talked as though they had penetrated the CIA." Goleniewski was also convinced that the Russians had found out about him through a leak from the CIA and that he had barely escaped with his life.

It was possible that his fears were exaggerated. It was also possible that the Russians had found out about him through some other source, perhaps through a penetration of British intelligence, which had worked closely with the CIA on the Goleniewski case. But there was one fact that made the conclusion that the KGB had penetrated the CIA all but inescapable. "A letter Goleniewski wrote us when he was still in Warsaw provided specific evidence that the Soviets knew of our intention to take a specific operational step," a CIA officer said. "For it to get into Goleniewski's letter, the Russians had to have told him about it within two weeks of its formulation in Washington." The operation, a CIA plan to recruit a Polish intelligence officer in Switzerland, "could scarcely have been more tightly held." How else could the Russians have known of it—unless they had penetrated the CIA?

The Agency had barely begun to digest the Goleniewski case when in December of 1961 a KGB officer named Klimov appeared without warning at the home of the CIA station chief in Helsinki, handed over a batch of documents, and announced that he wanted to defect.

Klimov's name had been Anatoli Golitsin when he had first come to the CIA's attention in 1954 as a young counterintelligence officer assigned to Vienna. One of his colleagues, Peter Deriabin, had defected and during his interrogation had listed the KGB officers most susceptible to recruitment by the CIA. Golitsin was second on Deriabin's list. Golitsin's wife had a loose reputation, Deriabin said, and that could be used to get under his skin. Golitsin was also vulnerable because he had an overblown notion of his expertise and was unpopular with his fellow officers, Deriabin told his interrogators.

Before the CIA could prepare a recruitment pitch for Golitsin, he was recalled to Moscow for a headquarters assignment in the Anglo-American department of the First Chief Directorate, the branch that conducted espionage operations against targets in the United States and Britain. Later he spent some months in a headquarters unit that processed reports from the KGB's spies inside

NATO. It was during this period, Golitsin later said, that he became fed up with the Soviet system and decided to offer his services to the other side. With that aim in mind, he began searching the intelligence reports for clues to the identities of the KGB's sources and memorizing the contents of documents pilfered from NATO files.

Golitsin's chance came in 1961, when he was given his new identity as Klimov and dispatched with his wife and child to the KGB station in Helsinki. The CIA did not draw the connection between the Golitsin of Vienna and the Klimov of Helsinki and again made no attempt to recruit him. Golitsin finally took matters into his own hands and defected. "It was quite a shock," a CIA officer said.

The CIA appeared to have been handed a major triumph in the espionage wars. Almost in spite of itself the Agency had latched onto a source who claimed to be capable of exposing Soviet spies throughout the Western world. There was the usual danger that Golitsin might be a KGB disinformation agent and not a bona fide defector, but his handlers quickly satisfied themselves on that score. "The amount of information we got from Golitsin in the first forty-eight hours of his interrogation established in most people's minds that he was for real," a CIA officer said. "We knew quite a bit about the Soviet Embassy in Helsinki, and we were able to check his information against what we already knew."

The biggest problem with Golitsin was not his bona fides but his behavior. Defectors are a notoriously difficult lot to handle, and Golitsin was no exception. "There is no such thing as a normal defector," a chief of the CIA's Soviet Bloc Division said. "He defects for a series of reasons usually having to do with serious psychological problems. There is something wrong with him in the first instance. The fact is that the guy is sick and temperamental. The Canadian government has spent something like seven million dollars trying to settle Gouzenko down. He's a drunk who would go out and spend hundreds of thousands of dollars. But he is also a showcase character who fled from terror, and the Canadians don't want the negative side to get out. He's been one of the biggest thorns in the side of the Canadian government they've ever had, but on the other hand, his information was great." The United States experienced similar though less costly problems with Goleniewski. According to Howard Roman, "Goleniewski got into quite a psychological tizzy during his interrogations. He used to play Victrola records of old European songs at top volume and drink booze." Goleniewski would later insist that he was the last of the Romanovs and that Henry Kissinger was a Soviet agent.

As for Golitsin, he was "diagnosed by a psychiatrist and separately by a clinical psychologist as a paranoid," said John Hart, a CIA officer who conducted an extensive review of the Agency's handling of defectors. Peer de Silva, the onetime chief of operations for the Soviet Bloc Division, called Golitsin "a total son of a bitch." An aide to Angleton put it more delicately: "Golitsin was a very difficult individual to accommodate." Another counterintelligence officer said that "at first SB [Soviet Bloc Division] handled him, but he just refused to cooperate with a whole series of SB case officers who he insisted were idiots. He demanded access to the highest levels of the U.S. government." John Hart said that Golitsin "basically insisted that he wanted to deal only with the President of the United States."

Finally, Golitsin was handed over to Angleton, commencing one of the most extraordinary relationships in the history of the secret war between the CIA and the KGB. In Golitsin, Angleton found a defector whose dire warnings of Soviet machinations conformed to his own vision of fiendishly subtle KGB plots. According to Hart, Golitsin's warnings "centered around the idea that the KGB had vast resources which it was using to deceive not only the U.S. government but other Western governments. This plot was masterminded by something called the KGB Disinformation Directorate, and this KGB Disinformation Directorate was able to deceive the West . . . because of the fact that it had penetrations at high levels, both within the intelligence services of these countries, including our own, but also in high places in the governments of the various countries." Coming so soon after the Goleniewski case and the arrests of Blake, Lonsdale, and Felfe, Golitsin's message was a compelling one, particularly for Angleton.

"Golitsin became the swami as far as Jim was concerned," de Silva said. "Angleton made a career out of Golitsin," a chief of the Soviet Bloc Division added. "He built his whole position on Golitsin." Assigned the cryptonym AE/LADLE, Golitsin became what one officer called "the prime interpreter of counterintelligence." Angleton arranged for Golitsin to meet with the President's brother, Attorney General Robert F. Kennedy. "An Attorney General who does not know the minutiae of the threat is a very poor Attorney General," Angleton said. Although Kennedy turned down Golitsin's audacious request for $30 million with which to conduct operations against the Soviet Union, the defector had finally gained the access he craved. When Golitsin warned that a KGB network with the code name SAPPHIRE was operating inside French intelligence and that even the French cabinet had been penetrated, the information was relayed to Paris in the form of a personal letter from President Kennedy to Charles de Gaulle.

Golitsin told of penetrations everywhere—in the United States, England, France, Germany, Austria, Canada, Australia, and on and on. Alerted to this new source, security officers from friendly intelligence services all over the world flocked to Washington to question Golitsin. He told the Canadians about a homosexual ambassador to the Soviet Union who had been blackmailed into working for the KGB, and he also warned the British about a "ring of five" Soviet agents.

Burgess and Maclean undoubtedly were two members of the "ring of five," and Philby was the leading candidate for the third. With all the circumstantial evidence against him, Philby must have been laboring under a tremendous psychological burden, particularly after George Blake was sentenced to forty-two years for spying. When Nicholas Elliott, the MI6 station chief in Beirut, confronted him anew with the evidence against him, Philby finally broke and gave what one officer described as "a very limited confession." Elliott flew to London for consultation about the next move, leaving Philby a free man in Beirut. On January 23, 1963, nearly twelve years after Harvey had first pointed an accusing finger, Philby fled to the Soviet Union. A year later, Sir Anthony Blunt, curator of the royal art collection, confessed to having spied for the Soviets during the war and to having helped Burgess and Maclean escape in 1951. Blunt did not have to follow Philby into exile. He was granted immunity in return for his confession. Meanwhile, security officers intensified their search for a fifth man, concentrating on several members of MI5 who had known Burgess. The deeper they dug, said one British investigator, the more Golitsin's "ring of five" looked like a "ring of twenty-five."

Angleton's search for Soviet spies in the CIA's ranks was not meeting with such spectacular results. According to Golitsin, the KGB had a source named SASHA who had penetrated the Agency's German-based operations. "Right in the middle of the SB [Soviet bloc] Division there was a staff officer named Sasha," a onetime head of the division recalled. Not only did the name match, but the description fit as well. In the early 1950s, the CIA's Sasha had been stationed in Germany running operations against the Soviet Union with Russian émigrés. "At first everyone became frantic," the division chief said, "but then cooler heads prevailed and said, 'Forget it, no one's going to name an agent by his true name.' " Besides, Golitsin had a better lead to source SASHA's true identity. He could not recall his name precisely, but he was certain that it began with the letter "K." An investigation of CIA officers whose names began with "K" and who had served in Germany failed to uncover any Soviet agents, although it did result in the resignation of one officer for mishandling of Agency funds.

Even as Angleton pressed the hunt for SASHA, Golitsin raised the specter of another, more deadly penetration of the Agency. He told of a trip made to the United States in 1957 by V. M. Kovshuk, head of the American Embassy section in the KGB's Second Chief Directorate. Kovshuk was too senior an officer to be dispatched to the United States unless it was a mission of the greatest import, Golitsin said. He suggested that Kovshuk had come to meet with a high-level mole, someone who had been recruited while serving in Moscow and who was now assigned to CIA headquarters in a sensitive position.

Golitsin warned Angleton that the Soviets would attempt to prevent the CIA from discovering the true purpose of Kovshuk's mission by sending disinformation agents to deflect the investigation. Golitsin's warning was quite specific. He predicted that the Soviets would send false defectors from both the KGB and the GRU. Within a few months of Golitsin's defection, as if he had known of their plans, one KGB officer and one GRU officer, both ostensibly members of the Soviet delegation to the United Nations, contacted the FBI and volunteered their services as spies against their country. The two agents were christened SCOTCH and BOURBON. The FBI was ecstatic over its sudden success. Angleton waited for the plot to unfold.

In June of 1962 a third Soviet agent, Yuri Nosenko, a KGB officer with the Soviet delegation to disarmament talks in Geneva, contacted the CIA and offered to sell information for 900 Swiss francs. Nosenko said he needed the money to replace KGB funds he had squandered on a drinking spree. Pete Bagley, a CIA case officer stationed in Bern, rushed to Geneva to handle the Agency's latest "walk-in," and a second officer, George Kisvalter, flew in from Washington to serve as interpreter.

Nosenko "took about an hour and a half before each meeting in order to be sure that he was not being tailed," according to John Hart, who later examined the case in detail. "This countersurveillance measure consisted of visiting a number of bars, in each of which he had a drink. He had one scotch and soda in each of four or five bars." When Nosenko arrived at the CIA safe house for his meeting with Bagley and Kisvalter, "he was then offered further liquor, and he continued to drink throughout the interrogation," Hart said. "I must tell you honestly that at all these meetings I was snookered," Nosenko later confided to Hart.

Kisvalter, who had been born in the former tsarist capital, St. Petersburg, conducted the interrogation. Nosenko said that he had joined the KGB in 1953 as a member of the Second Chief Directorate, which was responsible for the surveillance and recruitment of foreigners in Moscow. He had risen steadily within the directorate until in 1962 he was named deputy chief of the Seventh Department, in charge of operations against American tourists. Among other things, Nosenko revealed that the walls of the American Embassy in Moscow were honeycombed with electronic listening devices and that the KGB had recruited a homosexual employee of the British Admiralty.

On June 11 Bagley cabled headquarters: "Subject has conclusively proved his bona fides. He has provided info of importance and sensitivity. Willing to meet when abroad and will meet as often and as long as possible [until] his departure [from] Geneva on 15 June." At his final meeting with Bagley and Kisvalter, Nosenko warned them not to make any effort to recontact him in Moscow. Given his firsthand knowledge of KGB surveillance operations there, that seemed like a reasonable precaution. After providing Nosenko with a phone number and a password he could use whenever he wanted to get in touch, Bagley rushed to Washington, still flushed with the prospect of a major penetration of the KGB. "We had a big meeting here on Saturday, and Bagley thought he had the biggest fish of his life," Angleton said. "I mean he really did. And everything I heard from him, however, was in direct contrast from what we had heard from Golitsin."

Golitsin had suggested that V. M. Kovshuk, head of the KGB's American Embassy section, had come to the United States in 1957 to meet with a high-level Soviet penetration agent. Nosenko said the purpose of Kovshuk's trip was to contact an agent named ANDREY, an American serviceman who had been recruited by the KGB while serving in Moscow. ANDREY hardly sounded like a high-level penetration of the CIA. Remembering Golitsin's prediction that the KGB would send false agents to undermine his information, Angleton assumed that ANDREY was a straw man set up by Nosenko to lead the CIA away from the true purpose of Kovshuk's mission.

Nosenko, code-named AE/FOXTROT, had an all-too-reassuring answer to one other mystery: the blowing of Popov. At first the CIA had assumed that the FBI's heavy-handed surveillance of Popov's agent Tairova had been the cause of his undoing. But George Blake, the KGB's man inside MI6, claimed he had known about Popov long before the Tairova incident. Then Golitsin had raised the specter of a well-placed KGB source inside the CIA capable of blowing Popov or any other agent. Now Nosenko was maintaining that the KGB had found out about Popov through its routine surveillance of American personnel in Moscow. As Nosenko told it, the KGB had followed an American diplomat to a dead drop and then staked it out until the unfortunate Popov came along to empty it.

Nosenko's story fit nicely with a message Popov had passed to his CIA contact, Russell Langelle, at their final meeting. Popov had thrust upon Langelle six pages of notes scribbled on toilet paper, warning that his work for the CIA had been detected by KGB surveillance and that he was at that very moment under KGB control. Given the circumstances, the CIA had discounted Popov's note as a piece of disinformation fabricated by the KGB to disguise its real source. Besides, the diplomat was certain he had not been followed. Nosenko, however, provided new credibility for Popov's message. He even had an explanation for why the diplomat was so certain he had not been trailed. The KGB had applied a chemical substance to the diplomat's shoes that left an invisible trail that was easily followed at a distance, Nosenko explained. The chemical, which gave off a scent that could be detected only by a dog, had been applied to the diplomat's shoes by the Russian maid who cleaned his apartment.

If what Nosenko said was true, neither Kovshuk's mission nor Popov's capture had anything to do with Soviet penetration agents. Angleton didn't believe it—and neither did Bagley, once he was, as one officer said, "taken in hand by Angleton, who made all of the Golitsin material available to him." Exposed to Golitsin's information for the first time, Bagley began to see Nosenko in a different light. "Alone, Nosenko looked good," he recalled. "Seen alongside [Golitsin] . . . Nosenko looked very odd indeed. . . . Nosenko's information tended to negate or deflect leads by [Golitsin]." After a weekend spent poring over the files in Angleton's office, Bagley flew to New York for a meeting with Golitsin himself. In the name of security Bagley disguised Nosenko's identity by telling Golitsin that new information had come to the CIA through the mails. Golitsin laughed at Bagley's ruse and said the CIA was obviously in touch with a live source sent by the Russians to counteract him. By the time he returned to Switzerland, Bagley was convinced that Nosenko was a provocation, part of a desperate Soviet attempt to sidetrack the hunt for the mole.

Undeniably, something was wrong. The Popov and Goleniewski operations, the CIA's two best penetrations of Soviet intelligence, had been terminated within a year of each other. The Goleniewski case, in particular the leak to the KGB of the CIA's planned recruitment of the Polish intelligence officer in Switzerland, argued convincingly for the existence of a mole, a fear that Golitsin confirmed. Within six months of Golitsin's defection three Soviet intelligence officers—SCOTCH and BOURBON in New York and Nosenko in Geneva—had volunteered to serve as agents in place. Another "walk-in," Colonel Oleg Penkovsky of the GRU, was busy handing over 10,000 pages of highly classified documents on Soviet missiles. Suddenly, in the spring of 1962, the CIA was awash with penetrations of Soviet intelligence—more at one time than during its entire history. It strained credulity to think that all of these volunteers were genuine, particularly if the CIA was as deeply penetrated as the Goleniewski case indicated and as Golitsin said. The mole inside the CIA would have warned Moscow Center about these traitors and they would have been silenced as swiftly as possible—that is, if they were genuine. If they had been dispatched by the KGB in the first place, there would be no need to silence them.

Of the four—SCOTCH, BOURBON, Nosenko, and Penkovsky—only Penkovsky was silenced. He had had his first meeting with Western intelligence on the night of April 20, 1961, at the Mount Royal Hotel in London. He had been trying desperately to make contact for some time, stopping American and Canadian tourists on the streets of Moscow and asking them to relay a message, but his bold overtures had only aroused suspicions of a Soviet provocation. Finally, in the course of his official duties, Penkovsky met a British businessman named Greville Wynne, who specialized in arranging the exchange of trade delegations between East and West. As a GRU officer, Penkovsky had no interest in trade. His job was to insert as many intelligence operatives as possible into the Soviet delegations and supervise their work during their visits to the West. Penkovsky confided in Wynne, saying he must talk to people in the West "to tell them what conditions in the Soviet Union are really like." Wynne agreed to carry a letter to British intelligence, and when Penkovsky arrived in London at the head of a Soviet trade delegation, representatives of MI6 and the CIA, including the ubiquitous George Kisvalter, were waiting to greet him.

Outfitted with a Minox miniature camera and a transistor radio receiver, Penkovsky returned to Moscow to begin his work for the West. In May, Wynne flew to Moscow to resume his trade talks with the Soviet government. As his official host, Penkovsky met Wynne at Sheremetyevo Airport and during the drive into the city handed him twenty rolls of exposed film. That evening Penkovsky visited Wynne in his room at the Metropol Hotel and was given a packet of thirty fresh rolls of film. During the summer, Penkovsky paid another official visit to London and for nearly a month met regularly with Kisvalter and his MI6 counterparts. During this second stay in London, he was introduced to Janet Chisholm, the wife of an attaché at the British Embassy in Moscow and mother of three children, who would serve as his secret contact with the West in the coming months. Back in Moscow, Penkovsky happened upon the Chisholm children one day as they played in a sandbox along one of the city's broad, tree-lined boulevards. While Mrs. Chisholm watched from a nearby bench, a smiling Penkovsky gave the children a box of candy drops and walked on. Inside the box were four rolls of exposed film.

Penkovsky worked at a feverish pace, meeting openly with American and British officials at diplomatic functions in Moscow and secretly with Kisvalter during a Soviet trade visit to Paris. He would pass on photographs of top-secret documents in his brush encounters with Mrs. Chisholm or simply deposit them in a variety of dead drops scattered about Moscow. The West would acknowledge receipt of the film with a short radio transmission that Penkovsky could pick up on the receiver he had been given earlier in London.

On January 5, 1962, the first shadow crossed his path. During another hurried rendezvous with Mrs. Chisholm, Penkovsky spotted a car following him the wrong way down a one-way street. In April his Soviet superiors told him that a scheduled trip to the United States would have to be postponed. The surveillance became heavier and heavier until on July 5 at a meeting with Wynne in Moscow's Peking Restaurant the two men were literally surrounded by KGB agents. The end came on November 2. The phone rang in the Moscow apartment of Alexis Davison, an Air Force doctor assigned to the American Embassy. When Davison answered, the caller hung up. A short time later, the phone rang in the apartment of Hugh Montgomery, a CIA officer under diplomatic cover in the embassy. When Montgomery answered, the caller hung up. That was Penkovsky's signal that the dead drop on Pushkin Street, a matchbox taped behind a radiator in the entrance to an apartment building, was ready to be emptied. Davison confirmed the signal by checking a certain lamppost on Kutuzov Prospect. The black mark was there. Richard Jacobs, another CIA officer serving under diplomatic cover, headed for the radiator on Pushkin Street—and straight into a KGB trap. Eight British diplomats and five American officials were expelled from the Soviet Union. Wynne was apprehended by Soviet authorities in Budapest, flown to Moscow, and locked in Lubyanka prison. Penkovsky was shot.

Murder Corrupts

The counterintelligence maelstrom stirred by the fear of a Soviet mole had barely begun to swirl within the CIA when a crisis of major proportions struck from without. On April 17, 1961, just three days before George Kisvalter was to meet for the first time with Oleg Penkovsky, the Agency suffered the greatest debacle in its history with the abortive landing at Cuba's Bay of Pigs. Even as Kisvalter was sitting down with Penkovsky in a London hotel room, an enraged John F. Kennedy was ordering both a full-scale shake-up of the CIA and a renewed effort to overthrow Fidel Castro.

"There can be no long-term living with Castro as a neighbor," a secret eyes-only memo signed by the President's brother Robert warned. "If you can't stand up to Castro," Kennedy had said during his presidential campaign, "how can you be expected to stand up to Khrushchev?" His rhetoric took on a grim reality during two days of face-to-face meetings with Khrushchev in Vienna. "He just beat the hell out of me," a dazed Kennedy was quoted as saying afterward. "I think he did it because of the Bay of Pigs. I think he thought that anyone who was so young and inexperienced as

117

to get into that mess could be taken, and anyone who got into it and didn't see it through had no guts. . . . Until we remove those ideas, we won't get anywhere with him. So we have to act."

Kennedy began by getting rid of Allen Dulles. "Dulles is a legendary figure, and it's hard to operate with legendary figures," the President said. "I must have someone there with whom I can be in complete and intimate contact—someone from whom I will be getting the exact pitch. I made a mistake in putting Bobby in the Justice Department. . . . Bobby should be in CIA."

It was too early in his administration to be shuffling his cabinet, so the President brought in the hard-driving John McCone, a strait-laced, right-wing California businessman, to head the CIA. McCone moved at once to replace the collegial "old boy" atmosphere of the Dulles era with a strict, managerial regime. One of his first acts was to rip out an intercom system that had allowed senior officers to interrupt the Director at his desk with urgent matters. "Jolly John," as the crusty McCone was quickly dubbed, also had the door that connected his office directly with the Deputy Director's sealed off, ordering that the job be done overnight so that Marshall Carter would find a blank wall when he reported for duty the next morning. Realizing what had happened, Carter placed a fake hand on his newly paneled wall, as if it had been lopped off when the door slammed shut for the last time.

With similar decisiveness, McCone moved to wall off the lingering effects of the Bay of Pigs. Dulles's Deputy Director, Charles Cabell, had already been removed, the Deputy Director for Operations, Richard Bissell, seemed certain to follow, and the survivors were jockeying for position in the new order of things. Lyman Kirkpatrick, the Agency's Inspector General, saw a chance to rehabilitate a career that had been cruelly stunted. In 1952, at the age of thirty-five, Kirkpatrick had been slated for the number-two job in the Operations Directorate. Helms, Angleton, Harvey—they all would be working for him. But Kirkpatrick had been stricken by polio. For eight months he had lain in a hospital bed and watched helplessly as his job went to Helms. When finally able to return to work, Kirkpatrick was confined to a wheelchair, with only partial use of his right arm. To add to his torment, he was shunted aside to the Inspector General's office, a post divorced from operations and forever off the upward path. "The IG staff wasn't the way to go to fame and glory," one officer said. "It was where you put somebody who had blotted his copybook somewhere along the way."

Having suffered this fate through no fault of his own, Kirkpatrick was left with what one colleague called "a streak of bitterness, an attitude of vindictiveness toward the whole Clandestine Service operation as it evolved." By 1961 the Clandestine Service operation had evolved to the Bay of Pigs, and it fell to Kirkpatrick as Inspector General to determine what had gone wrong. By his own account, he produced "a very severe report," concluding that "the operation had been very badly handled in almost every respect." The report was immediately perceived by his detractors, who were legion, as "a hatchet job . . . reflecting his continuing ambition." It "was designed to be damaging to Richard Bissell and to be damaging to Allen Dulles," one officer directly affected said. The report's unstated premise seemed to be that things would not have gone so badly had Kirkpatrick been in charge. McGeorge Bundy, the President's national security adviser, who was so dispirited by the Bay of Pigs that he had offered to resign, took one look at the report and said, "Well, that casts quite a different light on things." But when Kirkpatrick tried to use the report to curry favor with McCone, it blew up in his face.

Angleton, who monitored the entire affair closely, described what happened. Kirkpatrick "either went to National [Airport] or he sent somebody" to give the report to McCone before he boarded a plane for Los Angeles, where he was still winding up his business affairs prior to assuming the directorship. McCone "read it on the way back to California, and when he got off the plane he obviously began to see that something was up." The Inspector General was attempting, in Angleton's words, to "double-cross his Director, carrying on a feud with the clandestine side." From California, Angleton continued, McCone "called Kirkpatrick and asked whether he had given a copy to Dulles. When the answer came 'No,' he became quite rude and ordered him to give a copy to Dulles since he was still the Director." A chastened Kirkpatrick admitted that "I probably handled it the wrong way." When McCone officially succeeded

Dulles, he ordered all copies of Kirkpatrick's report destroyed and kept the original locked in his private files.

Even so decisive an executive as McCone could not easily rid himself of the enduring legacy of the Bay of Pigs. A secret postmortem said that the invasion had been approved because "it offered what appeared to be a last chance to overthrow Castro by Cubans before the weapons and technicians acquired from the Communists and the repressive internal measures would make the task too hard without overt U.S. intervention." That "last chance" had been missed, but failure only intensified the President's determination to rid himself of Castro, despite the fact that the Bay of Pigs had crippled what small capability the CIA had for conducting covert operations inside Cuba.

The Agency had never been very successful at establishing a network of agents on the island. It was the inability to establish a working underground that had prompted the decision to attempt the Bay of Pigs invasion. "We never got to first base in Cuba in building an underground organization," Richard Bissell said. Supplies were parachuted in, but out of a half-dozen drops "we only had one where we were reasonably sure that the people the supplies were intended for actually got them." Agents were slipped in by boat under cover of darkness, but their survival rate was "appallingly small." Any agents who did survive were wiped out in the mass arrests and executions—Castro's "war on traitors"—that followed the Bay of Pigs.

The President was not interested in the CIA's problems. He wanted results. "The White House is always under enormous political priorities which completely obscure the long-range purposes of an intelligence service," one CIA officer grumbled. "They don't want to hear about how difficult spying is or how long it takes. They all want it done yesterday. As a result, you expend decades of assets for short-term gains." Bill Harvey, recently returned from the front lines in Berlin, was to become one of those expended assets.

Smarting from a tongue-lashing by the two Kennedy brothers for "sitting on his ass and not doing anything about getting rid of Castro," Bissell turned in November of 1961 to Harvey and the "application of ZR/RIFLE program to Cuba." Harvey had been working on the concept for ZR/RIFLE for several months in deepest secrecy under cover of his official title as head of Staff D, a small Agency component responsible for communications intercepts. D was the perfect cranny in which to tuck a particularly nasty piece of business like ZR/RIFLE, and Harvey was just the man to make sure that no one came poking around. At one time, all of the CIA's covert staffs had been designated simply by letters. Staff A was Foreign Intelligence, B was Operations, and C was Counterintelligence. The other staffs, even Angleton's Counterintelligence, gradually acquired more descriptive titles, but D retained its anonymity behind a door barred twenty-four hours a day by a Marine guard. There were three combination safes along the wall in Harvey's office, but that was not secure enough for him, so he brought in a one-ton safe of his own. At the outset of the Kennedy administration, Bissell assigned Harvey the task of creating a new capability for the Agency. "The White House had twice urged me to create such a capability," Harvey's notes quoted Bissell as saying. Bissell called it "executive action." Harvey called it "the magic button" and the "last resort beyond last resort and a confession of weakness." He made a note to himself never to call "executive action" by its true name. "Never mention word 'assassination,'" Harvey scribbled.

The CIA had tried once before to kill Castro—at the time of the Bay of Pigs invasion—but the attempt had disintegrated into what one of the plotters called "a Keystone Comedy Act." Colonel Sheffield Edwards, head of the Agency's Office of Security, had enlisted Robert Maheu, a former FBI agent turned private detective, to recruit members of the underworld for the job. Maheu turned to Johnny Rosselli, a former member of the Capone gang who had done time for a Hollywood shakedown scheme, and Rosselli contacted Sam Giancana and Santos Trafficante, two Mafia "dons" who had been singled out by the Attorney General as targets in his war on organized crime. Maheu soon suspected, however, that Giancana had bragged about the plot to his girl friend, singer Phyllis McGuire, who in turn might have gossiped to another boyfriend, comedian Dan Rowan. At that rate of exposure, the assassination plot would soon become a major motion picture. Maheu dispatched a private investigator to Las Vegas to install a wiretap on the phone in Rowan's hotel room, but he was discovered by a maid and had to be bailed out of jail by Rosselli. Meanwhile, the CIA's Technical Services Division was experiencing some difficulties in concocting the right weapon to be used against Castro. The first batch of poison capsules refused to dissolve in water.

The farce would have been laughable had not the plotters left a trail leading directly into the Oval Office and even the President's bedroom. Kennedy had actually met personally and publicly with one of the plotters, a Cuban exile leader named Tony Varona. The President's only purpose had been to assure Varona and several other leaders of the exile community that every effort would be made to rescue their comrades left stranded at the Bay of Pigs. But the mere fact that he had met with Varona would forever rob the administration of any moral authority should the plot become known. At the same time, Kennedy was carrying on an affair with a woman named Judith Campbell, who counted among her other beaus both John Rosselli and Sam Giancana. Not only was the liaison less than presidential in image, but it would also create the appearance that Judith Campbell was being used as a courier to shuttle information between the White House and the Mafia on the progress of the assassination plot.

The much more stringent requirements laid down for Harvey's "executive action" program were designed to avoid all such complications. "Maximum security" and "nonattributability" were the primary guidelines specified in the executive-action file. "KUBARK only," the file commanded, employing the cryptonym used internally to identify the CIA. There could be "no approach to other Govt. agencies" for assistance. Inside KUBARK, everything must be done by "word of mouth," "strictly person-to-person, singleton ops," "no projects on paper." Executive action would "require most professional, proven operationally competent, ruthless, stable, CE [counterespionage]-experienced ops officers." There were "few available," but Harvey was one of them. His first step would be the "search"—find and recruit the assassin—"Pretext: KUTUBE/D search." KUTUBE/D, the Agency's cryptonym for Staff D, was already conducting a search for agents who could be recruited to steal the code books of other nations. That would be used as the cover for the search for a killer. The KUTUBE/D search had been given the code name RIFLE, which, now that it served the ends of "executive action," was an entirely appropriate description of what was involved.

It would not be easy to find the right man. "No chain of connections permitting blackmail," the executive-action file directed. Extreme caution would be exercised so that no assassin could be traced back to the United States government. "No American citizen or residents or people who ever obtained U.S. visas" could serve as assassins. "Corsicans recommended," but not Sicilians. "Sicilians could lead to Mafia." It was imperative to "exclude organization criminals, those with records of arrests." As an added precaution, "planning should include provisions for blaming Sovs or Czechs in case of blow. Should have phony 201 in RG to backstop this, all documents therein forged and backdated." The 201—the basic personnel folder kept in Central Registry ("RG") on anyone, friend or foe, of interest to the Agency—would be "forged and backdated" so that the file of an agent recruited for murder would look like that of an enemy assassin in the hire of the "Sovs or Czechs." To further support the fiction that the CIA's assassin was an enemy agent, the 201 "should look like a CE [counterespionage] file." Harvey made a note to himself to talk with "Jim A."

To conduct the search, Harvey already had the perfect asset. "QJ/WIN is under written contract as a principal agent, with the primary task of spotting agent candidates." WIN, a European of a more than checkered past, had begun his government career in the late 1950s as an informant for the Bureau of Narcotics. "Files of this Bureau reflect an excellent performance by QJ/WIN," the CIA noted. He was, one of his CIA handlers said, a man capable of anything. "If you needed somebody to carry out murder," Richard Helms said, "I guess you had a man who might be prepared to carry it out." All for an annual salary of $7,200. According to a CIA memo, "QJ/WIN was recruited in Frankfurt 1 November 1960 to undertake a one-shot mission to the Belgian Congo," a mission that "potentially involved great risk." The memo was characteristically vague about what exactly the mission had been, although the author must have chuckled over his reference to "one-shot," since other documents left no doubt that WIN had been dispatched to arrange "the assassination of Patrice Lumumba."

The initial plan had been to inject a deadly virus into Lumumba's food or toothpaste. A syringe, a surgical mask, and rubber gloves were sent to the Congo through the diplomatic pouch, and an Agency scientist flew in with the virus in a vial. But the scheme foundered for lack of access to Lumumba's entourage. By the time WIN arrived on the scene, Lumumba had been ousted from his post in the Congolese government and was in the protective custody of United Nations guards. WIN was instructed to lure Lumumba out of UN custody so that he could be turned over to his Congolese rivals, who would surely do him in. WIN's control officer had serious moral qualms about poisoning Lumumba but had no objections to arranging his execution. "Murder corrupts," he said, but "I am not opposed to capital punishment." Lumumba died exactly as the CIA had planned, but the Agency for all its scheming, was not responsible. Lumumba evaded the UN guards by his own devices and was captured by his Congolese enemies, who, according to one version, ran him through with a bayonet.

The Agency had not had such good luck with Castro, and Bissell hoped Harvey could change that with ZR/RIFLE. On the day after he and Bissell discussed "the application of ZR/RIFLE program to Cuba," Harvey would have been somewhat bemused to hear President Kennedy tell an audience in Seattle, Washington, that "we cannot, as a free nation, compete with our adversaries in tactics of terror, assassination, false promises, counterfeit mobs and crises."

ZR/RIFLE was only a small portion of what the Kennedy administration proposed to throw against Castro. Two weeks earlier, a twenty-nine-year-old White House aide named Richard Goodwin had written a memo to the President urging a major new covert action program against Cuba. The objective, said Goodwin, would be to build a revolution inside Cuba. Agents would be infiltrated to make contact with what few pockets of political resistance remained after the Bay of Pigs and to build an insurgent movement gradually that would gather support from a population increasingly disgruntled with Castro's mismanagement of the economy, a mismanagement aided and abetted by economic warfare waged overtly with a trade embargo and covertly with sabotage. The program would require a government-wide effort, for which the President's brother "would be the most effective commander," Goodwin wrote.

Instead, Kennedy chose Brigadier General Edward Lansdale as his Cuba commander. Lansdale was a romantic figure of considerable proportions—the stuff of which two novels, Graham Greene's *The Quiet American* and William Lederer's *The Ugly American,* were made. Nominally an Air Force officer, Lansdale had been a CIA operaive waging unconventional war against Communist insurgents in the Philippines and Vietnam. He had returned to Washington the week before Kennedy's inauguration to write a gloomy twelve-page memo on "the downhill and dangerous trend in Vietnam." New departures were needed, Lansdale wrote, and they were needed at once. "The U.S. should recognize that Vietnam is in critical condition and should treat it as a combat area of the Cold War, as an area requiring emergency treatment." The memo so struck the President's fancy that he wanted to name Lansdale as his ambassador to Saigon, an appointment that Secretary of State Dean Rusk managed to block by threatening to resign. Now Kennedy needed to administer "emergency treatment" to another "combat area of the Cold War," and Lansdale was his man.

On November 30, 1961, the President secretly directed his cabinet to "use our available assets . . . to help Cuba overthrow the Communist regime." Lansdale was placed in command, and a special panel chaired by the President's military representative, General Maxwell Taylor, was created to oversee the operation. The roster of the Special Group—national security adviser McGeorge Bundy, CIA Director John McCone, Chairman of the Joint Chiefs of Staff Lyman Lemnitzer, Deputy Defense Secretary Roswell Gilpatric, and Under Secretary of State U. Alexis Johnson—clearly signaled that this was not just another box on the organization chart. The panel was augmented by the addition of one other member, the President's brother. Bobby Kennedy would give the panel both its official title—Special Group (Augmented)—and its sense of urgency.

In an effort to give the new Cuba operation an extra measure of protection from public disclosure, it was assigned a deliberately misleading CIA cryptonym. All Agency cryptonyms began with a two-letter "diagraph" that served as a geographic designator for the operation. "AM" was the diagraph for Cuba, but the CIA's cryptic reference officer was asked for a list of names beginning with "MO," the geographic designator for a part of the world far removed from Cuba. MONGOOSE was chosen. Apart from its descriptive merits, MONGOOSE would assure the curious that this was not another ill-fated Cuba operation.

No sooner had MONGOOSE been christened, one CIA officer recalled, than "out of the clear blue sky McCone suddenly names Helms as his new man on Cuba with Bissell sitting right there in the room." The time had come to cut Bissell loose. He was too closely associated with the previous Cuba fiasco. Helms, who had managed to stay clear of the Bay of Pigs, and had made no secret of his distaste for Bissell's methods, was not tainted by failure. Moving with sure bureaucratic instinct, Helms plucked Cuba from the doldrums of the Caribbean Division, where it had been languishing ever since the Bay of Pigs, and established a new Cuba task force. "Helms always managed to set up ad hoc task forces so when they blew up they didn't blow up in his face," an admiring colleague said. "He could see there was no profit whatever for the Agency in this thing."

MONGOOSE was doomed to fail from the start. The CIA's Board of National Estimates had already concluded that "it is highly improbable that an extensive popular uprising could be fomented" against Castro. Even Castro's death "would almost certainly not prove fatal to the regime." But the administration's obsession with overthrowing Castro was beyond the reach of reason. "We were hysterical about Castro," Defense Secretary Robert McNamara acknowledged. The CIA's pessimism was viewed as foot-dragging, one more indication that the Agency had not regained its nerve since the Bay of Pigs. The estimate "seems to be the major evidence to be used to oppose your program," Lansdale warned Bobby Kennedy.

Lansdale apparently envisioned Cuba as another Vietnam, a country where the insurgent forces could establish sanctuaries from which they would roam the countryside, offering a political alternative to the disaffected peasants. But Cuba was not Vietnam. As Lansdale himself pointed out, the Communists had spent decades preparing the battlefield in Vietnam, infiltrating their first agents into the stream of laborers imported by French plantation owners from Singapore in the 1920s. No such groundwork had been laid in Cuba. To think that it could quickly be laid down now was folly, for the island was rapidly becoming a satellite state of the Soviet Union. "Cuba had essentially the same type of controls, perhaps in some ways even tighter controls, over the people than does the Soviet Union," McNamara said. "The thing Lansdale couldn't realize was that he wasn't operating anymore in friendly territory," a member of the CIA's new Cuba task force said. "He was operating in enemy territory without a goddamn asset in the place."

The lament fell on deaf ears. "Overthrow of Castro is possible," Bobby Kennedy told Helms amid the controlled chaos of his fifth-floor office at the Justice Department. An aide to Helms wrote rapidly to keep up with the Attorney General's staccato cadence. "A solution to the Cuban problem today carried top priority in U.S. Govt. No time, money, effort—or manpower is to be spared. . . . Yesterday . . . the President had indicated to him that the final chapter had not been written—it's got to be done and will be done."

Helms's response was to place Harvey in charge of the Cuba task force. Two-gun Bill Harvey, foreman of the Berlin tunnel, that covert masterpiece of daring and imagination, was the CIA's heaviest hitter. Never mind, as Helms now realized, that the tunnel had been blown from the start. That little detail was best left in the files. Harvey's appointment, more than anything else Helms could do, would convince the Kennedy administration that the CIA meant business. Harvey would also serve as a buffer between Helms and the impatient demands of the White House. "Harvey didn't recognize until it was too late that he was being had by Helms," a CIA officer said.

Harvey welcomed the challenge. He was not happy in Staff D, which did little more than provide technical assistance for eavesdropping operations requested by the National Security Agency and run by the CIA's various geographical divisions. Although Staff

D was a perfectly logical assignment for the man who had supervised the biggest wiretap operation in the CIA's history, Harvey thought he deserved better. He longed to become head of the Soviet Bloc Division and made no secret about it. Perhaps if he performed well on the Cuba task force, his wish would not be denied a second time.

Helms sent out a "book message"—an all-points bulletin to every CIA installation in the world—announcing Harvey's appointment to what would be known within the Agency as Task Force W. Harvey, who had walked point for so many years against the Russians in Berlin, was once again at the CIA's cutting edge. Lansdale, for one, was suitably impressed. He introduced Harvey to the President as the American James Bond.

The President's enthusiasm for Ian Fleming and the improbable escapades of his British superagent, 007, was well publicized. After *Life* magazine listed *Dr. No*—an adventure in which Bond disposes of the diabolical dictator of a tiny Caribbean island—as one of Kennedy's ten favorite books, 007 was on his way to becoming the most popular fictional character of the decade. Bobby Kennedy was also a fan. After Fleming autographed his copy of *From Russia with Love,* he wrote a short thank-you note saying, "We can all hardly wait for your next contribution to our leisure hours." Lansdale must have been more than a little flattered when John Kennedy remarked to him one day that he was America's answer to Bond. Lansdale, with all due modesty, demurred, suggesting that the real American 007 was this fellow Harvey whom Helms had just put on the Cuba case. Naturally, the President wanted to meet the man, and before long Harvey and Lansdale were sitting outside the Oval Office, waiting to be ushered in.

As Lansdale told the story, he turned to Harvey and said, "You're not carrying your gun, are you?" Of course he was, Harvey replied, starting to pull a revolver from his pants pocket. Aghast at what the Secret Service might do if this strange-looking man were suddenly to draw a gun, Lansdale quickly told Harvey to keep the damn thing in his pants until he could explain to the agents that the gentleman would like to check his firearm. Harvey turned over the gun and was about to enter the Oval Office when suddenly he remembered something. Reaching behind him, he whipped out a .38 Detective Special from a holster snapped to his belt in the small of his back and handed it to the startled Secret Service agents.

The President left no record of his reaction to the sight of his American Bond—this red-faced, pop-eyed, bullet-headed, pear-shaped man advancing on him with a ducklike strut that was part waddle and part swagger. Harvey's deep, gruff voice must have restored the President's faith in 007 somewhat, but Ian Fleming would never read the same again. It was a light moment, Harvey later recounted. Kennedy said, "So you're our James Bond," and Harvey, acknowledging the disparity between fact and fiction, chuckled that as the President could see, he was not equipped for some of Bond's more daring sexual escapades. The President welcomed him aboard the Cuba operation, and the encounter ended.

Operation MONGOOSE had just begun. Harvey moved Task Force W into the basement of the CIA's new headquarters in Langley, Virginia, and set up the command bunker for operations against Cuba. Lansdale had already drawn up a list of thirty-two planning tasks that contemplated a spectrum of activities ranging from intelligence collection to developing a "schedule for sabotage operations inside Cuba" and the "use of U.S. military force to support the Cuban popular movement." To all that he added Task 33, a plan to "incapacitate" Cuban sugar workers with biological warfare agents during the upcoming harvest.

"He was an idea man," Maxwell Taylor said of Lansdale, "but to find an idea that was feasible was a different proposition." The CIA had been through this once before with Lansdale in Vietnam, where, among other things, he had conceived a plan to neutralize the Vietcong's communications network. The idea was to use direction-finding equipment to pinpoint an enemy transmitter and then send in a helicopter to wipe it out. The CIA dispatched a man from Japan to assist in the project, but his first briefing by electronics experts convinced him it wouldn't work. The direction-finding equipment could locate the Vietcong transmitters but only to within a two-mile radius. That meant the helicopter would have to search more than twelve square miles of jungle for a transmitter the size of a suitcase.

"He used to drive everybody crazy with his ideas," an aide to Helms said. "He'd bombard Harvey with a million goddamn papers all the time." Task 33 was typical Lansdale, a member of Task Force W recalled. The CIA didn't have a single agent in place who could perform the task by covert means, and any overt effort, such as spraying the sugar workers from the air like so many insects, would be traced immediately to the United States. "Reaction to such an attack would probably result in demonstrations and riots . . . throughout the world," a memo from the Joint Chiefs of Staff predicted. Another invasion of Cuba "could conceivably cause less furor in the international forum and perhaps be less detrimental to the long-term interests of the United States" than Lansdale's Task 33.

Lansdale's brainstorms spawned ever more fanciful schemes as CIA planners racked their brains for ways to implement his grandiose ideas. Operation BOUNTY called for a "system of financial rewards, commensurate with position and stature, for killing or delivering alive known Communists." Leaflets would be dropped over Cuba listing rewards ranging from $5,000 for an "informant" to $10,000 for "government officials." Castro would be worth only "2¢." Another plan, dubbed "Elimination by Illumination," called for nothing less than a reenactment of the Second Coming. According to Thomas Parrott, a CIA officer who served as secretary to the Special Group (Augmented), "This plan consisted of spreading the word that the Second Coming of Christ was imminent and that Christ was against Castro [who] was anti-Christ. And you would spread this word around Cuba and then . . . just over the horizon there would be an American submarine which would surface off of Cuba and send up some starshells. And this would be the manifestation of the Second Coming and Castro would be overthrown."

Undaunted, Lansdale turned out a "Basic Action Plan" for MONGOOSE designed to culminate in the "open revolt and overthrow of the Communist regime"—"the touchdown play," as he liked

to call it—by the end of October of 1962. The timetable was preposterous, especially coming from a man who lectured others on how
long it had taken the Communists to build an insurgency in Vietnam.
Members of Harvey's Task Force W decided that Lansdale's October
deadline had more to do with the November elections than with
the realities of insurgency. Even the Special Group (Augmented)
found Lansdale's "Basic Action Plan" excessive and issued guidelines stating that simple intelligence collection would be the "immediate priority objective of U.S. efforts in the coming months." Covert
actions should be kept on a scale "short of those reasonably calculated to inspire a revolt." Since there was virtually no chance that
any covert action could inspire a revolt against Castro, the guidelines
countenanced almost any havoc the CIA could wreak.

A total of four hundred CIA officers were assigned to Task
Force W. Foreign diplomats and businessmen traveling to Cuba
were recruited as spies; Cuban officials traveling abroad were pres-
sured to defect; and political-action programs were mounted to provoke other nations into severing diplomatic ties with Cuba. One
member of Task Force W went around the world attempting to
persuade firms whose products reached Cuba despite the trade embargo to sabotage their wares. Two other officers, outfitted with
phony Italian names, roamed the United States in search of members
of the Mafia who had had gambling interests in Cuba in the days
before Castro. "Task Force W was all out of proportion," one member said. "We had a force working on Cuba that was the equivalent
for an entire area of the world. I specifically was told that I could
have as many people as I wanted when I got my job."

JM/WAVE, the CIA's forward operations base in Florida, was
revitalized under the command of Ted Shackley, a thirty-four-year-
old protégé of Harvey's from Berlin. Unlike CIA stations overseas,
JM/WAVE did not have the benefit of an American embassy to
provide diplomatic cover for its operations, so it had to be run
under commercial cover. The sign over the entrance to the weather-
beaten clapboard building located in an abandoned corner of the
University of Miami's campus read "Zenith Technical Enterprises
Inc." Inside, the walls were cluttered with sales charts, business
licenses, even an award certificate from the United Givers' Fund

citing Zenith for its contributions to the annual fund-raising drive.

JM/WAVE soon became the largest CIA station in the world. "You can't imagine how many people were involved," an aide to Helms said. Operations included the overt interrogation of the three thousand refugees who arrived each week from Havana; the thinly veiled activities of the Gibraltar Steamship Corporation, which broadcast propaganda and coded messages over Radio Swan; and the secret training of commandos for missions into Cuba. Bases were scattered throughout the Everglades and Florida Keys; high-speed boats disguised as pleasure craft were moored at marinas up and down the peninsula; and safe houses were located in some of the poshest neighborhoods of Key Biscayne and Coral Gables. Scores of proprietary firms with such names as Paragon Air Service provided logistical support for the vast complex, while literally thousands of Cuban exiles worked for JM/WAVE as drivers, cooks, informants, boat captains, commandos, and case officers. It was impossible to tell where JM/WAVE left off and the myriad anti-Castro groups operating out of Miami began. If JM/WAVE did not actually direct their activities, its money made them possible. "As you look back upon the goddamn thing, so much of the goddamn stuff was really juvenile," an aide to Helms said. "And what it cost."

"We were running a ferry service back and forth to the island with agents," a member of Task Force W recalled. Teams of Cuban exiles were dispatched in the dark of the moon, setting out in 150-foot-long "mother ships" for the 90-mile run to Cuba. While still in international waters, the teams transferred to 20-foot fiberglass boats powered by twin 100-horsepower engines for the high-speed run to the beach, covering the last stretch of water in a rubber dinghy outfitted with a heavily muffled 25-horsepower motor. Once ashore, the teams sank the dinghies among the mangroves or deflated and buried them in the sand. Some of the teams simply left weapons caches for agents already on the island. Others headed inland toward their native provinces, where they could seek out relatives who might give them food and shelter while they went about the tedious task of building an underground network. The exiles sent out radio reports on the condition of the transportation and food-distribution systems, the status of power and water supplies, the schedules of police patrols, and all the other measures of Castro's grip on the island. They distributed leaflets informing the populace that the worm—or *gusano,* as Castro called the exile community—had turned. They urged their compatriots to commit minor sabotage such as leaving the lights on and the water running. They carried condoms filled with graphite to dump into an engine's oil system.

But minor sabotage "didn't appeal to the Cubans," Maxwell Taylor said. "They wanted to go in there and throw a bomb at somebody." The official records of Operation MONGOOSE contained only the slightest hint of the ferocity with which this secret war was waged. The code names the CIA assigned to some of its agents inside Cuba—names like BLOOD, WHIP, and LASH—were more expressive of the mayhem involved. "This demands a change from business-as-usual and a hard facing of the fact that we are in a combat situation," Lansdale said. "Cut off their heads and leave them in the trails," an aide to Lansdale chanted.

Sabotage missions were launched against bridges, power transformers, microwave towers, tank farms, and railroad lines within reach of the beach. The commandos set their mortars in the sand, lobbed a few shells inland, and retreated to sea. "Sometimes mortar rounds go long and they land in a village," the chief of Task Force W's paramilitary operations said philosophically. "People died," Harvey's executive assistant said, "no question of that." All to no avail. "To the best of my knowledge, there wasn't one damn thing that was accomplished of any note at all," the paramilitary chief said. "Absolute failure."

The rationale behind the sabotage was that it would result in economic dislocations that would sow discontent among the people and provide fertile ground for nurturing a resistance network. But the Special Group (Augmented) repeatedly balked at approving the kind of assault that would work any real economic hardship. As Tom Parrott, the secretary to the Special Group, explained, "Nobody knew exactly what they wanted to do. It had only been a year since the Bay of Pigs and nobody wanted to get into another one of those. What was our policy toward Cuba? Well, our policy toward Cuba was to keep the pot simmering." Over and over the phrase was used. "Keep the pot simmering." After a while, Harvey's paramilitary aide said, "it began to dawn on us that we were involved in a random event."

"What's the matter with these bastards?" Harvey groused to Parrott. "Why don't they get off their duffs and do something?" The matter was that the Special Group didn't trust Harvey. "Your friend Harvey doesn't inspire much confidence," Bundy snapped at Parrott. Harvey was terribly long-winded. He would drone on and on in his low-pitched monotone, oblivious to the fact that the Attorney General, whose own clipped phrases were the epitome of terseness, was drumming his fingers on the table. "Tell him not to mumble so much," one member of the Special Group said to Parrott. For all his mumbling, Harvey was not telling the Special Group what it wanted to know. "Bill had trouble getting down to the specifics some of the military people were demanding," Parrott said. "They would want to know exactly 'What are these guys going to do—what night are they going, what time, what are they going to hit, what's their disaster plan?' " Harvey preferred to talk concepts. "Look, Mr. Harvey," Maxwell Taylor interrupted, "we've got to have more specifics."

Everything had to be laid before the Special Group in "excruciating detail," Harvey griped. "It went down to such things as the gradients on the beach and the composition of the sand," Harvey's executive assistant said. The Special Group even wanted to know what rations the raiders would carry. "It was almost as if Bill and the rest of us were accused of trying to sucker them into another Bay of Pigs," Harvey's paramilitary aide said. "It was an insult to our professionalism," the executive assistant added, "and it was a useless exercise. What difference did it make if they were carrying a .38 or a .45?" Exasperated, Harvey complained to McCone. "To permit requisite flexibility and professionalism for a maximum operational effort against Cuba, the tight controls exercised by the Special Group and the present time-consuming coordination and briefing procedures should, if at all possible, be made less restrictive and less stultifying," he wrote in his typically long-winded fashion. "You could see trouble coming," Helms's assistant said.

Bobby Kennedy browbeat Harvey and his aides so relentlessly that after one session Taylor turned to him and said, "You could sack a town and enjoy it." The Attorney General would call a junior officer in the Task Force W bunker at Langley, bark out an order, and hang up, leaving the CIA man wondering whether he had just talked to the President's brother or a prankster. He gave one officer the name of "a man who was in contact with a small group of Cubans who had a plan for creating an insurrection." When the officer reported back that the Cubans did not seem to have a concrete plan, Kennedy ordered him to fly to Guantánamo and "start working and developing this particular group." The officer protested, saying that the CIA had promised the Defense Department not to work out of Guantánamo. "We will see about that," Kennedy snapped. Sometimes the Attorney General would take things into his own hands, and the CIA would not find out about it until after the fact. He sent Lansdale down to Miami in a futile effort to form a cohesive government-in-exile and kept the trip a secret from the CIA. "I felt you preferred informing the President privately," Lansdale said in a handwritten note to Kennedy. The Attorney General frequently dealt directly with some of the Cuban exiles who were supposed to be Harvey's agents. They would troop in and out of the Justice Department bearing firsthand reports of CIA ineptitudes. "One of these Cubans told him we were asking the refugees questions about what they thought of President Kennedy," Helms's aide said. "RFK raised a stink that this was getting JFK too closely involved."

It was vintage Bobby Kennedy, turning the bureaucracy upside down and shaking it by the heels. Such tactics served him well in most endeavors, but not when it came to the business of spying, with all its reverence for "tradecraft." Even the unorthodox Lansdale was taken aback by Kennedy's antibureaucratic instincts. Lansdale had taken some top-secret documents to Hickory Hill, where Kennedy lay sick in bed with the flu. Kennedy spread the papers over the covers, and the two men discussed the latest plans for Castro's overthrow while children played with a train set under the bed. "We were discussing these very sensitive matters," Lansdale recalled, shaking his head, "and this kid was going 'Choo-choo' around my feet."

To Harvey, it was all so much amateurish meddling. Soon he

started referring to Kennedy in private as "that fucker" and began suggesting that some of the Attorney General's actions bordered on the traitorous. It usually happened after he had been drinking, and it made his friends wince. "He had some things that he said of Bobby Kennedy that were unwise, which he couldn't support, but which were part of his dislike for the man," a friend said. "Bobby was wielding so much power, and Bill distorted this into intent to do harm." In short, the friend said, "he hated Bobby Kennedy's guts with a purple passion." For his part, Kennedy thought that Harvey was "not very good." The Berlin tunnel "was a helluva project," Kennedy conceded, "but he did that better than he did this. . . . [Harvey had] this great achievement and then he ended in disaster by working out this program." Stories began to circulate. One had it that Harvey had flatly refused a direct order from Kennedy, then slapped his gun down on the conference table and spun it around so the barrel pointed at the Attorney General. The story was almost certainly apocryphal, but its very existence signaled that something was drastically wrong.

Relations with Lansdale were no better. A clash between Lansdale, the guerrilla fighter, and Harvey, the espionage agent, was inevitable. Their instincts were as far apart as the jungles of Vietnam and the back alleys of Berlin. "People who'd been up against the Soviet types were always very strange to me," Lansdale said. "I'm sure they thought I was strange." Despite his long and storied background in Asian intrigue, Lansdale had an irrepressible naiveté about him. He could give such trailwise advice as "In a campfire, dry bamboo gives light, dry coconut shells (not husks) give cooking heat but little light," and in the next breath pronounce, "One of the precepts I wanted American officials to follow was the Golden Rule." James Symington, who in 1962 served as Bobby Kennedy's administrative assistant, came back from his first meeting with Lansdale and wrote a memo saying, "I have now met the All-American Boy Guerrilla Fighter." He meant it as a joke, but Kennedy didn't think it was funny. "Bob gave me a rather dour look and said, 'You don't seem to understand. This man is a very great warrior.' " After that, Symington kept his opinion of Lansdale to himself. "It just seemed to me he was a little wacky," he said.

To Harvey, Lansdale was worse than wacky. He was a security risk. "Harvey seldom really talked to me," Lansdale said. "He would never initiate conversations. It was very hard to get information from him. . . . I'd ask him for a full explanation, and I'd get one sentence back, and I'd say, 'You mean that's full?' He'd say, 'I'm trying to answer your question. . . . Everything's under control.' When I'd ask a question, he'd say, 'I just told you. Everything's under control.' Or, 'Well, I'm very busy here, and I can't go into details on every last thing.' . . . It used to burn me up. . . . If I was talking to Harvey and he got a phone call, he'd start talking code. After a while I caught on and realized he was talking about me. The son of a bitch. Why couldn't he have just told me he had something he wanted to discuss in private and ask me to step out for a moment? I would have understood that." Harvey displayed his contempt in other ways as well. At meetings he would "lift his ass and fart and pare his nails with a sheath knife," Helms's aide said. One day at the Pentagon, Harvey took his gun from his pocket, emptied all the ammunition on the table, and began playing with the bullets in an elaborate show of boredom. The incident caused such a ruckus that the CIA issued new regulations regarding the carrying of firearms by employees.

The final break with Lansdale came on August 13, 1962. Lansdale sent a memo to State, Defense, the CIA, and the USIA, laying out plans for the next phase of operations against Cuba. There, in black and white, Lansdale wrote, "Mr. Harvey: Intelligence, Political (including liquidation of leaders), Economic (sabotage, limited deception), and Paramilitary." Three days before, Harvey had sat silent in Dean Rusk's office while fifteen or so of the administration's leading lights—McNamara, Taylor, Bundy, McCone, Gilpatric, Lansdale, Goodwin, and others—briefly discussed the "liquidation of leaders," Castro in particular. "It was the obvious consensus of that meeting . . . that this was not a subject which has been a matter of public record," Harvey reported afterward to Helms. All mention of the liquidation of leaders had been expunged from the official minutes of the meeting, but three days later, Lansdale put it in writing and sent the memo all over town. As soon as McCone saw it, he called Harvey in and told him, "If I got myself involved in something like this, I might end up getting myself excommunicated." Harvey listened with a straight face, then stormed back to his basement office, scratched out the offending words from the memo, and called Lansdale to rage against "the inadmissability and stupidity of putting this type of comment in such a document." The CIA "would write no document pertaining to this and would participate in no open meeting discussing it," Harvey told Lansdale. Lansdale didn't know it, but he had stuck his big foot right in the middle of ZR/RIFLE.

Lansdale was the least of ZR/RIFLE's problems. At Helms's urging, Harvey had abandoned the intricate stratagem of using QJ/WIN in the KUTUBE/D search for a suitable assassin as the original executive-action file had specified. Instead, he had reverted to a more tightly controlled version of the "Keystone Comedy Act" that had been concocted for the Bay of Pigs. "This is an ongoing matter which I was injected into" on "explicit orders" from Helms, Harvey insisted. Helms acknowledged that "I had very grave doubts about the wisdom of this," but "we had so few assets inside Cuba at that time I was willing to try almost anything." Harvey summed up the liabilities of this "damned dicey operation" by saying that it carried the "very real possibility of this government being blackmailed either by Cubans for political purposes or by figures in organized crime for their own self-protection or aggrandizement."

To limit the potential damage as much as possible, Harvey dropped the ex-FBI agent Maheu and the two Mafia "dons," Trafficante and Giancana, as "surplus" and "untrustworthy" and began working exclusively with Johnny Rosselli. On April 21, 1962, Harvey and Rosselli met in the cocktail lounge at the Miami airport. The bulbous Harvey gulped his double martini while the sleek Rosselli, wearing a custom-tailored suit, alligator shoes, and a $2,000 watch, sipped Smirnoff on the rocks. Suddenly Harvey slapped his revolver down on the table between them. From now on, he commanded, Rosselli would be working for him and him only. He was to maintain contact with the Cuban Tony Varona but have no further dealings with Maheu, Giancana, or Trafficante. Harvey handed Rosselli four poison capsules and assured him that they would "work anywhere and at any time with anything." Rosselli said that Varona planned that the new pills would be used not only on Fidel Castro but also on his brother Raul and on Ché Guevara. "Everything is all right," Harvey responded. As a backup, Harvey and Ted Shackley, the JM/WAVE station chief, rented a U-Haul truck, filled it with $5,000 worth of explosives, detonators, rifles, handguns, radios, and boat radar, dropped it off in a parking lot, walked across the street, and handed the keys to Rosselli.

When Harvey returned to Washington, he reported to the Special Group that three more teams of agents had been infiltrated, bringing to seventy-two the number of CIA assets in place in Cuba, but he made no mention of Rosselli, Varona, the pills, or the U-Haul truck. Harvey kept the assassination plot "pretty much in his back pocket," Helms said. "There was a fairly detailed discussion between myself and Helms as to whether or not McCone should at that time be briefed concerning this," Harvey related. "For a variety of reasons which were tossed back and forth, we agreed that it was not necessary or advisable to brief him at that time." Helms explained that "Mr. McCone was relatively new to the Agency, and I guess I must have thought to myself, well this is going to look peculiar to him. It was a Mafia connection . . . and this was, you know, not a very savory operation."

Something more than mere silence was required to keep the Attorney General ignorant of the plan. Kennedy had only just learned about the original "Keystone Comedy Act" after the CIA explained to him the very compelling reasons why it would be unwise for the Justice Department to proceed with a prosecution of Giancana, Rosselli, and Maheu in connection with the abortive attempt to place a wiretap on Dan Rowan's telephone. That unenviable chore had fallen to Sheffield Edwards, the orchestrator of the plot, and Lawrence Houston, general counsel for the CIA. "I trust that if you ever do business with organized crime again—with gangsters—you will let the Attorney General know," Kennedy glowered. "If you have seen Mr. Kennedy's eyes get steely and his jaw set and his voice get low and precise, you get a definite feeling of unhappiness," Houston recalled. Houston and Edwards assured Kennedy that the plot to kill Castro had been terminated, a statement that Edwards knew to be a lie. To back up his lie, Edwards returned to the CIA and wrote a memo for the record stating that "Mr. Harvey called me and indicated that he was dropping any plans for the use of Subject [Rosselli] for the future." The memo "was not true," Harvey conceded, "and Colonel Edwards knew it was not true." But then, as General Carter, the Agency's Deputy Director, once said, "Memorandums [sic] for the record have very little validity in fact."

Rosselli soon reported to Harvey that the pills and guns had arrived in Cuba. They waited, but nothing happened. In June, Rosselli told Harvey that a three-man team was on its way to Cuba to do the job. Still Castro flourished. It had been a full eight months since Bissell had first mentioned to Harvey the "application of ZR/RIFLE program to Cuba" and since the President had recorded his decision to "use our available assets . . . to help Cuba overthrow the Communist regime." During that time, the only result that could be discerned was that the Russians had begun shipping vast quantities of military supplies to Cuba.

On August 8 the Special Group met to consider "stepped-up Course B plus," which was nothing more than a reversion to Lansdale's original "Basic Action Plan" for inspiring an internal revolt within Cuba by October. This time the Special Group reached the same conclusion that the CIA's Board of National Estimates had reached nearly a year before. It was no longer possible to overthrow Castro by clandestine means. On August 20 Maxwell Taylor told the President that the Special Group saw no likelihood that Castro could be overturned without direct United States military intervention. But MONGOOSE was not abandoned. On August 22, when the S.S. *Streatham Hill,* bound for the Soviet Union with 800,000 bags of Cuban sugar aboard, put into San Juan harbor in Puerto Rico for repairs, CIA agents contaminated the cargo with a harmless but unpalatable substance known as Bitrex. The next day, August 23, Bundy issued an action memorandum stating that at the President's direction "the line of activity projected for Operation MONGOOSE Plan B plus should be developed with all possible speed." Harvey was ordered to submit a list of all possible sabotage targets. Lansdale urged hitting "the Matahambre mine and various refineries, nickel plants." The CIA's agents should encourage "destruction of crops by fire, chemicals and weeds, hampering of harvest by work slowdown, destruction of bags, cartons and other shipping containers." The Pentagon began laying plans for "Contingency II"—a paratroop assault on Cuba. On Sepember 7 Harvey met again with Rosselli in Miami to find out what was holding up Castro's death.

A day later, on September 8, a naval reconnaissance aircraft on routine patrol over the Atlantic approaches to Cuba snapped a photograph of the Soviet freighter *Omsk* steaming toward Havana harbor. The pictures revealed two-and-a-half- and five-ton cargo trucks lashed to her decks, but tarpaulins stretched over her hatches concealed the cargo below. Built with extra-large hatches, the *Omsk* was designed to carry lumber, but lumber was not among the supplies that Russia was shipping to Cuba. Analysts decided the *Omsk* had been pressed into duty as a bulk carrier because of a shortage of ship bottoms. But there was something else about the ship. She was riding high in the water. Either her holds were partly empty beneath those tarpaulins—extremely unlikely, given the shortage of bottoms—or she was carrying a space-consuming cargo of large volume and low density.

On September 12, three days after the *Omsk* unloaded her mysterious cargo under cover of darkness, a forty-four-year-old Cuban accountant in a small town southwest of Havana looked up from his desk to see a large missile being towed through the streets. By coincidence, the accountant was wrestling with a problem that hinged on the dimensions of the property across the street. As the missile passed by, he was able to gauge its precise length. The accountant packed his bags and headed for Florida.

On September 18 the CIA's Board of National Estimates issued a secret report concluding that the Soviets would not install offensive missiles in Cuba. "The establishment on Cuban soil of a significant strike capability . . . would represent a sharp departure from Soviet practice, since such weapons have so far not been installed even in Satellite territory," the report said. "Serious problems of command and control would arise. There would have to be a conspicuously larger number of Soviet personnel in Cuba."

McCone disagreed. Ever since he had seen surveillance photographs of surface-to-air missiles (SAM) sites being erected in western Cuba, he was convinced that they were there for one reason only: to protect Soviet nuclear missiles from an American air strike. An ocean away, on the French Riviera where he was honeymooning with his second wife, McCone bombarded headquarters with messages—"the honeymoon cables"—urging that more weight be given to the possibility of Soviet missiles in Cuba.

On September 20, eight days after he had spotted the oversized missile outside his office window, the Cuban accountant reached the CIA's refugee-debriefing center at Opa-Locka, Florida. The dimensions he gave his interrogators matched exactly those of a Soviet medium-range ballistic missile (MRBM). The interrogators, who had been listening to exiles tell of Soviet missiles in Cuba for more than a year, were doubtful. The accountant was shown photographs and drawings of all types of missiles from around the world. The pictures had all been reduced to the same size so that he would have to rely on characteristics other than length in attempting to identify the missile he had seen. Without hesitation, he pointed to a picture of a Soviet MRBM.

The report was forwarded to Washington, where it was greeted with the same weary skepticism born of a thousand false missile sightings. "Doubt that this should be in meters, probably ought to be in feet," one analyst noted in the margin of the report, downgrading the missile from an offensive weapon capable of striking targets in the United States as far west as the Mississippi to a defensive SAM. But soon another agent's report reached CIA headquarters, this time in the form of a message in secret writing sent through the international mails, warning that all civilians had been evacuated from the area of San Cristóbal, fifty miles southwest of Havana. The timing and location were consistent with the accountant's sighting.

Early on the morning of October 14, a U-2 reconnaissance aircraft left the airspace over Florida, proceeded to the Isle of Pines, fifty miles off Cuba's southern coast, turned, and headed north across Cuba. Within five minutes it had traversed the island. The U-2's cameras had picked out a total of fourteen, 73-foot MRBMs lying in various stages of readiness in a heavily wooded area near San

Cristóbal. When the photos came back from the National Photographic Interpretation Center, Walter Elder, McCone's executive assistant, immediately dialed a number in Seattle, Washington, where McCone was attending the funeral of his stepson, who had been killed in an automobile accident. Speaking guardedly over the long-distance connection, Elder told McCone, "That which you and you alone said would happen, did."

On October 16 the photos were shown to the President and his advisers. "I for one had to take their word for it," Bobby Kennedy said. "I examined the pictures carefully, and what I saw appeared to be no more than the clearing of a field for a farm or the basement of a house." The photo analysts could both pick out the missiles and judge with considerable precision their readiness. Working with Russian maintenance and operations manuals that had been provided to the CIA by Colonel Oleg Penkovsky, the analysts estimated that the first MRBM could be ready for launch within eighteen hours. It was Penkovsky's last and greatest service.

The presence of nuclear missiles in Cuba signaled the final futility of MONGOOSE. Yet on the same day he saw the photographs, Bobby Kennedy told Helms that he was going to give MONGOOSE "more personal attention in view of the lack of progress." According to Helms's notes, Kennedy expressed the "general dissatisfaction of the President" with MONGOOSE and "pointed out that [MONGOOSE] had been underway for a year . . . that there had been no acts of sabotage and that even the one which had been attempted had failed twice."

There had been acts of sabotage, but nothing that amounted to much. The Agency had tried twice to knock out the Matahambre copper mines, developing elaborate plans that included the erection of a full-scale model in the Florida Everglades. Both times the operation had been aborted—once because the boat had conked out on the way to Cuba, and the second time because the raiders had encountered a Castro patrol. On October 16, even as Kennedy complained about these past failures, a team of eight commandos left their base at Summer Land Key for Cuba and another raid on the Matahambre. They hit the beach on the nineteenth but again were spotted by a Cuban patrol. Six of the commandos made it back to the boat. For three nights they hovered close to shore, looking for the two who were missing. On the third night their vigil was broken by the voice of President Kennedy coming loud and clear over the boat's radio as he informed the nation of the presence of Soviet missiles in Cuba and of the blockade that he had ordered against the island. The team returned to Florida minus two of their comrades but jubilant that Kennedy, at long last, was really going to do something about Castro.

In the heat of the moment, Harvey ordered ten more teams dispatched to Cuba, not for sabotage but to be in place with beacons and flares that could light the way if the President ordered a military invasion. The Attorney General learned of the order by accident when "one of the fellows who was going to go . . . got in touch with me and said . . . we don't mind going, but we want to make sure we're going because you think it's worthwhile." Kennedy ordered the missions scrubbed, but Harvey said that three of the teams were beyond recall. "I was furious," Kennedy later related. "I said, 'You were dealing with people's lives . . . and then you're going to go off with a half-assed operation such as this.'" On whose authority had Harvey dispatched no less than sixty of these brave men into Cuba at a time when the slightest provocation might unleash a nuclear holocaust? Kennedy demanded to know. "[Harvey] said we planned it because the military wanted it done, and I asked the military and they never heard of it." Kennedy demanded a better explanation and said, "I've got two minutes to hear your answer." Two minutes later Harvey was still talking. Kennedy got up and walked out of the room. That evening when McCone returned to CIA headquarters in Langley, he told Ray Cline, his Deputy Director for Intelligence, "Harvey has destroyed himself today. His usefulness has ended."

McCone was furious, not only with Harvey but also with Sherman Kent, head of the Board of National Estimates, which had failed to predict the presence of the missiles in Cuba despite the urgings of "the honeymoon cables." One at a time, McCone called Harvey and Kent into his office. "I've just been made a charter member of the bleeding asshole society," Kent said afterward, "but Bill Harvey's the president." McCone replaced Harvey as head of

Task Force W with Desmond FitzGerald, chief of the Agency's Far East Division. FitzGerald was a man of considerable wealth, sophistication, and charm who sprang from the same Boston Irish roots as the Kennedys. He would be able to deal with the White House as a colleague, not an adversary. To fill the hole left by FitzGerald in the Far East Division, McCone picked an intense, unflappable fellow Catholic named William Colby. FitzGerald descended to the Task Force W vault, and Harvey moved into a nearby cubicle, where he tidied up his papers and waited for the officials on the seventh floor to decide what to do with him.

There was one loose end still dangling from the Cuba operation that required Harvey's personal attention. He flew to Los Angeles to advise Rosselli that the plot to kill Castro had. been terminated. By now it was nothing more than a formality, since Harvey had long ago given up any hope that the deed would be done. During the months they had shared their little secret, Harvey, the former FBI agent, and Rosselli, the ex-con, had developed a genuine fondness for one another. Harvey saw in Rosselli a man much like himself, a dedicated anti-Communist whose motive in wanting to kill Castro was nothing more complicated than patriotism. Rosselli had never requested a cent for his services, not even money to cover his expenses, although Harvey must have realized that the gangster had maneuvered himself into an excellent position from which to stave off with threats of blackmail any future criminal prosecution by the Justice Department. The two men also shared a hatred for Bobby Kennedy—Rosselli because of the Attorney General's war on organized crime, Harvey for Kennedy's meddling with his precious tradecraft.

Rosselli flew to Washington for a farewell dinner at Harvey's home. Harvey picked him up at National Airport, where they were placed under surveillance by FBI agents assigned to keep tabs on Rosselli. Not recognizing Harvey but sensing that he was something more than an underworld crony, the agents contacted Sam Papich, the FBI's liaison with the CIA, reaching him at Angleton's dinner table. Angleton and Papich immediately identified Harvey from the physical description given by the agents. Papich later told Harvey that his consorting with organized crime would have to be brought to Hoover's attention, which immediately raised the prospect that it would get back to McCone. That would require some rather complicated explanations to a man who had said he might be excommunicated if he became involved in assassination. Harvey and Helms discussed the wisdom of briefing McCone and again decided against it.

Figuring out what to do with Harvey had become something of a problem for Helms. Harvey suggested Laos, but Helms gently deflected that idea, citing Harvey's weight and thyroid problems. The truth was that Harvey would never again be allowed near an operation in which the White House was likely to take an active interest. Helms decided to send him to Rome as station chief. The assignment was stunning in its incongruity. The tough-talking, hard-drinking, gun-toting Harvey would be serving in a post whose chief duties were liaison with the Italian intelligence services. Having offended almost every high-ranking national security official in the Kennedy administration, he would now have a chance to offend almost every high-ranking national security official in the Italian government. "They couldn't have picked a bigger bull for a better china shop," one CIA officer snorted. But Harvey had to be got out of the country fast, and Rome was the first available slot for an officer of his rank. The irony cannot have escaped Harvey that it was he, the loyal government servant, and not Rosselli, the Mafioso, who was being deported to Italy.

"He lost his self-confidence for the first time in his life," Angleton said of Harvey. Angleton tried to cheer him up by handcrafting a small leather holster for Harvey's .38 Detective Special. The task force threw a party for him. "It was a tearful kind of thing," one participant said. Everybody there felt Harvey had been "shafted." Instead of being relieved of his command, they felt, he should have been decorated for having put together the worldwide intelligence network that had discovered the missiles in time. "We went to great pains to try to buoy him up because he was bitter, very bitter—and hurt," a member of the task force said. There were mock presentations: a stuffed mongoose (in fact a ferret, since Washington taxidermists did not carry so exotic an item) and a roll of toilet paper with every sheet stamped "PSM" for "Please See Me," Harvey's standard way of summoning subordinates. And there were speeches—a satire on Shakespeare's *Julius Caesar* in which Harvey was Caesar, stabbed in the back. When Harvey's turn came, he picked up the cue. "Brutus was Bobby," he said.

No Innocent Explanation

7

With the notable exception of Harvey, the CIA emerged from the Cuban missile crisis with its honor restored. MONGOOSE had been a disaster, but the Agency's intelligence-collection apparatus had spotted the missiles in time, blending human and technical intelligence into an accurate picture of Soviet capabilities that enabled the President to call the Soviet hand. It would be a long time, if ever, before the system worked so well again, for deep within the Agency, in his heavily curtained second-floor office, James Angleton had fallen under the spell of the defector Golitsin, who warned that a KGB mole had penetrated the secret corridors of the CIA. Angleton had as yet been unable to track down Golitsin's leads, but the strange appearance of three Soviet "walk-ins"—SCOTCH, BOURBON, and Yuri Nosenko—in what seemed like a deliberate KGB scheme to discredit Golitsin, had convinced him that he was on the right path. As the world let out its breath at the news that the Soviet Union had begun to dismantle its nuclear missiles in Cuba, Angleton set off down that path, heading deeper and deeper into the wilderness of mirrors.

After his initial debriefings, the difficult Golitsin had grown increasingly aloof, refusing to deal with anyone but Angleton or his assistant, Raymond Rocca, and demanding that he be allowed to live in England. The CIA had already gone to the trouble and expense of providing him with a new identity, John Stone, and a $40,000 home in suburban Washington, complete with color television, but Golitsin insisted that he be in England by January of 1963. The Agency procrastinated, but it could hardly hold him against his will, so in March of 1963, after persuading Rocca and a fellow defector named Nicholas Shadrin to watch over his two German shepherds, Golitsin boarded an ocean liner bound for Britain.

It had been fifteen months since Golitsin knocked on the door of the CIA station chief in Helsinki. During that time he had caused consternation in the ranks of Western intelligence with his warnings about Soviet spies in virtually every capital of the free world. To test his claim that whole volumes of NATO's most sensitive documents were available in Moscow, interrogators had shown Golitsin classified NATO files interspersed with a number of bogus papers. All of the papers he claimed to have read in Moscow were authentic NATO documents.

So far, however, Golitsin's tantalizing information had produced only limited results. He had directly named only one Soviet penetration agent, Georges Pacques, a deputy press officer at NATO headquarters in Paris. He had aroused suspicions about the possibility of a Soviet penetration of the British Admiralty, but it was not until Nosenko provided additional details to his CIA handlers in Geneva that investigators were able to identify William John Vassall as the culprit. His warnings about Soviet penetration of British intelligence had provided the occasion for the final denouement of the Philby case, but Golitsin had not added one iota of evidence against Philby. Besides, the final unmasking of Philby had little effect on the secret balance of power between Soviet and Western intelligence, since his career as a high-level penetration agent had been brought to an end twelve years before by Harvey's memo. Compared to Goleniewski's information, which had led swiftly to the arrests of George Blake, Heinz Felfe, Gordon Lonsdale, and a multitude of accomplices, Golitsin's contribution had been a modest one. But his contribution had only just begun. In July of 1963 his English idyll was broken by a news report that a high-ranking Soviet defector named "Dolnytsin" was hiding somewhere in Great Britain. The garbled account struck too close for comfort. Stirred from his lair, Golitsin returned to the United States, bearing new and timely warnings of KGB machinations.

The recent ideological rupture between the two Communist giants, China and the Soviet Union, was a fraud, Golitsin cried, a massive disinformation campaign designed to lull the West into a false sense of security. Beyond his infinite faith in the devious capabilities of the KGB's Disinformation Directorate, the only evidence Golitsin could produce to support his claim was the identities of certain KGB officers and Soviet scientists who remained in China despite the split. Operatives and experts of that caliber would not stay on in Peking unless the Russians were still in league with the Chinese, Golitsin said. Angleton was persuaded and urged Helms to arrange for Golitsin to meet with a panel of CIA experts on Sino-Soviet affairs. The panel was singularly unimpressed. "He did not adduce anything of a factual nature to support his theory," one member of the panel said. "He had no evidence that it was a fabricated affair. He simply posited that the split was a fake. He couldn't conceive of it being anything else. . . . It was strictly a hypothesis, very forcefully presented. . . . He got angry and overbearing because we didn't agree with him. . . . He shifted the burden of proof to us. We had to prove that it was true. He demanded to see every classified report with true source identification that reported on the split. He proposed to show that all these reports were deceptive. . . . He wanted to know who the sources were by name so he could discredit them. . . . We, of course, couldn't do that." Angleton was as upset with the panel's incredulity as Golitsin and harshly reprimanded one member who circulated a report debunking the defector's claim.

Golitsin's message about the Sino-Soviet split was only one of several urgent warnings he brought with him from England. He recalled that the chief of KGB operations in Northern Europe had once told him of a plan to kill the leader of an opposition party in the West. The only opposition leader in Northern Europe to die in the interim had been Hugh Gaitskell, head of Britain's Labour Party, who had unexpectedly succumbed to a massive infection of the heart, kidney, and lungs. Golitsin was convinced that the KGB had poisoned Gaitskell in order to promote the new leader of the Labour Party, Harold Wilson, who Golitsin said was a Soviet asset.

Then came the assassination of John F. Kennedy in Dallas on November 22, 1963. For Angleton and the small coterie of American and British intelligence officers privy to Golitsin's suspicions about Gaitskell's death, the President's murder could only have brought visions of a KGB plot of unspeakable malevolence. For Harvey and the even smaller number of officers aware of the CIA's own plot to kill Fidel Castro, the President's murder must have appeared as dreadful retribution. There was a wealth of circumstantial evidence linking Lee Harvey Oswald to both the Cuban and Soviet governments. Oswald had defected to the Soviet Union in 1959 and had taken up the cause of the Fair Play for Cuba Committee when he returned to the United States in 1962 with his Russian wife, Marina. In late September of 1963, less than two months before Kennedy's murder, Oswald had visited both the Cuban and Soviet embassies in Mexico City, ostensibly seeking a visa to return to Moscow by way of Havana. The CIA station in Mexico, through its routine surveillance of Communist embassies, had intercepted a phone call that Oswald made from the Cuban to the Soviet Embassy, demanding in his broken Russian to speak to "Comrade Kostikov" about his visa application, a curious request since his visa application was on file with the Soviet consulate in Washington. Valery Kostikov and his boss, Pavel Yotskov, chief of the embassy's consular section, who was later overheard to say that he had actually met with Oswald, were both "known officers" of the KGB, a CIA memo reported.

Immediately after the assassination, headquarters at Langley cabled Mexico City for the names of all contacts of Yotskov and Kostikov. Early on the morning of November 24 the Mexico City station cabled its response. One of the names on the list was Rolando Cubella, a high-ranking Cuban official and confidant of Fidel Castro. Cubella was already known to the CIA as AM/LASH, the prime asset in yet another Agency plot to overthrow Castro, this time under the direction of Desmond FitzGerald, head of the Special Affairs Staff (SAS), successor to Harvey's Task Force W. The chief of SAS counterintelligence had warned FitzGerald that Cubella's "bona fides were subject to question," meaning that AM/LASH might be a double agent sent by Castro.

At a meeting with his CIA case officer in São Paulo, Brazil, AM/LASH had stated that he wanted American support in attempting an "inside job" against Castro, a reference the case officer took to mean the "execution" of Castro as the first step in a coup. AM/LASH's bold proposal was cabled to CIA headquarters on September 7, 1963. That evening, Castro walked into a reception at the Brazilian Embassy in Havana and warned a startled reporter that "United States leaders should think that if they are aiding terrorist plans to eliminate Cuban leaders, they themselves will not be safe." Even to those unaware of the eerie coincidence involved in Castro's choice of the Brazilian Embassy so soon after the meeting in São Paulo, the threat represented what Angleton's aide Rocca called "a more-than-ordinary attempt to get a message on the record in the United States."

FitzGerald, one of the few who knew enough to appreciate the Brazilian coincidence, did not get the message. On October 29 he flew to Paris to assure AM/LASH personally that his efforts had the backing of the President's brother, Bobby Kennedy. When Fitz-Gerald returned to Washington he authorized the case officer to tell AM/LASH that the rifles, telescopic sights, and explosives he had requested would be provided. Another meeting was set with AM/LASH for November 22. At that meeting, the case officer gave AM/LASH a ball-point pen fitted with a hypodermic needle and suggested it be used with Blackleaf-40, a deadly poison commercially available. A CIA report later noted that "it is likely that at the very moment President Kennedy was shot, a CIA officer was meeting with a Cuban agent . . . and giving him an assassination device for use against Castro."

The implication was inescapable—the AM/LASH operation was known to Castro and had provoked him to order Kennedy's death. FitzGerald sized up the problem at once and ordered AM/LASH's case officer not to include any mention of the poison-pen device in his contact report for the November 22 meeting. The operational file on Cubella, which contained the details of the plot, was withheld from the investigators who had turned up his name in running down the contacts of the two KGB officers, Yotskov and Kostikov, in Mexico City. None of the information about AM/LASH, or any of the other CIA plots to kill Castro, was turned over to the Warren Commission.

One month after the assassination, the Agency's Western Hemisphere Division prepared a report for President Lyndon B. Johnson summarizing the findings to date. Other than his contacts with the Cuban and Soviet embassies, Oswald's activities during the five days he had spent in Mexico remained largely unknown. Even less was known about his two and a half years in the Soviet Union. Much more work needed to be done before the United States could satisfy itself on the question of foreign involvement in the President's murder. Late in December, Angleton suggested and Helms agreed that the Counterintelligence Division should take over the investigation for the duration of the Warren Commission's inquiry.

Angleton's timing was exquisite, for a potential solution to the riddle of Oswald's years in Russia loomed just over the horizon in the person of Yuri Nosenko, who was expected to reemerge from the Soviet Union in January as the KGB security officer with the Soviet delegation to the disarmament talks in Geneva. As a former member of the American Department of the KGB's Second Chief Directorate, Nosenko was in a perfect position to provide information on Oswald's stay in the USSR. Angleton was convinced that Nosenko was a disinformation agent dispatched by the KGB in 1962 to sidetrack the CIA's hunt for the mole, but that did not diminish his value as a potential source of information about Oswald. The lies he told could be as revealing as the truths. On December 19 Nosenko's case officer, Pete Bagley, who had recently been promoted to chief of counterintelligence for the Soviet Bloc Division, circulated a twelve-page memo on the subject, recommending that if Nosenko recontacted the CIA upon his return to Geneva, he should be regarded as under Soviet control.

That was a harsh judgment to render against someone who

had helped the CIA uncover two major KGB penetrations. Nosenko had warned that the KGB had blackmailed a homosexual in the British naval attaché's office, a tip that led directly to the arrest and conviction of William John Vassall, and he had revealed that small, pencillike listening devices were imbedded in the wall behind each radiator at the American Embassy in Moscow. They had been placed behind the radiators, he explained, so that the tiny pinholes that channeled the sound to the bugs would not be painted over. In the world of counterintelligence, however, it was easy enough to pass these two leads off as "giveaways," penetrations that the Soviets assumed to be blown already and that could be given up to establish an agent's bona fides without damage to ongoing operations. According to Bagley, both Vassall and the bugging operation had been compromised prior to the appearance of Nosenko. In fact, they had been compromised by Golitsin—two more instances of the uncanny overlap of information provided by Russian intelligence officers who had ostensibly served in entirely different branches of the KGB. Although Golitsin had not known Vassall's name, he had revealed enough to make his uncovering "inevitable," Bagley maintained, a fact that the KGB recognized by severing its contacts with Vassall immediately after Golitsin's defection. Nosenko's information merely "permitted [Vassall] to be caught sooner, and that is all," Bagley said. As for the bugs in the embassy, Golitsin "had given approximate locations of some of the microphones six months earlier. . . . The actual tearing out of the walls . . . would have been done, and the microphone system found, without Nosenko's information."

Nosenko arrived in Geneva as expected on January 20, 1964, along with the rest of the Soviet delegation. After checking into his hotel, he went to a pay phone, dialed the telegraph office, and dictated a brief, innocuous message. Within hours Bagley and Kisvalter were on a plane to Switzerland. Three days later they were sitting in a CIA safe house in the suburbs of Geneva listening to Nosenko's assurances that the KGB had never had anything to do with Lee Harvey Oswald and most especially had not recruited him to kill Kennedy. Nosenko said he had personally examined the case when Oswald defected to Moscow in October of 1959, and had determined that he was too unstable to be taken on as an agent. The KGB had not even wanted to accept Oswald as a defector, Nosenko said, but had relented when he attempted suicide. As for Oswald's wife, Marina, Nosenko said that she was stupid, uneducated, and possessed "anti-Soviet characteristics." When she and Oswald asked to leave the Soviet Union for the United States, the KGB was perfectly content to see them go. Summarizing Nosenko's first session with Bagley and Kisvalter, Angleton wrote that "the thrust of Source's account was that neither Oswald nor his wife had at any time been of any interest whatsoever to Soviet authorities, that there had not ever been thought given to recruiting either of them as agents and that, in fact, the Soviets were glad to get rid of them both."

One week later Nosenko slipped away for another session with Bagley and Kisvalter. "No matter how I may hate anyone," he said, "I cannot speak against my convictions and since I know this case I could unhesitatingly sign off to the fact that the Soviet Union cannot be tied into this in any way." Nosenko said that within hours of Kennedy's assassination he had been called in to examine Oswald's file and assess the KGB's liability in the President's death. Nosenko insisted that the only KGB involvement had been to ask Marina's uncle, a colonel in the Ministry of Internal Affairs (MVD), to persuade Oswald not to spread anti-Soviet propaganda upon his return to the United States. Nosenko also claimed to know all about the visit Oswald paid to the Russian Embassy in Mexico City in quest of a visa to return to the Soviet Union. The embassy cabled Moscow for instructions, Nosenko related, "and we said absolutely not because he is completely undesirable—there was no interest in him whatsoever."

Quite apart from the preexisting suspicion that he was under KGB control, Nosenko's story defied belief. Such categorical assurances of Russian innocence, coming so soon after the assassination, seemed too convenient for comfort. As Bagley put it, the CIA was "unbelievably lucky" to have found such a source. "Of the many thousands of KGB people throughout the world, CIA had secret relations with only one, and this one turned out to have participated directly in the Oswald case. Not only once, but on two separate occasions: when Oswald came to Russia in 1959 and again after the assassination when the Kremlin leadership caused a definitive review of the whole KGB file on Oswald."

Nosenko's contention that the KGB had not even bothered to debrief Oswald, an ex-Marine who had been stationed at a U-2 base in Japan, flew in the face of everything that was known about the KGB's handling of defectors. "Here was a young American," Bagley said, "just out of the Marine Corps, already inside the USSR and going to great lengths to stay there and become a citizen. The KGB never bothered to talk to him, not even once. . . . Can this be true? Could we all be wrong in what we've heard about rigid Soviet security precautions and about their strict procedures and disciplines . . . ? Of course not." Helms stated flatly that "no person familiar with the facts . . . finds Nosenko's statements about Lee Harvey Oswald and the KGB to be credible."

Nosenko told Bagley and Kisvalter that he wanted to defect, a sharp reversal from eighteen months before when he had said he could never abandon his family in Moscow. Bagley, by his own account, was "stupefied." "Why?" he asked Nosenko. "Didn't you tell us you never would?"

"Well, I think they may suspect me," Nosenko replied vaguely. "I have decided to make a new life."

"How about your family?" Bagley asked. Nosenko said they would be all right.

Ordinarily, a suspected disinformation agent would not be accepted as a defector, but this was an extraordinary case. True or false, Nosenko was crucial to the Warren Commission's investigation. As Richard Helms later explained it, "If his information were to be believed, then we could conclude that the KGB and the Soviet Union had nothing to do with Lee Harvey Oswald in 1963 and therefore had nothing to do with President Kennedy's murder. . . . If Mr. Nosenko was giving us false information about Oswald's contacts with the KGB in 1959 to 1962, it was fair for us to surmise that there may have been an Oswald-KGB connection in November, 1963, more specifically that Oswald was acting as a Soviet agent when he shot President Kennedy."

Either way, Nosenko was the best witness the CIA was likely

to find. "You couldn't possibly turn this one down," a CIA officer said. "It was decided that although the Agency was intensely suspicious of him—perhaps more than suspicious, they had concluded that he was being dispatched to mislead the U.S. government— nevertheless we must not tip our hand," John Hart, an expert on the Nosenko case, explained. "We must not let Nosenko know that we suspected him, because Nosenko would then report back to his superiors that we knew what they were up to. Thus Nosenko was treated with a maximum of duplicity."

"The only thing I want to know, and I ask this question, what should I expect in the future?" Nosenko inquired of Bagley in his broken English.

"The following awaits," Bagley replied. "As I presented it, you wanted to come to the United States to have some job, some chance for future life which gives you security, and if possible, the opportunity to work in this field which you know. Is that correct?"

"Absolutely," Nosenko responded.

"The Director has said yes, flatly, absolutely yes. In fact, I would say enthusiastic. That is the only way to describe it," Bagley assured him. "We talked about the means by which you can have a solid career with a certain personal independence. Because of the very great assistance you have been to us already and because of this desire to give you a backing, they will give you a little additional personal security. We want to give you an account of your own, a sum at the beginning of just plain $50,000, and from there on, as a working contract, $25,000 a year. But, in addition, because of [the Vassall] case, which would have been impossible without your information, we are going to add at least $10,000 to this initial sum."

Nosenko warned Bagley that they would have to move quickly. He feared that his superiors were on to him. He had just received a telegram recalling him to Moscow on the next day, February 4. On that day Nosenko once again slipped away from the rest of the Soviet delegation and, dressed as an American Army officer, was driven across the German border to a CIA safe house near Frankfurt. Three days later David Murphy, chief of the Soviet Bloc Division, arrived in Frankfurt and repeated to Nosenko the promises

Bagley had made in Geneva. "First, I assured Subject that I was satisfied that he was genuine," Murphy recorded. "Based on this and assuming his continued 'cooperation,' I said we would proceed to make arrangements to bring him to the States. Second, I confirmed our agreement to pay him $25,000 for each year in place [$50,000 to cover the period since Nosenko's initial contact in June of 1962] plus $10,000 for [the Vassall case] and our readiness to contract for his services at $25,000 per year. Third, I explained the polygraph he would be expected to take as final proof of his bona fides."

In fact, Murphy was certain Nosenko was lying, at least about Oswald. "I did not believe that it would be possible for the Soviet intelligence services to have remained indifferent to the arrival in 1959 in Moscow of a former Marine radar operator who had served at what was an active U-2 operational base." It was possible that the Soviets had not made the connection between Oswald's assignment and the U-2, but that would not deter them from debriefing him. If nothing else, "they will talk to a Marine about close order drill," Murphy said. Upon his return to Washington, Murphy drafted a memo that revealed his true opinion of Nosenko, namely, "that Subject is here on a KGB-directed mission," and urged that "Subject must be broken at some point if we are to learn something of the full scope of the KGB plan."

Nosenko arrived in the United States on February 11. Afraid—with good reason—that the CIA's promises would evaporate, he drowned his anxieties in drink. "He got to the point where he was starting out the day with a drink and was continuing to drink more or less continually throughout the twenty-four hours," Hart said. "He didn't want to do anything except drink and carouse," Helms recalled, adding that one binge ended with "an incident in Baltimore where he started punching up a bar."

Had he known what Golitsin was saying about him, Nosenko might have taken to drink with an even greater vengeance. Consulted about Nosenko's bona fides, Golitsin "felt in general that there are indeed serious signs of disinformation in this affair," a CIA memo reported. "The purpose of Nosenko's coming out, he thought, would be to contradict what [Golitsin] had said, and also possibly to set [Golitsin] up for kidnapping, also to divert our attention from investigations of [Golitsin's] leads by throwing up false scents, and to protect remaining Soviet sources."

A case in point was the still unsolved mystery of V. M. Kovshuk's mission to the United States. At his first meetings with Bagley and Kisvalter in 1962, Nosenko said that Kovshuk had come to meet with an American serviceman whose Soviet code name was ANDREY. After his defection Nosenko provided additional clues to ANDREY's identity. He had been recruited during the early 1950s while serving as a mechanic in the motor pool at the American Embassy in Moscow, Nosenko said. That quickly led the FBI to an Army sergeant who admitted meeting with the Soviets in Moscow and even with Kovshuk in the United States. But an Army mechanic would have no information of any conceivable intelligence value to the Russians. An official as important as Golitsin said Kovshuk was would not have come all the way to the United States just to meet with ANDREY. Golitsin insisted that Kovshuk had come to meet with a much more important source, perhaps the KGB's mole inside the CIA, and that Nosenko's story about the meeting with ANDREY was merely a cover for Kovshuk's real mission.

A similar pattern existed in the case of SASHA, the KGB spy who Golitsin said had penetrated the CIA's operations in Germany. Although a number of suspects had been investigated, the CIA had made no progress in identifying SASHA until Golitsin dredged up from his memory some additional leads to specific operations SASHA had blown in Berlin. Combing the files of the Berlin Operations Base, investigators came upon "a whole series of operational disasters." The common denominator in all of the failed operations was a CIA contract agent named Igor Orlov, "barely over five feet tall, a little china doll of a man," who had served valiantly as a Russian agent behind the German lines in World War II and had defected to the West after the fighting stopped. Throughout most of the 1950s Orlov had been a "principal agent" of Bill Harvey in Berlin. As a native Russian, he had been the perfect vehicle for maintaining contact between the American CIA officers and their agents in the Soviet sector of Berlin. If he were working for the Russians, however, Orlov would have been the perfect vehicle for blowing the cover of each and every CIA agent he dealt with. One of his handlers estimated that Orlov could have blown as many as twenty CIA agents.

Nosenko's already suspect credibility was badly damaged by the SASHA case. Although Orlov denied the charge, Golitsin had been proved right, and Nosenko wrong. Nosenko had intimated to his interrogators that SASHA was an Army officer, an inaccurate lead that momentarily sidetracked the CIA's investigation just as it was closing in on Orlov. Here was one more instance to support their thesis that Nosenko had been sent to undermine Golitsin's information. There was still another case in which Nosenko's version of events seemed designed to assure the CIA that, regardless of what Golitsin said, it had not been penetrated by the KGB.

Nosenko said that in November of 1963 he had traveled to Gorki, a major industrial city on the Volga River, as part of a nationwide manhunt for a traitor, one Cherapanov, a former KGB officer who had passed a packet of classified documents to the American Embassy in Moscow. Cherapanov was well known to the CIA, since several years before he had made an unsuccessful attempt to defect to the Americans in Yugoslavia. According to Nosenko, Cherapanov had lost his job with the KGB as a result of his abortive defection and had been exiled to a functionary's position in a state-run publishing enterprise. Cherapanov was serving as a guide for an Indiana bookseller and his wife, who were touring the Soviet Union, when he handed them a package wrapped in old copies of *Pravda* and *Izvestia* and asked them to deliver it to the American Embassy. The Indiana couple did as Cherapanov asked, handing the bundle to the political counselor, Malcolm Toon, who immediately concluded that this was a setup. Two weeks earlier in Warsaw, an American Army attaché had been declared *persona non grata* for accepting a map of rocket sites thrust upon him by a Polish intelligence officer in a deliberate provocation. Members of the CIA station in Moscow argued with Toon that the Cherapanov case was different, that the documents, which among other things contained detailed KGB surveillance reports, were too damaging to be an intentional plant. Toon refused to reconsider, and the documents were returned to the Ministry of Foreign Affairs. According to Nosenko's version, Soviet security agents immediately identified Cherapanov as the source of the documents, and after a brief chase he was apprehended and shot.

By Nosenko's account, Toon had made a rash decision that cost Cherapanov his life, but a counterintelligence analysis suggested that perhaps Toon had done the right thing for the wrong reason. Once Cherapanov had tried to defect in Yugoslavia, the KGB would never have allowed him to come in contact with United States citizens again except for some deliberate purpose. Furthermore, the documents Cherapanov had handed to the Indiana bookseller fairly reeked of disinformation. Before returning them to the Soviets as Toon had ordered, the CIA took the precaution of photographing the documents for further study, and one of them, a detailed KGB analysis of the movements of FBI surveillance teams in New York City, provided new evidence in the Popov case. The KGB analysis showed that the FBI was concentrating on a special surveillance at precisely the time that Popov's agent Tairova had arrived in New York. If it was genuine, the document lent considerable weight to the thesis that the FBI's indiscreet handling of the case had led to Popov's downfall. By relating the details of the KGB's pursuit of Cherapanov, Nosenko seemed to be vouching for the authenticity of a document that said in effect that Popov had not been blown by George Blake in 1955 but had remained a trustworthy CIA agent until the Tairova case in 1959. From the Soviet point of view, the Cherapanov document served the dual purpose of further confusing the question of Popov's bona fides and of sowing a few seeds of discord between the CIA and FBI.

Suspicions of Nosenko's story were heightened by the fact that it contained a deliberate and demonstrable falsehood. At the time of his defection in 1964, Nosenko claimed that he was a lieutenant colonel in the KGB and offered as proof of his rank a travel document that he said had been issued to him for his trip to Gorki during the hunt for Cherapanov. The document listed his rank as lieutenant colonel, but under questioning Nosenko admitted that he was merely a captain in the KGB. It was not surprising that Nosenko would inflate his rank in order to convince the CIA of his importance, but the fact that the inflated rank was confirmed by the KGB travel document suggested that Nosenko had had help in concocting his ruse.

More suspicious still, Nosenko's bogus rank was backed up by a second Soviet source—SCOTCH, the KGB officer at the United Nations who had volunteered his services to the Americans around the time of Golitsin's defection. SCOTCH also confirmed the story Nosenko had told Bagley and Kisvalter just before his defection in Geneva about receiving a telegram recalling him to Moscow at once. But an analysis by the National Security Agency of the radio traffic between Moscow and Geneva found no indication that such a message had been sent. Like the inflated rank, the recall telegram was an understandable lie told by a would-be defector eager to convince his handlers of the importance and urgency of his case. But the fact that SCOTCH should vouch for the lie was not understandable unless the KGB was purposely channeling disinformation to the CIA in an effort to build up Nosenko's story. Again, Golitsin's warnings seemed the only believable explanation. He had said that the KGB would send false agents to discredit him, and now both SCOTCH and Nosenko appeared to be playing that very game.

On April 2, 1964, Helms, accompanied by Murphy and Lawrence Houston, the Agency's general counsel, met with Deputy Attorney General Nicholas Katzenbach to determine Nosenko's legal status. According to a memo written by Houston, Katzenbach said that Nosenko was technically on parole to the CIA until the question of his bona fides could be settled and that the Agency was free "to take any action necessary to carry out the terms of the parole." Until now, Nosenko had been treated like any other defector. His interrogators had behaved cordially toward him and had not confronted him with any of the contradictions in his story. Under these laissez-faire conditions, it was impossible to pin him down. He was drunk much of the time, and when sober, "he deflected questions, changed the subject, and invented excuses not to talk, even about isolated points of detail," Bagley said. "It became clear that if he were to be questioned at all, some discipline had to be applied." Given the implications Nosenko's bona fides held for Soviet involvement in Kennedy's death and for KGB penetration of the CIA, "it was our duty to clarify this matter," Bagley said.

"Anything less would have been . . . dereliction of duty."

On April 4, two months to the day after his defection, Nosenko was given his first lie-detector test—"fluttered," in Agency parlance. In an effort to trick him into abandoning his charade, Nosenko was to be told that he had failed the test regardless of the outcome. The polygraph did in fact detect "significant reactions" indicating that Nosenko was lying, although the validity of the test was undermined by the intimidation tactics that preceded it. "An artifact which was described to him as an electroencephalograph was attached to him and he was told that in addition to all the other sensors, we were going to read his brain waves," Hart recounted. "Now there was no purpose for this except—as the documentary evidence shows—except to raise his tension. He was made to fear this polygraph in every way he could." It was impossible to tell whether the "significant reactions" were measures of Nosenko's fear or his prevarication.

In a deposition given to a congressional committee years later, Nosenko described what happened after he was fluttered. "An officer of CIA . . . started to shout that I was a phony and immediately several guards entered the room. The guards ordered me to stand by the wall, to undress, and checked me. After that I was taken upstairs in an attic room. The room had a metal bed attached to the floor in the center of this room. Nobody told me anything—how long I would be there or what would happen to me. After several days, two officers of CIA . . . started interrogations. I tried to cooperate and even in evening hours was writing for them whatever I could recollect about the KGB. These officers were interrogating me about a month or two months. The tone of interrogations was hostile. Then they stopped to come to see me until the end of 1964. I was kept in this room till the end of 1964 and beginning of 1965." Nosenko was forced to rise every morning at six A.M. and was not permitted to lie down again until ten P.M. "The conditions were very poor and difficult. I could have a shower once in a week and once in a week I could shave. I was not given a toothbrush and toothpaste and food given to me was very poor. I did not have enough to eat and was hungry all the time. I had no contact with anybody to talk. I could not read. I could not smoke, and I even could not have fresh air to see anything from this room. The only window was screened and boarded. The only door of the room had a metal screen and outside in a corridor two guards were watching me day and night. The only furniture in the room was a single bed and a light bulb. The room was very, very hot in summertime."

According to Hart, "the guards at the house were given instructions that there must be no physical mistreatment of him but that they were not to talk to him, they were not to smile at him." The guards passed the time by watching television, but they wore earphones so that Nosenko could not hear the sound. A CIA memo explained the purpose of Nosenko's solitary confinement. "The interval in isolation will be extremely valuable in terms of allowing subject to ponder on the complete failure of his recent gambits." Besides, now that Nosenko realized that the CIA did not believe him, he had to be kept confined for fear that he would redefect to the Soviet Union before the true dimensions of the KGB's disinformation plot could be uncovered.

Hostile interrogation had only deepened the CIA's suspicions of Nosenko. "Before, we suspected Nosenko might be a plant," Bagley said. "Afterwards we had come to think moreover that he might never have been a true KGB officer and that he surely had not held certain of the positions in the KGB which he claimed." Under questioning, "Nosenko was unable to clarify any single point of doubt. Brought up against his own contradictions and other independent information, he admitted that there could be no innocent explanation . . . or he would remain silent, or he would come up with a new story, only to change that, too." The contradictions could not be explained away by mere loss of memory. As Bagley pointed out, Nosenko "was supposedly talking of things he'd lived through—the KGB files he'd seen, the officers he'd worked with. If these were real experiences, he need only recall them and his reports would, all of themselves, come out the same way each time." Nosenko admitted that he "looked bad," even to himself.

Helms met privately with Chief Justice Earl Warren to inform him of the CIA's doubts about Nosenko's bona fides. Other members of the Warren Commission and its staff were told flatly that "Nosenko is a KGB plant." The problem was that no one in the CIA was willing to take the next step and declare that Nosenko had been sent to cover up KGB complicity in Kennedy's murder. That step could be taken only if the CIA could "break Nosenko and get the full story of how and why he was told to tell the story he did about Oswald." There was, the CIA conceded, "no certainty that we can ever do this." Moreover, even if Nosenko could be definitively exposed as a liar, it did not necessarily follow that Oswald had been ordered by the KGB to kill Kennedy. Bagley speculated that Oswald might have been carried on the KGB's rolls as a sleeper agent to be activated for sabotage in time of war. After all, Bagley pointed out, the KGB could not have expected too much from an agent whose cover was so thin as to permit a Soviet wife. Under such circumstances, Bagley said, "they would be absolutely shocked to hear their man had taken it upon himself to kill the American President."

For the moment, therefore, Nosenko's testimony would have to be discounted entirely and all references to him excised from the commission's final report so that his interrogation could proceed in secret. The commission was left with little more to go on than Oswald's diary of his stay in Russia and the few official documents provided by the Kremlin. Neither, of course, gave any hint of Soviet complicity in the President's death. When the commission issued its final report on September 28, 1964, it was no closer to resolving the doubts about Soviet involvement than it had been ten months before, and the CIA was no closer to solving the Nosenko riddle than on the day in June of 1962 when he had first made contact.

The conviction of Helms, Murphy, Bagley, and, of course, Angleton that Nosenko had been sent by the KGB to dissemble was, almost by definition, beyond challenge. When it came to espionage operations against the Soviet Union, they were the four most powerful men in the CIA. A serious disagreement with them might well damage an officer's career. Besides, very few officers outside their circle knew enough about the case to form an independent judgment. The facts were held very tightly, Bagley explained, because "if Nosenko was a KGB plant, there was a KGB spy within CIA. This is not the sort of thing one wants to spread widely." The logic was flawless, but the extreme secrecy that resulted effectively quenched any dissenting opinions.

As the years passed, however, and the circle of knowledge inevitably expanded, a small school of Nosenko believers began to develop. Invariably, they were men who scorned the double-cross school of counterintelligence and were satisfied that the KGB would never deliberately give away as many secrets as Nosenko had. Nosenko had given up the Soviet spy Vassall, the bugging of the American Embassy in Moscow, and a host of leads to such Americans as ANDREY. He had also confirmed Golitsin's warning about the homosexual Canadian ambassador to the Soviet Union.

After listening to Golitsin, Canada's RCMP was convinced that he could only be describing John Watkins, a close friend of Prime Minister Lester Pearson and a noted academician, who had served in Moscow during the 1950s. With only Golitsin's information to go on, however, the RCMP was reluctant to accuse such a distinguished and well-connected man of treason. But Nosenko seconded the story, adding so much convincing detail that it could no longer be ignored. According to Nosenko, Watkins's KGB case officer had arranged in 1955 for then Foreign Minister Pearson to meet with Khrushchev at his dacha in the Crimea. Nosenko told of a drunken dinner party at which Khrushchev raised toast after toast of vodka to his Canadian guests. As his tongue loosened, Khrushchev began to mock Watkins with thinly veiled remarks about his homosexuality. During a toast to women, he leered at Watkins and said that not everybody present loved women. Nosenko's account of the dinner party was later partially confirmed by no less a source than Pearson, who wrote in his memoirs that "Khrushchev was determined . . . to put us all 'under the table' " and that while "the atmosphere became mellower and mellower John Watkins . . . looked less and less happy." Acting on Nosenko's testimony, the RCMP rousted Watkins from retirement in Paris and placed him under intense interrogation. He confessed his homosexuality but steadfastly denied that he had ever been recruited by the KGB. Just as the RCMP was about to abandon the interrogation, Watkins suffered a heart attack and died. Though he never confessed, there was little doubt within the RCMP or the CIA that he had been blackmailed into doing the KGB's bidding.

Would the KGB really direct a defector to reveal so much in order to establish his bona fides? "There is no precedent that we know of for the Soviets giving information of this sensitivity away," John Hart insisted. George Kisvalter, the Agency's premier case officer, who had handled Popov and Penkovsky, the best agents the CIA ever had, argued that the Russians "would be crazy to give [Vassall] up . . . the precedent of giving up such an agent would be almost anathema to the future recruitment of agents."

Such homilies made little impression on the double-cross disciples for whom the quality of the intelligence given up was merely a measure of the magnitude of the deception to come. "It is a straightforward counterespionage technique," Bagley insisted, citing a captured KGB document as his source. "It stated that just catching American spies isn't enough, for the enemy can always start again with new ones," he recalled. "Therefore, said this KGB document, disinformation operations are essential. And among the purposes of such operations . . . is 'to negate and discredit authentic information the enemy has obtained.' I believe that Nosenko's mission in 1962 involved just that—covering and protecting KGB sources threatened by [Golitsin's] defection." Yet there had to be some point at which the double-cross equation went off the graph, some truth the KGB would not give up in the name of deception. The case of Sergeant Robert Lee Johnson seemed to be that point.

Nosenko told the CIA that prior to his defection there had been rumors circulating in Moscow Center of a tremendous new penetration in France. A friend of his in the KGB's technical services division had actually gone to Paris to help process the take, Nosenko said. He assumed that the penetration was in some way related to the KGB's recent development of an X-ray device capable of reading combination locks, the brainchild of a grotesque squad of safecrackers who had lost all their teeth to the radiation it emitted. Nosenko's rumors became fact on November 25, 1964, when Sergeant Johnson confessed to the greatest wholesale compromise of military secrets in the nation's history.

As the case was later reconstructed in an authoritative exposé of the KGB by John Barron, Johnson left his guard post at the Armed Forces Courier Center near Paris a few minutes past midnight on Sunday, December 15, 1962, carrying a blue Air France flight bag crammed with secret documents. He drove his crotchety Citroën to a service road near Orly Airport where a gray Mercedes waited. Johnson handed the flight bag to Feliks Ivanov of the KGB and received in return an identical blue bag filled with wine and food. Within five minutes he was back at his post while Ivanov sped toward the Soviet Embassy in the center of Paris, where a team of KGB technicians flown in from Moscow via Algeria waited in a third-floor room. For one hour the technicians worked with hushed intensity, photographing the contents of the flight bag. At fifteen minutes past three, Ivanov parked his Mercedes on a dirt road next to a small cemetery five miles from Orly. Johnson drove up, exchanged flight bags with Ivanov once again, and returned to the Courier Center to await his relief at six A.M. On the way home that morning, Johnson stopped at a telephone booth to leave a pack of Lucky Strike cigarettes with an X penciled on the inside, the sign that the documents had been safely returned.

That clockwork maneuver was the product of nine years' perseverance by the KGB which had begun in 1953 when a disgruntled Johnson left his Army post in West Berlin, took the tram to the Karlshorst stop in East Berlin, and offered to defect. The KGB gently deflected Johnson's offer and instead maintained a desultory, mostly unproductive contact with him until March of 1961, when he was transferred to the Courier Center, the funnel point for all classified documents passing between Washington and NATO command posts in Europe. The center was one of the most enticing and impregnable espionage targets in the free world. An armed guard was on duty around the clock, and two steel doors barred the entrance to the vault that housed the documents. The first door was secured by a metal bar with combination locks at each end. The second had a key lock. No one could open the vault without the key and both combinations. No one was allowed inside the vault alone. On weekends a single guard was left to watch the vault, but both doors were locked and the guard had neither the key nor the two combinations needed to open it.

Coached by the KGB, Johnson managed to make a clay impression of the key and to retrieve the combination to one of the other locks from a piece of scratch paper carelessly thrown into a wastebasket. The final combination eluded him until the fall of 1962, when he volunteered for weekend guard duty. Alone in the center from six P.M. Saturday until six A.M. Sunday, Johnson worked with a portable X-ray machine that when fitted over the lock revealed the combination. The final barrier overcome, Johnson and his KGB accomplices managed to loot the vault on seven separate occasions before he was finally transferred to another post in the fall of 1963.

Nosenko knew none of these details. His information had not been specific enough to pinpoint Johnson as even a suspect in the case. Johnson had done himself in. At the end of his mental tether, he had gone AWOL, then surrendered to police in Reno, Nevada, and confessed. Still, Nosenko had told the CIA of a major penetration in Paris, a penetration that until his defection had gone totally undetected. Surely the KGB would not deliberately have alerted an unsuspecting United States to such a hemorrhaging of secrets. There were other ways to establish Nosenko's bona fides.

No sooner was this argument made in favor of Nosenko than a counterintelligence analysis of the Johnson case suggested that the KGB had long since given up the operation as blown. After his seventh entry into the vault, Johnson had fallen asleep and failed to return to the cemetery at the scheduled time to retrieve the documents from his KGB controller, Ivanov. If the documents were not returned to the vault before Johnson was relieved at six A.M., the game would be over. Shortly after five A.M., Johnson woke up, looked at his watch, realized what had happened, and dashed frantically out the door to his car. The flight bag full of documents was sitting on the front seat, left by Ivanov in a last-ditch effort to save the operation. Johnson returned the documents to the vault, completing the job only seconds before his relief arrived. Unwilling to admit to Ivanov that he had nearly ruined so valuable an operation by falling asleep, Johnson concocted a story that an officer had arrived without warning to pick up some documents, making it impossible for him to break away for the rendezvous—

a story that conflicted with the fact that withdrawals from the vault were never made on weekends and that two commissioned officers were required to sign for all documents. Sensing a trap, the KGB terminated the operation.

According to this analysis, the KGB had every reason to believe that the operation had been blown and that Johnson had switched his allegiance back to the United States. As far as the KGB was concerned, Nosenko had told the CIA nothing it didn't already know. The fact that the KGB was mistaken did not detract from the force of the argument.

Angleton and his staff, so quick to discount Nosenko's give-aways, ignored the fact that the same calculus could be used against much of Golitsin's information. It was true that Golitsin had provided leads that narrowed the search for the KGB's source SASHA to the diminutive Igor Orlov, but by then the CIA had already terminated Orlov's services. He had become a handling problem and had been brought back from Germany and resettled in Washington. Orlov acknowledged having had a couple of run-ins with West German police, but insisted that the reason his CIA career ended was that he had accused an officer of stealing from one of his agents. In either case, Orlov was out of the spy business. Anyone who suspected him of being a KGB agent would logically have to entertain the possibility that he was just another giveaway.

All such conjecture aside, the simple truth was that for all Golitsin's alarms about moles and disinformation campaigns, Nosenko had provided the CIA with at least as many confirmed leads to Soviet penetrations as Golitsin—if not more. Hart asserted flatly that "quantitatively and qualitatively, the information given by [Golitsin] was much smaller than that given by Nosenko." Yet Nosenko languished in solitary confinement while Golitsin served as what one officer called "a trusted contract agent being paid a very respectable sum." Golitsin "was given access to all the debriefings of Nosenko . . . to the tapes themselves . . . [and] allowed to think up questions which were to be asked Nosenko," Hart said. "Angleton will apply certain standards to other people that he was never willing to apply to his pet," a chief of the Soviet Bloc Division grumbled.

The interrogation of Nosenko was resumed at the end of 1964.

"The first day they kept me under 24 hours interrogation," he later testified. "All interrogations were done in a hostile manner. . . . I . . . asked how long it would continue. I was told that I would be there 3,860 days and even more. . . . I was taken by guards blindfolded and handcuffed in a car and delivered to an airport and put in a plane. I was taken to another location where I was put into a concrete room with bars on a door." According to Hart, Nosenko's new prison had been "built especially to house him" and resembled nothing so much as "a bank vault." It "was a very expensive construction because it consisted of heavy steel reinforced concrete." As Nosenko described it, his cell was furnished with "a single steel bed and a mattress—no pillow, no sheet and no blanket. During winter it was very cold and I asked to give me a blanket which I received after some time. I was watched day and night through TV camera. Trying to pass the time a couple of times I was making from threads chess set. And everytime when I finished those sets immediately guards were entering in my cell and taking them from me." According to Hart, "He also made himself a calendar out of lint from his clothing. . . . He was desperately trying to keep track of the time. . . . But in the course of his having been compelled to sweep up his room or clean up his room, why these calendars were of course ruined, so he had to start all over again." Nosenko said, "I was desperately wanting to read, and once when I was given a toothpaste I found in a toothpaste box a piece of paper with description of components of this toothpaste. I was trying to read it under blanket but guard noticed it and again it was taken from me." After nearly two years in the vault, Nosenko was granted thirty minutes a day for exercise in a small yard next to his cell. "The area was surrounded by a chain-link fence and by a second fence that I could not see through," Nosenko said. "The only thing I could see was the sky."

Officially, this inhuman treatment was referred to as "highly secure conditions" that were required "to permit extensive and prolonged debriefing." But of the 1,277 days Nosenko was held captive, he was questioned on only 292. Memos danced around that fact by referring to "the additional need to provide Mr. Nosenko with continuing personal protection since there was the distinct possibility that he would be targeted for execution if the Soviets should discover his whereabouts." That last was an especially disingenuous piece of rationalization, since those who had directed Nosenko's confinement were convinced that he was still working for the KGB.

Through it all, Nosenko stuck to his story no matter how many holes his captors were able to poke in it. He said, for example, that during the early 1950s he had spent a great deal of time trying to recruit a military attaché assigned to the American Embassy in Moscow. But Nosenko could not identify the officer's photograph and did not know that he had subsequently been expelled from the Soviet Union after he was caught receiving documents from a Russian citizen. Nosenko also said that in early 1961 he had received daily reports on the KGB's surveillance of a CIA dead drop in Moscow. But CIA records showed that the dead drop, which had been used for communications with Penkovsky, had not been set up until late 1961. Nosenko, who maintained that his primary intelligence target had been the American Embassy, did not know which floors were set aside for classified work. And the man who claimed he had been assigned to Moscow Center from 1953 until his defection in 1964 could not describe the KGB cafeteria.

At one point, Bagley thought Nosenko was about to break. When he was unable to provide any details about a case he had supposedly run for the KGB, Bagley asked why he wouldn't admit he hadn't handled the case. Nosenko sat silent for a moment and then said that if he admitted he hadn't handled the case he would also have to admit that he was not the man he said he was. There was another pause, and then Nosenko pulled himself together and went on.

Finally, in August of 1966, Helms lost patience and gave the Counterintelligence and Soviet Bloc Divisions sixty days in which to conclude their case against Nosenko. He rejected a request to interrogate Nosenko under the influence of sodium amytal, forcing the interrogators to resort once again to polygraph. Nosenko had already failed the polygraph once, but the results were worthless because of the intimidation to which he had been subjected. The second test was no better. According to Hart, Nosenko's examiner began by telling him "that he was a fanatic and that there was

no evidence to support his legend and your future is now zero."
During the examination, Nosenko was left strapped to the chair
for hours on end while his interrogators took "lunch breaks." One
"lunch break" lasted three hours and fifteen minutes; another, four
hours. "There was no intention that this 1966 series of polygraphs
would be valid," Hart said. Bagley's handwritten notes revealed
the true intent: "To gain more insight into points of detail which
we could use in fabricating an ostensible Nosenko confession . . .
[which] would be useful in any eventual disposal of Nosenko." Bagley was willing to contemplate almost anything to avoid what he
called the "devastating consequences" of awarding Nosenko his
bona fides. He jotted down, "for my fleeting use only," a list of
"alternative actions" that could be taken "to liquidate and insofar
as possible to clean up traces of a situation in which CIA could
be accused of illegally holding Nosenko." Fifth on the list was
"liquidate the man." Number six was "render him incapable of
giving coherent story (special dose of drug et cetera). Possible aim,
commitment to loony bin." Number seven was "commitment to
loony bin without making him nuts."

Bagley compiled a report more than 900 pages in length, which
detail by eye-glazing detail dissected the discrepancies in Nosenko's
story. "Nosenko claimed that his operational success during 1959
earned him a commendation from the KGB chairman," Bagley
wrote on page 127. "He has since retracted all claims to any awards
during his KGB service." Nosenko claimed to have "thoroughly
reviewed Oswald's file within hours of Kennedy's assassination,"
Bagley noted on page 307. But "Nosenko later told CIA on one
occasion that he 'only skimmed the file' and on another that he
had it in his possession about 20 minutes." Nosenko was not aware
that Oswald and his wife had sent visa requests to the Soviet Embassy in Washington, Bagley continued. "Nosenko's apparent ignorance of Oswald's communications with the Soviet Embassy in
Washington discredits his claim to complete knowledge of all aspects
of the KGB relationship with Oswald." On and on for 900 pages.
All told, said Bagley, there were "hundreds of specific points of
doubt such as had never arisen in any of the scores of defections
of Soviet Bloc intelligence officers before Nosenko." A decade after

compiling the report, Bagley would still remember "at least 20 clear cases of Nosenko's lying about KGB activity and about the career which gave him authority to tell of it, and a dozen examples of his ignorance of matters within his claimed area of responsibility, for which there is no innocent explanation." Bagley's conclusion was that Nosenko had held none of the jobs he said he had held, and that he was not the man he claimed to be.

Bagley forwarded his report to Angleton's Counterintelligence Division, and now Angleton found himself in something of a dilemma. Although he had never deigned to meet with Nosenko, Angleton had from the start been the guiding light behind Bagley's suspicions. It was he who first initiated Bagley into the dark world of Golitsin and planted the notion that Nosenko had been sent to protect the KGB's mole. But despite his conviction that Nosenko was a dispatched disinformation agent, Angleton could not accept Bagley's report because it implied that "his pet," Golitsin, was not totally reliable. For all his warnings about "serious signs of disinformation in this affair," Golitsin had at least confirmed that Nosenko was a bona fide KGB officer. "He did give evidence confirming that Nosenko had had certain jobs, which was in agreement with what Nosenko told us he had done," Hart said. Bagley's report would not concede even that small point, and Angleton balked. "Chief CI said that he did not see how we could submit a final report . . . if it contained suggestions that Golitsin had lied to us about certain aspects of Nosenko's past," a staff memo recorded. The Counterintelligence and Soviet Bloc divisions bargained Bagley's "thousand-pager," as it came to be known, down to 447 pages.

No matter how long the report, no matter how strongly Angleton and Bagley felt, the CIA could not bring itself to declare Nosenko a dispatched agent of the KGB. The consequences were too grave. A man's life was at stake. If Nosenko were wrongly sent back to the Soviet Union as a false defector, the CIA would be sending an innocent man—a man who had provided valuable intelligence to the United States—to his death. Beyond that, the repudiation of Nosenko, the bearer of assurances that Oswald was not a Soviet operative, would logically require a reopening of the investigation into Kennedy's death. Angleton's staff had assigned an 85 percent probability to the likelihood that Nosenko was a false agent. Given the consequences, 85 percent wasn't enough.

Curiously, Angleton and his assistants seemed to have overlooked the single most basic and telling point about Nosenko's bona fides. If the CIA was as deeply penetrated as Goleniewski and Golitsin said it was, as Angleton and his aides believed it was, word of Nosenko's first meetings with Bagley and Kisvalter in Geneva in June of 1962 would have gotten back to Moscow Center. From that moment on, Nosenko would either be under KGB control or dead. The mere fact that he should reappear in Geneva was persuasive evidence that he had been sent to deceive. "If you accept the fact that there was high-level penetration of the CIA," an Agency officer said, "it's out of the question that Nosenko could have returned from Moscow a genuine article." Even had the point been raised, however, it would not have clinched the case against Nosenko, since proof of a high-level penetration of the CIA was as elusive as Nosenko's bona fides.

Casting about for some way out of the quandary, Helms called for a review of the entire affair. Bruce Solie, a senior member of the CIA's Office of Security who had expended considerable time and energy over the past five years tracking down Nosenko's leads, was assigned to write a critique of Bagley's report. Solie took the straightforward view that a defector's bona fides should be judged by the quality of his information, and in the case of Nosenko he felt that too much attention had been paid to breaking his story down and not enough to finding out everything he could tell the CIA about KGB operations. Despite the 1,277 days of confinement and the 292 days of interrogation, Solie concluded that Nosenko had not been thoroughly debriefed. Until he was, and until all his leads could be run down, Nosenko's bona fides remained an open question.

In November of 1967 Nosenko was taken from his cell and "transferred blindfolded and handcuffed" to a safe house near Washington, D.C., where at last, Nosenko said, "I had a room with much better conditions." For the first time since his defection, Nosenko was in an atmosphere unclouded by the dark murmurings of Golitsin and the double-cross theories of counterintelligence. Now

Solie commenced an interrogation that was to last without letup for nine months.

"I was interrogated on this case . . . several times," Nosenko lamented. "It was very, very strictly put, everything, everything."

"Yes," Solie responded, "but what I want from you is—not strictly put—I want you to put it in your own words."

Solie's aim, unlike Bagley's, was not to break Nosenko but to elicit information from him. The results of his interrogations were forwarded to the FBI, which later reported "that a minimum of nine new cases have been developed as a result of this reexamination and that new information of considerable importance on old cases not previously available resulted from this effort." Commenting on all these neglected leads, CIA Deputy Director Rufus Taylor told Helms, "Before we are through with this the FBI just might level official criticism at this Agency for its previous handling of this case."

In August of 1968 Nosenko was given a third lie-detector test, minus all the intimidation of the first two. This time he passed. In October Solie submitted a 283-page report that disputed Bagley's "thousand-pager" and concluded that "Nosenko is identical to the person he claims to be." Solie went further and specifically ruled out the possibility that Nosenko had been dispatched by the Soviet government to give false information about Oswald.

Solie's report was immediately branded a "whitewash" and "despicable" by members of Angleton's staff, but the Agency's Deputy Director bought it. "I am now convinced that there is no reason to conclude that Nosenko is other than what he has claimed to be, that he has not knowingly and willfully withheld information from us, that there is no conflict between what we have learned from him and what we have learned from other defectors or informants that would cast any doubts on his bona fides," Rufus Taylor assured Helms in writing. "Most particularly, I perceive no significant conflict between the information Nosenko has provided and the information and opinions Golitsin has provided. Thus, I conclude that Nosenko should be accepted as a bona fide defector."

Taylor convened a meeting that one participant described as "a final effort to get all of these warring factions to sit down and see if we could get a consensus," but "nobody gave an inch." The Counterintelligence Division still refused to accept Nosenko as genuine. Giving Nosenko the benefit of every doubt, there still seemed no innocent explanation for why SCOTCH, the KGB agent at the United Nations, had corroborated for the CIA the false elements in Nosenko's story about his inflated rank and the nonexistent recall telegram. "There still remains a disagreement as to his bona fides," Howard Osborn, the CIA's Director of Security, reported to Helms. "But at least it has been agreed by all concerned that the problem of Nosenko's bona fides and his rehabilitation and resettlement can be considered separately. . . . Nosenko is becoming increasingly restive and desirous of obtaining freedom on his own. After nearly five years of varying degrees of confinement, this desire, including that for feminine companionship, is understandable," Osborn continued. "Something had to be done with Nosenko physically," the head of the Soviet Bloc Division said. "You just couldn't leave him in a cage." As a first step, Nosenko was permitted a two-week "vacation" in Florida under the watchful eyes of two CIA guards. Meanwhile, Angleton was preparing a new set of questions to be put to Nosenko upon his return.

Helms, still deeply suspicious, signaled an end to the dispute by awarding Solie a medal for his work in rehabilitating Nosenko. Resettling Nosenko "was the only viable option left to us," Helms said later. Freedom for Nosenko would remain a relative thing, however. "We will occupy contiguous quarters and . . . he will be required for an undetermined period to let us know where he is going and when he leaves these quarters," a CIA memo on "the Rehabilitation and Resettlement of Nosenko" said. "We will, initially at least, provide for technical coverage of his telephone and living quarters and will, within the extent of our capability, cover him through surveillance when he leaves these quarters." Nosenko was provided with a new identity, and in March of 1969 he was hired by the CIA as a consultant and eventually paid all of the money Bagley had originally promised him in 1964.

Looking back on the affair, Helms later said, "I don't think there has ever been anything more frustrating in my life." That was a considerable admission for a man who had spent his entire adult life wrestling with the inevitable uncertainties of intrigue. So much depended on Nosenko's bona fides. There was, of course, the question of Soviet involvement in Kennedy's murder, but beyond that there was the mystery of the mole. The passage of time might ease the controversy surrounding the President's death. But time only made more pressing the need to know whether Nosenko had been sent to sidetrack Angleton from Golitsin's leads to the KGB's man inside the CIA. Kennedy was gone, beyond avenging, but the mole—if he existed—would still be burrowing deeper and deeper toward the heart of the CIA. So the question burned even brighter than before, but the answer was receding farther and farther into the maze of transcripts, analyses, and memos, of inaccuracies, contradictions, and lies, that surrounded the investigation of Nosenko. The CIA had erected its own wilderness of mirrors. Whatever Nosenko had been to begin with, the fear that he might be a disinformation agent had become a self-fulfilling prophecy. The same could be said about the hunt for the mole.

Ides of March

Bill Harvey, the man who had fingered Kim Philby, played no part in the hunt for the mole. MONGOOSE and his confrontation with the President's brother had destroyed his career. Events seemed to mock Harvey. His career had reached its peak in 1961 when he was placed in charge of the Cuba task force and introduced to President Kennedy as the American 007, yet that same year he discovered that his greatest triumph—the Berlin tunnel—had been blown from the start by George Blake. His career had plummeted in 1963 with his sacking from the task force and his exile to Rome, yet that same year Philby had fled to Moscow, providing the ultimate proof of the case Harvey had made twelve years before. Nor could it have escaped Harvey that while he had been assigned to assassinate a foreign leader for the good of his country, it was his own President who had been murdered. Now, once again, on the evening of October 22, 1966, events trumped Harvey.

Sean Bourke stood in the pouring rain, clutching a pot of pink chrysanthemums. A passerby would have thought he was waiting for the start of visiting hours at London's Hammersmith Hospital just across the street. Behind Bourke was a twenty-foot brick wall, which encircled Wormwood Scrubs Prison. Inside, the men in cell block D were in the midst of their evening's entertainment, gathered about a television set, jeering a professional wrestling match. Remarking to a guard that the match was obviously fixed, George Blake, the most heavily sentenced prisoner in the British Isles, left the raucous crowd, ascended to the second tier of cells, and stood gazing out a large window that overlooked the main entrance to the cell block. The noise he made as he shattered the glass and kicked out a cast-iron bar was drowned in the hubbub from below. He wriggled through the opening, dropped to a canopy that covered the entrance, and from there to the ground. He sprinted twenty yards to the wall, climbed up a waiting rope ladder, and jumped to the ground next to Bourke. The two men sped away in a waiting car, leaving the rope ladder behind. An hour later the entertainment period ended, and the prisoners filed back to their cells. When Blake failed to answer the roll call, the grounds were searched and the ladder, its rungs reinforced with knitting needles, was discovered. By the time prison authorities notified police, Blake had an hour-and-a-half head start.

According to the official inquiry that was later conducted, Blake had given "every appearance of being a cooperative prisoner who was showing remarkable resilience in accepting his unprecedentedly long sentence." That resilience had no doubt been based on his confidence that the Soviets would quickly trade him for a captured British spy—a traditional practice between East and West. Within a year of Blake's sentencing, for instance, the Americans had given up the notorious Soviet spy master Rudolf Abel for Francis Gary Powers, the downed U-2 pilot. But Blake's confidence in an early exchange must have been badly shaken in April of 1964, when the Russians traded businessman Greville Wynne for Gordon Lonsdale, the bogus Canadian sentenced to twenty-five years for his theft of British naval secrets. Wynne, who had acted as the West's chief courier to Penkovsky, was Moscow's prize catch. The Russians had played their best card on Lonsdale instead of Blake. Their decision had nothing to do with the relative worth of the two spies.

The simple fact was that Lonsdale was a native Russian and Blake was not.

His best chance for an early exchange gone, Blake moved into action on his own, enlisting Bourke, a thirty-two-year-old Irishman who had spent nearly a third of his life in prison, as his chief accomplice. When Bourke met Blake at Wormwood Scrubs, he was nearing the end of a seven-year sentence for mailing a bomb to a policeman. Once released, Bourke laid the groundwork for Blake's escape, maintaining communications first by letter and then by a two-way radio that he managed to smuggle in to Blake.

The escape went off as planned, the only mishap being a broken wrist suffered by Blake in his leap to freedom. While Scotland Yard scrambled to cover all exits from Britain, Blake and Bourke watched television in a rented flat less than four minutes' drive from Worm-wood Scrubs. Seven weeks later, while police still had nothing more to go on than "the clue of the pink chrysanthemums," Blake hid in the back of a van and was driven aboard the Dover-to-Ostende ferry by two of Bourke's friends. Twenty-four hours later the van stopped on the autobahn leading through East Germany, and Blake alighted in friendly territory.

In Moscow, Blake was awarded the Order of Lenin, Russia's second highest decoration, an honor not even Philby had been accorded. The only other foreigner to have been so honored was the German Richard Sorge, the Soviet spy in Tokyo during World War II whose assurances that Japan would not attack Russia had enabled Stalin to transfer badly needed troops to the Western Front. Blake's canonization was presented to the Russian people in the form of two lengthy interviews published in *Izvestia*. Having so thoroughly duped the British both before and after his capture, Blake could scarcely refrain from gloating. The sharpest taunts seemed aimed at Harvey and his tunnel. "Many people made a career for themselves in connection with this notorious tunnel," Blake said with a bitter irony detectable only by those who knew the hard times on which Harvey had fallen.

"He was an utter disaster in Rome," a high-ranking CIA officer said of Harvey. "He was a fish out of water in Rome," the head of the CIA's Western Europe Division said. Harvey was as out of place in Rome as his Bavarian gun rack was in the elegant fawn-colored villa he inherited atop one of the Eternal City's seven hills. There was no more implausible sight than Harvey being attended by his white-gloved manservant. "Italians are highly sophisticated, smooth, and slow-going," a member of the Rome station said, describing attributes guaranteed to clash with the blunt, hard-charging Harvey. "I had the impression that he would be at a disadvantage in dealing with the Italians," sniffed the officer Harvey relieved. "He could be very brusque with Italians," another officer said. "He hated 'the goddamn wops,' as he called them," still another reported. His command of the language was nil. "Harvey would not have taken the trouble to learn the language of people he despised," said an officer who spoke the language fluently. Besides, "his sound in English could not possibly be converted into Italian." Another officer said that "Harvey and his wife were very fond of Germany, and they didn't like anything about Rome." A sympathetic friend said that "this was just not the kind of milieu Bill Harvey prospered in. He preferred the dark alleys of Berlin." Still, said an aide to McCone, "he would have been able to carry out his assignment had he not impaired his effectiveness with drink."

"When he first came to Rome, he tried to be very careful about his drinking," a member of the station staff said. "At cocktail parties he would drink iced tea." But soon "he was hitting the bottle very hard early in the morning," another colleague reported. "By noon, Bill was no longer Bill." One officer said, "I never tried to do business with him in the afternoon when he was back on the sauce. You could not call him drunk. He was sleepy and not alert." When a colonel in the local carabinieri took him on a tour of checkpoints along the border with Yugoslavia, Harvey slumbered drunkenly through the entire trip. When Harvey had an altercation with Italian police after one of several traffic accidents, the American ambassador, Frederick Reinhardt, cabled Washington that he hoped the station chief would be "less visible" in the future. When Reinhardt called an emergency meeting one Saturday, Harvey arrived "blotto" and fell asleep slumped over the arm of his chair. His gun fell out of his shoulder holster and onto the floor. "For Christ's sake," snapped Reinhardt, "who sent him to this town?"

Helms and Angleton had sent Harvey to Rome for a number of reasons. After his run-in with Bobby Kennedy, Harvey had to be got out of the country fast. But he was not to be demoted. The failure of MONGOOSE had not been his fault, and there was a feeling that Harvey had been "unfairly treated" by the White House. Rome was "the assignment Helms could find at the time that was high-level enough to accommodate him," one participant in the decision said. "I got him the job," Angleton stated flatly.

Although it had been more than fifteen years since he had been stationed in Rome, Angleton still exercised considerable control over Italian operations. He remained as well connected in Italy as the most seasoned Italian hand. Tom McCoy, a CIA officer who served in Rome during the 1950s, said that "Jim had a couple of people in Italy who did work for him and did not work for the station, including a source in the Vatican, although I could never prove it." Another CIA officer said that Angleton dealt directly with three CIA agents inside the Italian government whom he and his assistant, Ray Rocca, had recruited in the postwar years. "They were all three in very high-level and very sensitive positions," a CIA officer who knew their identities said. One was an official in the Ministry of Interior; another, code-named DELANDA, worked in the Ministry of Foreign Affairs. The third agent, code-named DETECTOR, was a major in the carabinieri who during the war had been chief of Italian counterintelligence in Switzerland. "He was very helpful in specific counterintelligence cases," an American said of DETECTOR. "He knew where all the skeletons were buried." Over the years, Angleton's "three big kills" had furnished valuable intelligence on the inner workings of the Italian government, among other things "pinpointing the areas where money could best be funneled," an Italian hand said. "Since Angleton and Rocca had recruited them, Angleton and Rocca were running the show. If anybody back there [in Washington] could speak about what was going on [in Italy] with any degree of confidence, it was Angleton and Rocca."

In Angleton's eyes, the land of his youth was about to disappear down the Communist maw. During the 1950s William Colby, the

CIA station chief in Rome, had annoyed him by his persistence
in keeping lines open to the left. "We were supporting and engaged
in operations with some left-wing elements that Angleton held highly
suspect because his police [carabinieri] friends held them suspect,"
said Tom McCoy, Colby's deputy in Rome. Now the Kennedy
administration was actively supporting an "opening to the left"
that would bring the Socialist Party into the ruling coalition government. To Angleton, who viewed the Socialist Party as nothing more
than a Communist front, the policy was tantamount to surrender.
Most disturbing of all, he suspected that the chief administration
proponent of this suicidal alliance with the left, White House aide
Arthur Schlesinger, was a Soviet agent. A member of the Soviet
Embassy in Caracas had been overheard saying that he had learned
the date of the Bay of Pigs invasion from someone in the White
House, and Angleton had settled on Schlesinger, a former member
of the OSS and the only administration official to oppose the Cuban
operation, as the likely culprit.

Everywhere he turned, Angleton saw the hand of the KGB at
work in Italy. Golitsin had described to him a KGB penetration
of NATO offices in Paris in terms that fit a very senior official in
the Italian Foreign Ministry. As far as Angleton was concerned,
the CIA station in Rome wasn't doing its job. It wasn't able to
ferret out low-level Communist agents within the Socialist Party,
much less a well-placed mole within the government. The station
relied on the Italian services for its intelligence on Soviet agents,
but "there was no help from the liaison services, who were afraid
of antagonizing the Soviets," an Italian hand said. "This was a
serious mistake from the very beginning. We put all our eggs in
the liaison basket." As a result the CIA was "getting nothing but
what the Italian government wanted to give it," the head of the
CIA's Western Europe Division said. The situation cried out for
a hard-nosed operative like Harvey who would install some
"plumbing" of his own—surveillance teams, wiretaps, bugs, and
all the other paraphernalia of espionage. Whatever else had happened to him, Harvey certainly had not gone soft. When a longtime
friend in the Rome station wrote him a warm letter of congratula-
tions on his appointment, Harvey reported the man to the Office

of Security for discussing classified material in the open mails.

Harvey was a cold slap in the face. "There were members of the Rome station who had been in the area for a long time, enjoying life and not being heckled too much and this new man comes in and tries to rekindle fires," one member of the station recalled. This new man was a queer bird indeed. When a veteran of twenty years in Italy went out to dinner with the new station chief, Harvey insisted on sitting in a corner with his back to the wall and his eye on the door. As Harvey seated himself, he cleared his coat-tails away from the revolver at his waist for a quicker draw. Thinking this was some kind of joke, the old hand asked if he could count on Harvey to cover him, but he suddenly realized that Harvey was dead serious.

"Harvey tried to turn the station around from a largely overt mission to an increased clandestine effort against the Soviets," one officer said. "Bill Harvey knew nothing about the Italian situation," said a CIA man who had been there since the war. "He was after the Russians and the KGB." Over drinks, Harvey told one old-timer, "I know you know a lot about Italy, but I know a lot about the Soviets. We'll get along fine." They didn't. "It was a period of extreme confusion and bewilderment," one officer said. "The station was turned upside down to recruit a Russian." No longer relying on the timid efforts of the Italian services, Harvey formed his own surveillance teams to track the Russian operatives. Officers who had made their living over dinner with Italian politicians found themselves pounding the pavement at all hours of the night. "People had to work a hell of a lot harder," one officer said, but "I don't think we succeeded in recruiting any Russians."

Relations with the Italian services grew steadily worse under Harvey's heavy hand. "He pushed too hard," a veteran officer said. "If only he'd had a little more tact. . . . Harvey forgot that we were dealing with the owners of the country." When the head of one of the Italian services—CIFAR—died, Harvey defied tradition by lobbying for the promotion of the chief of the counterintelligence division to the top job, which had long been considered the province of the military. The maneuver was successful, but it was not worth the wrenching of Italian sensibilities. Once in office the new chief of CIFAR turned out to be his own man. "We were trying to manipulate and run him," a veteran of sixteen years in Italy said, "but it's a myth, this idea that you recruit the chief of service." By the time Harvey's tour in Italy was over, the chief of CIFAR would inform the CIA that all eavesdropping operations against Eastern European embassies in Rome had been terminated.

Harvey's relations with his own Director were scarcely better. "McCone was never happy with that appointment," an aide to the Director said. To begin with, McCone had not been pleased with Harvey's previous performance on the Cuba task force. "When you take a plant supervisor and make him president of the company, it doesn't always work out," McCone said of Harvey's tour as chief of Task Force W. Harvey's assignment to Rome "had been approved in his absence and he didn't like it," McCone's aide said. "McCone is something of a snob and a puritan, and Harvey just wasn't his cup of tea." Once a year McCone, a devout Catholic, would visit Rome for an audience with the Pope, and Harvey would have to entertain him. "When McCone would come to Rome, Harvey would go to pieces with his drinking," a sympathetic officer remarked. "McCone was a difficult guest. . . . He demanded the best room in the best hotel. . . . He would insist on playing golf at a certain time. . . . His wife would want handworked leather bags picked up for her and shipped home." When McCone came to dinner, Harvey, pistol jammed into his belt, kept nodding off at the table while McCone's aide kicked desperately at his shins. When the aide called on Harvey at his office at ten-thirty in the morning, "Bill said, 'I'm thirsty,' and sent out for Campari and soda." At lunch that day he had five martinis. "I've never seen anybody drink as much in my life," the aide said. When he asked other members of the station how things were going, they cautiously responded, "I would not ask for another tour at this station under this man."

Soon the "horror stories" began to filter back to Washington, stories of his walking into a glass door or running over a roadside kiosk. "You heard about the time the gun went off in his office, didn't you? The girls in the outer office were afraid to open the door. They were afraid he'd blown his damn brains out. When they finally opened the door, there was Harvey sitting there as if nothing had happened." At first the reports were discounted as the petty spite of a small clique of officers who had grown too accustomed to the good life. "The gentlemen who were trying to pull him down in Italy were gnats buzzing about a bull," Harvey's immediate superior in Washington said. The KGB seemed to add its own menacing buzz to the swarm. Harvey would find the air let out of his tires or be awakened in the middle of the night by anonymous phone calls. One morning two sewer rats were found hanging from his front door with their heads chopped off.

Harvey suffered a heart attack. Two Agency doctors were sent from Germany to minister to him. After the crisis had passed, they warned him that he would have to stop drinking and smoking and keep regular hours. "Things looked up for a while," the chief of the Western Europe Division said. "He developed a couple of not spectacular but useful operations. He began to gain a little confidence." But the drinking resumed. "Then came a cable saying he wanted a number of officers recalled." Headquarters temporized by asking for more information. "Harvey responded with stiff messages" alleging that "these guys were not on the team, not sympathetic to changes he was trying to make." Harvey's wrath focused on one officer in particular, Mark Wyatt, who was in charge of liaison with the Italian services. Urbane, sophisticated, bilingual, independently wealthy, Wyatt was everything Harvey was not. "Harvey submitted a special fitness report which really tore this guy limb from limb."

Desmond FitzGerald, who had become head of the Operations Directorate, arrived in Rome for a firsthand look. "I got an ultimatum from Wyatt that either Harvey went or he went," a senior officer who accompanied FitzGerald said. "So I said, 'In that case, I'm relieving you as of now.'" Wyatt asked to be allowed to stay through the spring so that his children could finish the school year, but "we shipped him right out of there." After seeing Wyatt off on a ship to America, a member of the station recalled, "I said to a friend that Harvey wouldn't last long after Wyatt got back to Washington. . . . I made a bet that 'Before the Ides of March, Caesar will fall.' "

FitzGerald had supported Harvey against Wyatt, but at the

same time he had concluded, in the words of the officer who accompanied him, that "Harvey was not in a condition to continue as chief of the station. . . . He was sick and coming apart at the seams." FitzGerald cabled a lengthy report to Helms, and Helms ordered Harvey relieved of command. "I got the job of going back to Rome and relieving Bill Harvey," FitzGerald's companion said. "FitzGerald was very happy he didn't have to do it. . . . It was a night I shall not soon forget." For seven hours he sat across from Harvey, explaining that he was through. "Harvey was drinking brandy with a loaded gun in his lap . . . paring his nails with a sheath knife." Harvey never threatened him, but the barrel of the gun was always pointing directly at him.

The cable from the chief of station announcing that he would be returning to Washington went out to all CIA installations in Italy on the Ides of March. There was not the slightest hint that Harvey was going home in disgrace. He threw a farewell party for himself in the ballroom of the Rome Hilton complete with a flowing fountain of champagne, an excessive display by any standard and particularly for a supposedly anonymous CIA man. "By God, he was going to make a success out of this thing even if it wasn't," one disapproving officer said.

At CIA headquarters in Washington, Helms convened a meeting of FitzGerald, Angleton, and Lawrence "Red" White, the Agency's executive director, to decide what to do with Harvey upon his return. The idea was to find "something he could work at on his own time where he wouldn't have anybody to supervise or any operations to run," one participant in the meeting said. He was placed in charge of something called the Special Services Unit, where his job was to study countermeasures against electronic surveillance. FitzGerald told Harvey he hoped this would be only a brief interlude until he could regain his health and return to the front lines. "Red" White was assigned to watch over him.

"You and I have never had any problems," White said to Harvey. "As far as I'm concerned, the slate is clean."

"I'm sorry if I've embarrassed the Agency in any way," Harvey responded. "If I ever embarrass you or the Agency again, I will resign."

Before long, "we began finding gin bottles in his desk drawer," one of the CIA's most senior officers said. White called in Harvey, who reminded him of what he had said about resigning the next time he embarrassed the Agency.

"That would probably be the best thing to do," White said.

"At your pleasure," Harvey replied.

He was finished.

The Great Mole Hunt

The downfall of Harvey, the CIA's most aggressive clandestine operator, was symbolic of the fate that had befallen the Agency's espionage operations against the Soviet Union. Both were totally incapacitated. Operations were "dead in the water," a member of the Soviet
Bloc Division said, brought to a standstill by Golitsin's warning
that a KGB mole had penetrated to the highest levels of the CIA.
David Murphy, head of the Soviet Bloc Division, sent a message
to all CIA stations, directing them to pull back from their clandestine
Soviet sources. Since they had all been blown by the mole, any
sources still cooperating with the CIA must be under KGB control,
Murphy warned.

The CIA would continue to observe the Soviet Union as closely
as possible, but it would no longer attempt to penetrate the Kremlin.
The Agency continued to collect and analyze the great masses of
data that even a closed society spews forth—wheat crops and missile
silos were still photographed by reconnaissance satellites; Western
businessmen returning from Russia were still debriefed; official delegations to and from Moscow were still logged in and out; *Pravda,*

Izvestia, and all the other Soviet publications were still translated into English. But the effort to recruit an agent who could give meaning and form to all the other data, who could reveal the designs and intentions, the motives and methods of the Soviet government, had all but ceased. The KGB had emasculated the CIA. Or had the CIA emasculated itself? Was the mole or the fear of the mole to blame?

"Golitsin comes out and says there's a penetration," a disbelieving officer recalled, his voice dripping with sarcasm. "The next step is that nothing can happen in the United States government that the KGB doesn't know within twenty-four hours." Murphy was overreacting, his critics said, swallowing the double think propounded by Angleton and Bagley and playing right into the KGB's hands. One member of the Soviet Bloc Division became so incensed that he accused Murphy of being a Soviet agent.

To the counterintelligence officer there was, quite apart from what Golitsin was saying, "extensive evidence that a mole had penetrated to a sensitive point." Hadn't the KGB known about one CIA operation—the planned recruitment of the Polish intelligence officer in Switzerland—within two weeks of its inception? "Popov, Goleniewski, Penkovsky—the best the CIA ever had—all were compromised, and the KGB went to great lengths to mislead us as to the nature and timing of the compromise. In each instance, they gave us several choices." That was the most disconcerting thing of all. It was as if the KGB knew at any given moment exactly what the CIA was thinking.

In the spring of 1966, while the CIA and the FBI were still trying to extract from Igor Orlov a confession that he had been the KGB's source SASHA in Berlin, a second Igor suddenly arrived in Washington with additional evidence against Orlov. The new Igor jumped into the CIA's lap with an early morning phone call to the residence of Richard Helms, and by one o'clock that afternoon he was closeted with a CIA case officer at an Agency safe house. Igor was not unknown to the CIA. He had briefly flirted with the Agency once overseas. Now, Igor said, he was angling for an assignment to the KGB station in Washington, where he and the CIA could do business on a regular basis. But, he continued, his assignment depended on the success of his present mission, which was to recruit Nicholas Shadrin, a Soviet destroyer captain who had defected to the United States in 1959 and was now living in the Washington suburbs and serving as a consultant for the Office of Naval Intelligence. If the CIA would persuade Shadrin to accept recruitment, Igor explained, it could be the start of a beautiful relationship.

As proof that he could return a favor, Igor revealed that the suspect Orlov had just paid a visit to the Soviet Embassy, a tidbit confirmed by a review of the Bureau's photographic surveillance of the embassy. Orlov's visit did not prove anything. He insisted that he was merely trying to obtain the address of a relative in Russia. But coming on top of all the botched cases with which he had been associated in Berlin, it served to confirm existing suspicions—as if the KGB knew at any given moment exactly what the CIA was thinking.

The FBI was impressed by Igor's tidbit. The CIA, Angleton in particular, was convinced that Igor was a KGB trick. Although Igor's information confirmed Golitsin's leads to the identity of SA-SHA, that seemed to be nothing more than the further discrediting of an already suspect source—a "giveaway" designed to establish Igor's credentials as a prelude to deception. However, both the CIA and the FBI agreed for different reasons to play along with Igor, now code-named KITTY HAWK, and put him in touch with Shadrin. If the FBI was right about Igor, American intelligence could use Shadrin to funnel phony data to the KGB and at the same time promote the career of its new agent KITTY HAWK. As far as the CIA was concerned, feeding an unwitting Shadrin to Igor would at least keep the game alive by allowing the Russians to think that the Agency had fallen for their ploy.

In order to protect the gambit, Angleton ordered that the KITTY HAWK file be kept from the CIA's Soviet Bloc Division, which he believed to be penetrated by the KGB. The result was that the division of the CIA most directly responsible for the collection of clandestine intelligence reports on the Soviet Union remained ignorant of what the FBI considered to be potentially the most valuable penetration since Penkovsky. Espionage operations against the Soviet Union had indeed gone "dead in the water." The road map of intelligence had disintegrated into the maze of counterintelligence.

At the center of the maze stood Angleton and Golitsin, the chief of counterintelligence and his prize defector—"the Black Knight," as Angleton was sometimes called, and his charger. Without Golitsin, without Angleton's championing of Golitsin, the fear of KGB provocation, disinformation and penetration would never have taken control. Angleton was the only officer who possessed the command of fact, the strength of personality, the force of conviction needed to overcome the disbelief that traditionally greeted warnings about Soviet plots. Even so forceful a personality as Harvey had continually been frustrated by what he so long ago had called "the ineffectiveness of the overall Government program in dealing with Communists and Communist espionage." Angleton would not and could not be ignored. Where Harvey had raged against the Soviet threat with *basso profundo* and six-shooter, Angleton seduced with a hypnotic blend of brilliance and mystique. Angleton was the Italian stiletto to Harvey's German Luger. Yet it had been Harvey, the blunt, blustering cop, and not Angleton, the devious, enigmatic counterspy, who had stitched together the case against Kim Philby, the KGB's prize penetration agent. There, said Angleton's friends, lay the root cause of his fervor. Never again would he permit himself to be so badly duped. He would trust no one.

Sherman Kent, head of the CIA's Board of National Estimates, told colleagues of the time he dropped by Angleton's office to pick him up for a lunch date. Kent stood in front of Angleton's desk, waiting for him to lock his papers in his safe. Angleton gathered up the papers from his desk, but before placing them in the safe, he asked Kent to leave the room. Kent realized that Angleton was afraid he might be peering over his shoulder. Another CIA officer recalled the time that Angleton had briefed him on a particularly sensitive case. After swearing the officer to eternal secrecy, Angleton began to describe the case in hushed tones. It sounded very familiar to the officer, and when he peered across the desk, he realized that Angleton was reading from the officer's own handwritten notes. Friends of Angleton could always pass off such displays by saying that "anybody who works in counterintelligence should be given a few extra points for paranoia." Besides, a government official told a friend at the CIA, "I don't agree with a thing Jim says, but sometimes I wake up in the middle of the night thinking, 'What if he's right?' " What if Angleton were right about Golitsin and about the mole?

Golitsin had already provided the leads that pointed toward Igor Orlov as the prime suspect in the search for SASHA, and he was eager to provide more. According to a CIA officer, "Golitsin's line became: 'I gave you this penetration who ruined everything you ever did in Berlin but what the KGB really wants is to get at your own people. Give me a list of your people who ran this agent, and I will find among them the Soviet agents in the CIA.' " SASHA's handlers either had been in league with him from the start or had been recruited by the KGB through SASHA at some point in their relationship, Golitsin contended.

Angleton gave Golitsin access to the CIA's files on the case officers who had handled SASHA, about a dozen men in all, and the hunt was on. "This is what I distrust," one CIA division head said. "How the hell could anybody in his right mind give a KGB officer enough information [from CIA files] to allow him to make a valid analysis?" Said another officer, whose file was among those turned over to Golitsin, "To give Golitsin your personnel files, including going all the way back to your first Personal History Statement which you give when you join the Agency, it seems to me that that's outrageous, way beyond where Angleton should have gone." In fact, Angleton went even further in his hunt for the mole. If a man spoke Russian or had served in Moscow or was involved in any of the other cases that had gone sour, his file, too, was given to Golitsin. If Golitsin's eye picked out a suspicious pattern, the name would be entered in Angleton's list of "serials," or leads to possible Soviet agents, and a full investigation would begin.

Number one on Angleton's list was Richard Kovich, a case officer of Yugoslav descent assigned to the Soviet Bloc Division. "Golitsin named Kovich on the basis of his analysis of material we supplied him with," a CIA officer said. To Golitsin, everything about Kovich looked suspicious. He had handled SASHA, he spoke Russian, and he came from Eastern Europe. Kovich also associated openly with known KGB officers, joining them on picnics and family outings in what he maintained was a calculated effort to know the enemy. Angleton and Golitsin put the probability that Kovich was a Soviet agent at 100 percent. From his reading of the file, Golitsin even professed to know the precise moment at which Kovich had been recruited.

Kovich had been sent to Paris to handle a GRU officer named Federov, who had volunteered his services to the CIA. From the start, Federov had the smell of a Soviet provocation. He said that he was a GRU "illegal" who was being staged through Paris to his ultimate destination in Mexico. The name he gave for his GRU control turned out to be an office partner of Popov's in East Berlin, but his description of the office did not match that given by the trusted Popov. No sooner had he made contact with Kovich than Federov began to lead him a merry chase. Abandoning his mission to Mexico, he returned to Moscow and reappeared in Paris with the news that he had to go to the south of France to meet with another GRU illegal who was to take his place in Mexico. Kovich trailed Federov south. It was there, Golitsin said, while he was on his own with no one watching his back, that Kovich had been recruited by Soviet intelligence. Once again Federov was recalled to Moscow, this time, he claimed, by way of Frankfurt and Berlin, but the CIA followed him to Bern, down through the Simplon Tunnel to northern Italy, and back to the French Riviera. At his next meeting with Kovich, the now thoroughly suspect Federov announced that he was to be assigned to the Soviet Embassy in Stockholm. Then he returned to Moscow once more, reemerging a short time later in Berlin, but instead of going on to Stockholm, he went back to Moscow and was never heard from again. The most intriguing aspect of the entire affair was that Federov had returned to Moscow for the final time at almost precisely the same moment that Popov had been recalled for the interrogation that led to his final demise. In some way, Federov seemed linked to the end play in the Popov case.

Pawing through the files, Golitsin spotted another case that he felt reflected badly upon Kovich. Ingeborg Lygren, who was secretary to the Norwegian ambassador in Moscow and whom Kovich had handled as a CIA agent, had been working for the Russians all along, Golitsin said, suggesting that Kovich could have used her as a go-between with his KGB controllers. The Lygren case became a scandal of major proportions in Norway, although ultimately it would tell more about Angleton than Kovich.

By the time Golitsin identified Lygren as a Soviet agent, she had returned from Moscow to Oslo and was serving as secretary to the head of military intelligence, Colonel Wilhelm Evang, Norway's chief liaison with the CIA. Angleton flew to Oslo and told the head of Norway's internal security service about Lygren without bothering to inform Evang. The resulting flap "buggered up the CIA's dealing with both services for many years," the head of the CIA's Western Europe Division said. Evang and his aides "considered the fact that Angleton had gone to the police and not to Evang a stab in the back. The results were bad as far as liaison was concerned." Another CIA officer explained that "when you are in such close contact with the head of one service, and you have a security case that goes to the heart of his business, you don't go to the head of a rival service and then keep the resulting investigation secret from your principal liaison. The way it was handled blackened the name of CIA from then on." The damage was for naught. Lygren was found innocent, given her job back, and voted an indemnity by the Norwegian parliament. Twelve years later, the real spy, Gunvor Haavik, was caught passing documents to the Russians.

Golitsin's identification of Kovich as a Soviet agent proved no more accurate than his naming of Lygren. "Kovich was cleared of any evidence that he was a controlled agent of anybody else," one of his superiors said. "Nevertheless, he was injured because prior to the time that that determination was made he had to be removed from an active role in ongoing sensitive operations." Kovich was transferred out of the Soviet Bloc Division to a dead-end job in Central America. "What happened to Kovich was what any professional officer would expect," his superior said. His career was ruined. Although officially cleared, he remained in limbo, never rising above the rank he held when Golitsin first named him. According to Kovich's friend, George Kisvalter, "Angleton wiretapped him and blocked any promotions for him for ten years." Finally, Kovich quit the CIA in disgust.

Neither Kovich nor any of the other suspects identified by Golitsin were ever told that their loyalty was being questioned. By the time they realized what had happened and demanded a chance to rebut the charge, their careers had been damaged beyond repair. "When do you find out?" one suspect asked rhetorically. "You find out when you're the oldest living GS-16 in the building. You find out when old colleagues start turning the papers face down on their desk while they're talking to you, not taking any phone calls when you're in the office, pretending not to see you in the corridor, and shying away from you in the men's room."

The suspicions sowed by Golitsin spread far beyond individual officers at the CIA to infect all of Allied intelligence. Philippe de Vosjoli, the Washington representative of French intelligence, described Golitsin's debilitating effect. "Our team would do some preliminary work at home and return to Washington with a number of names, any one of which might fit the necessarily meager network of facts MARTEL [Golitsin's French cryptonym] had offered. But MARTEL could never answer with absolute assurance either yes or no about any of them. The problem in this for me—and, in fact, for the whole French intelligence system—lay in the fact that each session with MARTEL was also attended by American representatives, and each time our people dropped a name in front of MARTEL, that person automatically became suspect to the Americans. Small wonder, but as the list of clouded reputations lengthened, my professional contacts with the Americans . . . began to dry up, even on routine matters."

Golitsin's leads produced hundreds of suspects but virtually no spies. He "took everyone back to the days in the early twenties when the Soviets first allowed Western enterprise into the country and began recruiting agents," a senior officer said. "Battalions of people researched back. They came up with identities that fit the facts but never proved anything." By another officer's count, Golitsin's information produced more than a hundred cases of suspected espionage against Americans, nearly as many against the British, tens of cases involving the French, and a dozen or so in Germany, plus assorted leads to Soviet agents in Canada, New Zealand, Australia, Austria, Greece, and Norway. "This not only tied up all of your proper counterespionage functions, it tied up much of the security services of Allied nations," the senior officer continued. "It was also very stultifying to the positive, offensive operations of ourselves, the British, etc., because if you got a good case, got some good information, it was immediately written off as 'It's got to be a phony.' People didn't trust one another. You couldn't deal with another service because they were 'penetrated.' " The fears aroused by Golitsin and spread by Angleton seemed more devastating than real Soviet agents could ever have been.

No one was safe from Golitsin. David Murphy, head of the Soviet Bloc Division and a fervent believer in Golitsin, was listed in Angleton's "serials" as a "probable" Soviet agent. Murphy suffered from the same guilt by association as Kovich. He was of Polish descent, spoke fluent Russian, and was married to a White Russian. He had been with military intelligence at the outbreak of the Korean War and had crossed paths in Seoul with George Blake, who had had an affair with the wife of one of Murphy's agents. As the CIA chief in Munich, Murphy had directed the handling of SASHA and had even arranged for SASHA's transfer to Berlin. Later, as chief of the Soviet branch in Berlin, Murphy had met secretly with Popov. Afterward, George Blake claimed to have known all along about "Dave Murphy's big operation" with Popov.

Murphy was "accident-prone," one officer said. In Vienna he had had a beer thrown in his face by a Russian he was trying to recruit, and in Tokyo he had been beaten up by a KGB goon squad. "There was not one single Soviet case which this guy touched which didn't turn to shit," a fellow officer said. To some, Murphy's past performance smacked of deliberately destructive behavior. To others, it seemed unlikely that the KGB would purposely stain the record of its own man.

Murphy was removed from his job as head of the Soviet Bloc Division and assigned to Paris as station chief. He suspected nothing untoward. The Paris job was a plum. It also conveniently required an interim period of several months while Murphy attended the

Foreign Service Institute and studied French. During those months he was cut out of operations entirely and was under intensive investigation. "He wouldn't have gone [to Paris] if he hadn't been cleared," a senior officer said. Investigators "went over Murphy from stem to stern and concluded that he was clean." Angleton, however, was not convinced. After Murphy arrived in Paris, Angleton took the head of French intelligence aside and warned him that the CIA's new station chief was a Soviet agent. Such calumny was devastating to Murphy's effectiveness in Paris, but in the end Angleton would become the principal victim of his own warning.

Murphy was replaced as chief of the Soviet Bloc Division by Rolf Kingsley, formerly head of the Agency's Western Europe Division. Kingsley was an outsider with no better solution to the mystery of the mole than anyone else. But something had to be done to remove the paralysis of doubt that had brought operations against the Soviet Union to a standstill. "In order to get on with the darn job, we finally resorted to extreme measures," a senior member of the Soviet Bloc Division said. Kingsley purged the division of anybody who could conceivably be the mole. "He brought people in who couldn't have possibly been the penetration because they'd been a thousand miles away at the time," an officer explained. "In effect, Kingsley said, 'If a penetration is there, prove it. In the meantime, you can be damn sure he's not there right now.' He wanted it clear that the penetration was somewhere else." With Kovich in Central America and Murphy headed for Paris, Pete Bagley, now the deputy chief of the division, was sent to Brussels, an assignment that he had conveniently requested. Leonard McCoy, a reports officer who had become so upset by the handling of Nosenko that he bypassed the chain of command and barged into Helms's office to protest, was transferred out of the division. Another officer who had fallen under suspicion for his handling of SASHA was assigned to the CIA training base at Camp Peary, Virginia. And so it went: "If you couldn't find the guy, you could at least emasculate him."

But nothing could dispel the miasma of suspicion pervading the Agency's corridors. "Bill Harvey used to be a good man," Angleton mused to a colleague. "There must be something seriously wrong with him." It seemed that Angleton was suggesting that Harvey might have been recruited by the KGB, but "none of the many counterintelligence leads ever applied to Harvey," a CIA officer said. When Lyman Kirkpatrick, the embittered Inspector General, quit the Agency after his arch-rival Helms had been selected for the Director's job, a rumor that he was about to defect sent a ripple of panic through the seventh floor. Kirkpatrick had left Washington without telling anyone where he was going. When the CIA finally tracked him down by phone at a motel in El Paso and discreetly asked his intentions, Kirkpatrick explained huffily that he was on his way to Mexico to divorce his wife and marry his secretary. Meanwhile, the FBI directed its field offices "to obtain information concerning American students in attendance at Cambridge University from 1931 to 1937 who might have known Philby, Burgess, or Maclean or might have been engaged in subversive activities in college."

If the cases against Murphy and Kovich and all the other suspects did not stand up, then perhaps Golitsin's leads applied to someone else. The next to fall under suspicion was Bagley. Golitsin had not named Bagley, but he had given his interrogators one piece of information that aroused suspicion. Golitsin said that in Moscow he had seen copies of the CIA's debriefings of Peter Deriabin, the KGB officer who had defected in Vienna in 1954. Bagley had personally conducted that debriefing in Salzburg, Austria, and was an obvious candidate to be the source who had provided the KGB with a copy of the Deriabin transcript. Bagley was also at the center of the case that in 1959 had given the CIA hard evidence of a penetration in its ranks. He was the case officer who had been slated to make the recruitment pitch to the Polish officer in Switzerland, a gambit that Goleniewski's letters revealed had leaked to the Russians almost as soon as it had been conceived. Clearly, Bagley merited a closer look. But a case against Bagley, the chief accuser of Nosenko, did not make sense. If he was the Soviet mole, why would he work so hard to discredit the one source who said there was nothing to Golitsin's warnings about a penetration?

The mirrors of counterintelligence suggested an answer. Perhaps Nosenko was something more than just a disinformation agent, as Angleton, Bagley, and Golitsin maintained. Perhaps he had been dispatched to be discovered as a disinformation agent and thereby advance the career of his principal accuser, Bagley. During the course of the Nosenko affair, Bagley had risen from a case officer in Bern to deputy chief of the Soviet Bloc Division and heir apparent to the top job in the division until Kingsley was brought in to clean house. Bagley's zealousness in attempting to expose a KGB plot had earned for him the suspicion that he was part of the plot. Such was the quality of justice in the wilderness of mirrors. A man's successes could be used against him by suggesting that he must have had help from the other side, while his failures could be brought forward as evidence of deliberately destructive behavior. A man's entire past, as reflected in the counterintelligence files, became a potential weapon against him.

Bagley's past—the Nosenko case, along with the leak of the Deriabin transcript and of the planned Polish recruitment—was set down in painstaking detail, but the case was thrown out. The cloud passed over Bagley as quickly as it had formed, but the notion that Nosenko had been sent to be discovered had taken root. If not to advance Bagley's career, then whose? The only other person whose status had been noticeably enhanced by the discrediting of Nosenko was Golitsin, who had predicted that the KGB would attempt just such a ploy to undermine his information. Nosenko's attempt to discredit Golitsin had served to convince the Counterintelligence and Soviet Bloc Divisions of his importance. But a KGB plot to build up Golitsin, who threatened to expose the Soviet mole, made no sense—unless he, too, had been sent. Perhaps the KGB had dispatched Golitsin in a deliberate effort to sow the fatal seed of suspicion that the CIA had been penetrated by a Russian mole. "If you take the thesis of the KGB dispatching a defector to carry out a disinformation program and tie the CIA into knots," said a chief of the Soviet Bloc Division, "the absolute classic operation would be Golitsin."

The CIA and much of Western intelligence had been turned upside down and still the mole had not been found. Everybody from the lowliest case officer who had ever handled SASHA up to the chief of the Soviet Bloc Division had been investigated and cleared. While Golitsin's leads had been pursued to their mainly fruitless conclusions, no less than fifty leads provided by Nosenko had never been followed up on the grounds that they were false scents laid down to throw investigators off the track. "But the leads turned out to be very real," said a member of the Soviet Bloc Division. Angleton's counterintelligence staff could respond only that the leads were "giveaways," worthless spies willingly betrayed by Nosenko in order to protect the mole. "If Nosenko is giving all these throwaways in order to protect something much bigger," a senior officer in the Soviet Bloc Division commented, "this mythical character had to be pretty damn big."

Angleton and Golitsin rose to the occasion with the astonishing Project DINOSAUR, the code name for the investigation of W. Averell Harriman, who had been ambassador to the Soviet Union and the United Kingdom, governor of New York, and Secretary of Commerce, and who had just been named by President Johnson to negotiate an end to the Vietnam War. Golitsin described an agent who had been recruited by the KGB in the 1930s while he was in the Soviet Union on business. The KGB had supplied the agent with women, and an illegitimate son had resulted, Golitsin said. He even claimed to know the boy's name. The agent had had a falling out with his Soviet controllers, Golitsin continued, but during the 1950s he had returned to the fold. In honor of the agent's return to covert duty, Golitsin related, the Soviets had commissioned a play about the son of a capitalist prince by one of Moscow's leading playwrights, but when the agent attended the premiere he was so flabbergasted by the similarity between himself and the chief protagonist that he angrily warned the KGB that his cover might be blown. Angleton concluded that Golitsin's description matched no one but Harriman. The former ambassador had visited the Soviet Union as recently as 1959 and had written a book about his journey in which he thanked his guide, Vasili Vakrushev, who was none other than the illegitimate son named by Golitsin. A check of Harriman's itinerary showed that he had not been in Moscow on any of the nights that the play about the son of a capitalist prince was performed, but such details did not deter Angleton, who vigorously pressed the new Director, Richard Helms, to warn the President about Harriman. Helms declined.

People were growing weary of the world according to Golitsin. His leads to the mole had produced nothing but paralyzing suspicion, and his warnings about Soviet disinformation operations appeared more and more fanciful with the passage of time. His claim that the Sino-Soviet split was a ruse looked ridiculous in the face of U-2 photographs of the massive military buildup along Russia's border with China. "Events began to catch up," one senior official said. "People began saying, 'If he's so far wrong on this, what about all the other stuff?' " When Angleton proposed to convene a gathering of academics to hear Golitsin propound his theory about the Sino-Soviet split, it was immediately dubbed "the Flat Earth Conference." Never did Golitsin look more ridiculous than in 1968 at the time of Alexander Dubček's rebellion in Czechoslovakia. "Golitsin said Dubček and the Czech rebellion were completely staged for Western benefit to create an impression of great unrest behind the Iron Curtain and to suck us into trying to exploit the unrest," a senior officer in the Soviet Bloc Division said. "Up until the morning they invaded Czechoslovakia, Golitsin maintained that this was a deception and that the Soviets had no intention of invading Czechoslovakia."

Harriman, Czechoslovakia, and the Sino-Soviet split—no wonder, as one officer said, "the audience was getting smaller all the time." But it was one thing to say that Golitsin was creating his warnings out of whole cloth and quite another to conclude that he was a dispatched agent. Defectors were known to resort to "spinning" after their hard core of intelligence had been exhausted, concocting ever more astounding stories in an effort to remain the center of attention. The difference in Golitsin's case was that Angleton continued to believe him.

There were a few shreds of circumstantial evidence capable of supporting the idea that Golitsin had been sent. The defector Deriabin had placed Golitsin's name second on a list of KGB officers in Vienna who were vulnerable to recruitment by the CIA. By Golitsin's own account, that transcript had somehow fallen into

KGB hands. Knowing that the CIA had had its interest in Golitsin piqued by Deriabin, the KGB might have "dangled" him in Helsinki, hoping to foist a double agent on the unsuspecting Americans. When the CIA failed to rise to the bait, the KGB could then have taken matters into its own hands and ordered Golitsin to defect. To add to that wisp of speculation, there was the trip Golitsin had made to England in 1963. He had supposedly gone to live there permanently, but he had returned to the United States within five months. That brief interlude divided his career as a defector into two clearly distinct phases. The first had lasted from December of 1961, when he defected in Helsinki, until March of 1963, when he left the United States for England. During that period, it was accurate to say, as Angleton frequently did, that the information that Golitsin supplied had never been faulted. It was only after he returned from England in August of 1963 that Golitsin began leading Angleton on the mad hunt for the mole and telling his stories about Harriman, Czechoslovakia, and the Sino-Soviet split. It was as if Golitsin, having established his bona fides during his first stay in the United States, had returned to carry out his disinformation mission.

How could the KGB even dream of pulling off so convoluted a scheme? "Helms and I have talked about this many times," a high-ranking officer said. "I do not believe that any son of a bitch sitting in Moscow could have any conception that he could dispatch Golitsin here and disrupt the Allied intelligence services to the extent he did. Nobody could have expected Angleton to buy it, lock, stock, and barrel." And no one sitting in Moscow could have predicted with any certainty that Nosenko would be fingered as a plant and thereby build up Golitsin. Furthermore, it seemed incredible that the KGB would entrust to an agent whose mission was to be discovered as a fraud the message that the Soviet Union had not had a hand in Kennedy's death. Such a plot could only fuel suspicions of Soviet complicity. It was true that Angleton's counterintelligence staff, although convinced that Nosenko was lying, had concluded that there was no evidence to support the contention that Oswald was working for the Russians when he killed Kennedy. But surely the KGB could not control the workings of the counterintelligence staff with so fine a hand.

Could not—unless they already had a man inside the counterintelligence staff who could influence the handling of the case. Who controlled the counterintelligence staff? Who had directed the handling of both Golitsin and Nosenko, championing Golitsin, denigrating Nosenko, yet stopping short of the conclusion that the KGB had ordered Kennedy shot? Who but James Jesus Angleton?

Such a case had indeed been outlined. It had the attraction that all conspiracy theories possess. It provided a cause commensurate with the effect. "The effect of Golitsin was horrendous," a chief of the Soviet Bloc Division said, "the greatest disaster to Western security that happened in twenty years." Now, for the first time, the possibility arose that the entire fiasco was not a self-inflicted wound but the work of an infernal Soviet machination. Who better to cast as the villain than Angleton himself? Two men who had headed the Soviet Bloc Division at different times, neither aware that an effort had been made to develop a case against Angleton, would make the same point in almost identical terms. "If I were to pick a Soviet agent at the Agency, it would be Angleton for all the harm he's done," said one. "There is just as much reason to say Angleton could be the guy because he has done so much to be destructive," said the other. Popov, Goleniewski, Penkovsky, Golitsin, Nosenko. Everything that had gone wrong could plausibly be traced to Angleton. Complexity became simplicity. With Angleton as the mole, the KGB could dispatch any number of false defectors confident that they would be handled according to plan. "He is the guy who is perfectly placed," one of the Soviet Bloc chiefs said. "He's even better to have than the Director." The Soviets had penetrated the counterintelligence operations of the British with Kim Philby and of the Germans with Heinz Felfe. Why not the CIA with Angleton?

To others, the suggestion was outrageous on its face. "I've known him for thirty-five years and worked with him for thirty, and I find any suggestion of treason or intentional destruction absolutely ridiculous," said Thomas Karamessines, who directed the CIA's Operations Directorate in the late 1960s and early 1970s. "Jim did make enemies. There's no question about it. It was in the nature of his work. But he performed his work with distinction, and this country ought to be very proud of him." Richard Helms, looking back on his many years with Angleton, praised him for making "a really very significant contribution in showing what Soviet spies were doing. If he overdid it, maybe he did, but that's a difficulty inherent in the job."

Angleton had never aspired to anything higher than chief of counterintelligence. With the exception of J. Edgar Hoover, probably no other senior official in the United States government had held the same job for so long. In the two decades Angleton had headed the Counterintelligence Division, there had been no fewer than six directors and seven heads of the Operations Directorate. Angleton had chosen his station and remained at it. Promotion would only have taken him from the depths of espionage to the shallows of administration. There was no one to whom Helms delegated more authority. He knew that Angleton would always be a collaborator, never a rival. He knew that the leadership of the Counterintelligence Division would not change and that operations entrusted to Angleton would not be passed along from successor to successor until the circle of knowledge became so wide that the secret was no longer safe. Privately, Helms would call Angleton a "strange, strange man," but counterintelligence was a strange, strange business, and there was no one better suited to its practice.

Angleton. Even the name suggested labyrinthine conspiracies. His body seemed stooped and cocked to one side in a way that hinted of both deformity—as if his very frame had been twisted out of shape by machinations—and conspiracy—as if he were perpetually bending toward someone's ear to whisper a secret. He spoke in a voice so low of tone, so slow of pace, so absent of modulation that it seemed he had been fitted with a speech alteration device. In a secret agency, he was the most secretive of men. All CIA officers adopted an alias for communications between headquarters and the field—Angleton's was Hugh Ashmead—but when he traveled abroad he carried a private set of code pads in his belt to give his cables to headquarters even greater security. His aura of clandestine genius drew people into his web of intrigue, prompting them to entrust him with their most intimate confidences, as if the secret would somehow be safer in his care than in theirs. Even the diary and letters of a woman who had had a brief liaison with President Kennedy were entrusted to Angleton for safekeeping. He had so worked his spell on the Washington liaison officer of the French intelligence service that his superiors in Paris concluded he had been recruited by Angleton as an agent.

Angleton had dedicated his life to the CIA and the craft of counterintelligence. In his leisure hours he would use his considerable talents as a goldsmith to make personalized cuff links for the heads of foreign intelligence services. He cultivated rare orchids and sent them to his allies in the secret war against Russia. Like his passion for fly-casting with handcrafted lures, his fascination with orchids seemed an allegory of his chosen profession—cultivating plants for years until they burst into brief but glorious bloom. Angleton had even attempted to dedicate his property to the CIA, offering to donate a tract of land he owned along the Potomac River to the Agency as a site for the Director's house.

There was a certain poetic justice to be found in suspecting Angleton of being the KGB's mole. It was nothing more than he had done to others. But whether the suspicion was outrageous or deserved, the only question that mattered was whether it was true. Certainly such a grave allegation had to be based on something firmer than speculation about the bona fides of Golitsin and Nosenko. In the wilderness of mirrors, the ground was soft and treacherous. Footprints were everywhere. Which way did they lead?

Upon his defection, Golitsin had beat a path straight for Angleton, refusing to cooperate with any of the case officers assigned to him until he was handed over in frustration to the counterintelligence staff. Had the KGB "targeted" Golitsin for Angleton, or was it merely a coupling of kindred souls? If it had been by design, it had worked to perfection. Careers had been ruined, espionage operations against the Soviet Union paralyzed, and relations with several friendly intelligence services crippled. Through it all, Angleton's faith in Golitsin never wavered. When Golitsin said David Murphy was a Soviet agent, Angleton passed the warning on to the French, even though CIA investigators had satisfied themselves about Murphy's loyalty. When Golitsin suggested that Averell Harriman was a Soviet agent, Angleton badgered Helms to warn the President, even though the case fell of its own weight.

When other defectors made equally startling and unlikely claims, Angleton chose to ignore them. He did not take it upon himself to advise the FBI, for instance, when Michal Goleniewski claimed that Henry Kissinger, then at the height of his Middle East shuttle diplomacy, was a Soviet agent. No one was going to build a case of treason on the basis of Angleton's lassitude in the face of a warning about Kissinger, particularly since Goleniewski was by then claiming to be the last of the Romanovs. The case of Leslie "Jim" Bennett of the Royal Canadian Mounted Police seemed more to the point.

Bennett was the guiding force within Canadian counterintelligence, much like Angleton in the United States. Like Angleton, he had spent almost his entire career in counterintelligence and had no hesitancy about suspecting even the most respected government official of disloyalty. Where Angleton suspected Averell Harriman, the onetime American ambassador to the Soviet Union, Bennett suspected John Watkins, the onetime Canadian ambassador to the Soviet Union. He had personally confronted Watkins with the evidence provided by Golitsin's and Nosenko's lurid tales of homosexual blackmail, but his attempt to extract a confession ended with Watkins's fatal heart attack. Now, in the spring of 1972, doubts were raised about Bennett's loyalty. If they were well founded and if Watkins had indeed been working for the KGB, Bennett's interrogation of the ambassador had been an extraordinary event—one KGB agent promoting his career over the body of another.

Angleton was outraged to learn that the RCMP had begun an investigation of Bennett without his knowledge. The two men had worked closely together in pursuing Golitsin's leads to KGB penetrations in Canada. Once he learned of the case, Angleton took an intense interest in it, making Golitsin available to review and analyze the RCMP's findings. Golitsin concluded that the case was well founded, but that was of little help to the RCMP in developing the kind of evidence that could support a legal prosecution. Finally, Bennett was confronted with the evidence against him and interrogated for four days. At the end of his interrogation, he was given a "medical discharge" from the RCMP.

The Bennett case resembled the Philby affair of twenty years before. Much as Angleton would have liked to take credit for developing the case, he could not. Had Angleton been duped again? Had he been so busy raising suspicions against members of his own service that he had allowed himself to be taken in by a senior member of an allied service? Or was something more sinister afoot? The Bennett case was considerably more ambiguous than the Philby affair. At least Philby could be said with certainty to have been a Soviet agent. Bennett had admitted nothing. The Solicitor General of Canada assured Parliament that "there is no evidence whatsoever that Mr. Bennett was anything but a loyal Canadian citizen," and Bennett himself filed a libel suit when a transparently fictionalized account of his case appeared in print. Nevertheless, the FBI was sufficiently concerned about Bennett's loyalty to conduct a review of the American cases that he might conceivably have blown to the Soviets.

One such case was that of Nicholas Shadrin, the Soviet defector whom the CIA and the FBI had been running as a double agent since 1966, when he had been fed to Igor, the bold KGB officer who had approached Helms with an offer to spy for the United States. In 1971, Shadrin had traveled to Montreal for a meeting with his Soviet control, and the CIA had asked the RCMP to provide surveillance of the meeting. If Bennett was working for the KGB, he might have warned Moscow that the CIA knew all about Shadrin's secret meeting. In a way, speculation about whether Bennett had exposed Shadrin's game was irrelevant since Angleton's conviction that Igor was a Soviet provocation agent assumed that Shadrin had been compromised from the start. Whether blown in 1966 or 1971, Shadrin would later be sent to Vienna to continue his clandestine meetings with the KGB, an act which displayed a cavalier attitude toward Shadrin's safety but which was explained by the fact that his Soviet contacts had given him a "burst" transmitter. For the Soviets to entrust Shadrin with a sophisticated communications gadget which American intelligence had badly wanted to get a look at was seen as an encouraging sign that they suspected nothing, although the double-cross school contended that the transmitter was just one more indication of how far the KGB was willing to go to deceive the CIA. In the event, the CIA got its hands on the transmitter, and Shadrin disappeared without a trace in Vienna. Igor, despite his success in recruiting Shadrin, never received the Washington assignment he claimed to covet. He continued to meet sporadically with the CIA overseas in what Angleton characterized as the most sophisticated provocation the KGB had ever mounted. Provocation or not, Igor was scheduled to meet with the CIA in Vienna on the very weekend that Shadrin disappeared.

All of this was what one CIA officer called "more grist for the counterintelligence mill," but it hardly provided convincing evidence against Angleton. Even an ironclad case against Bennett was something less than an ironclad case against Angleton. It was merely one more in a string of anomalies in his career. Similar irregularities could probably be found in any career subjected to the same microscopic examination as Angleton's. Even the simplest life became complex under scrutiny, and Angleton's had been complex to begin with. How many anomalies added up to a sinister pattern? How many anomalies could Angleton explain away if he were confronted with them? In his private vault there were files that no one else was permitted to see. Perhaps they contained the answers to the troubling questions about his career. But it was impossible to see the files without Angleton's permission, which would surely alert him to the fact that he had fallen under suspicion. Like all those before him, Angleton was never told that his loyalty was in doubt.

By the spring of 1974, after nearly three years of searching through the files, all leads were exhausted. The paper case against Angleton would never be any more or less convincing than at that moment. Barring an unexpected windfall, such as a high-level defector or a communications break, any further progress would require a full-scale investigation of Angleton, subjecting him to electronic and physical surveillance. That kind of investigation of so senior an officer would have to be authorized by the Director, and he would first have to be convinced that the paper case established probable cause to suspect Angleton of treason.

Angleton's fate was now in the hands of William Colby, who had been unexpectedly propelled into the directorship by resignations and firings from the troubled Nixon administration. A colorless but decent man, Colby seemed the model of the faceless but faithful government servant. He had never aspired to the Director's office. By his own account, he was "stunned" to learn that he had been picked for the top spot. In his sudden assumption of power, Colby seemed the clandestine replica of Harry Truman, even down to the clear-rimmed spectacles. Just as Truman had been faced with the insubordination of the legendary General Douglas MacArthur, so Colby was confronted with the covert legend of James Jesus Angleton.

"I spent several long sessions doing my best to follow his tortuous conspiracy theories about the long arm of a powerful and wily KGB at work, over decades, placing its agents in the heart of Allied and neutral nations and sending its false defectors to influence and undermine American policy," Colby related. "I confess that I couldn't absorb it, possibly because I did not have the requisite grasp of this labyrinthine subject, possibly because Angleton's explanation was impossible to follow, or possibly because the evidence just didn't add up to his conclusions; and I finally concluded that the last was the real answer." Colby had first tried to get rid of Angleton early in 1973, when as head of the Operations Directorate he had urged Director James Schlesinger to fire the counterintelligence chief on the ground that "his ultraconspiratorial turn of mind had, at least in recent years, become more of a liability than an asset to the Agency." Schlesinger—"clearly fascinated by Angleton's undoubted brilliance"—balked, but Colby did force a suspension of HT/LINGUAL, Angleton's cherished but unproductive mail-opening project.

When Colby succeeded Schlesinger, the decision on Angleton's fate at last "was mine to make." But Colby procrastinated despite Angleton's refusal to bend to the will of his new chief. Privately, Angleton called Colby a "fool," and to his face told him he was liable to a taxpayers' suit for the damage his naiveté was doing to CIA assets. If Colby needed any further prompting, it came during a trip to Paris when the head of French intelligence confronted him with the fact that Angleton had told him that David Murphy was a Soviet agent. "After I recovered from the shock and looked into the case," Colby said, "I discovered that . . . the matter had been exhaustively investigated several years before and the officer, a brilliant and effective one at that, was given a totally clean bill of health." Colby wrote a memo for the record, expressing "total confidence" in Murphy and "resolved that I just had to get rid of Angleton."

Colby began by proposing to take the Israeli account away from Angleton, hoping that he "might take the hint and retire." Angleton fought back, arguing that the Israeli account was too valuable to be entrusted to the bureaucracy. "I yielded," Colby confessed, "in truth because I feared that Angleton's professional integrity and personal intensity might have led him to take dire measures."

Nothing Colby feared could have been as dire as the news that William Nelson, the new Deputy Director for Operations, had received a mammoth report prepared by Clare Edward Petty, a member of the counterintelligence staff, detailing the evidence that suggested that Angleton was a Soviet agent. Starting from the assumption that the Agency had been penetrated, Petty's report outlined the proposition that both Golitsin and Nosenko had been sent, all under the guidance of the real penetration agent, Angleton. It recounted in endless detail the anomalies in Angleton's career— the Philby and Bennett cases; his irrational pressing of theories about Harriman and the Sino-Soviet split; the damage done to liaison with friendly intelligence services by his unilateral and inaccurate accusations against such innocent people as David Murphy and Ingeborg Lygren. Almost as an afterthought, Petty noted that Angleton's three top aides—Ray Rocca, Newton Miler, and William Hood—although completely unwitting and totally beyond suspicion of any treachery, were so under his influence that they should be removed from the Counterintelligence Division.

"The case against Angleton was a great compilation of circumstantial material," Petty said. "It was not a clear-cut case." Calling his investigation "a long and unpleasant solitary effort," Petty retired from the CIA immediately after submitting his report.

To Colby, the report was an epitome of the "ultraconspiratorial turn of mind" that he disliked so much in Angleton. "There was a lot of supposition, factual situations which were subject to varying interpretations," one of Colby's assistants said. "You could draw conclusions one way or the other, and we felt the conclusions by the fellow who was making the case were overdrawn." Petty "was a very intense person," this officer continued. "He was seized with this theory, and like all people in this field, once they get seized with this thing, you wonder whether they're responsible or not."

Petty had been "seized" by other theories in the past, and in at least one striking instance his theory had proved correct. He had been the author of the original analysis pinpointing Heinz Felfe as the Soviet penetration agent inside the West German BND long before Goleniewski's letters provided enough hard evidence to warrant a criminal investigation. "He made quite a reputation on it," one officer said of Petty's case against Felfe. This officer had conducted a postmortem of the Felfe case and had interviewed Petty at great length. "I got to know the guy quite well," he said. "I would say he was levelheaded. I didn't like him terribly much, but I always found Petty to be reliable."

Petty was the second man to suspect Angleton of being a Soviet agent. Bill Harvey had harbored a similar though much more spontaneous and not nearly so detailed suspicion many years before. Harvey, too, was a very intense person who had once been seized by a theory about Kim Philby. Angleton stood twice accused by the two men in the CIA who had a proven record for spotting Soviet agents, but Colby saw no need to authorize an investigation. "I have absolutely no belief or suspicion that Angleton was a Soviet agent," he said.

Yet Colby had made up his mind to fire Angleton for essentially the same reasons that lay behind Petty's more sinister interpretation of events, namely that Angleton's pursuit of Golitsin's leads was doing more harm than good. In December of 1974, as the scandal over the CIA's spying on antiwar protestors broke in *The New York Times*, Colby demanded Angleton's resignation. At the same time, he informed Angleton's three top aides, Rocca, Miler, and Hood, that they would have to take jobs elsewhere in the Agency. All three chose to follow Angleton into retirement. The coincidental timing of the departure of Angleton and his aides would be inextricably linked in the public mind with the *Times* exposé. "No one in the world would believe [Angleton's] leaving was not the result of the article," Colby said. No one who knew about Petty's report would believe that the departure of Angleton and his three aides was not related to the suspicion that he was a Soviet agent. It was as if Colby had used one scandal as a cover for disposing of an even greater one. That was not the case, Colby insisted. "I can absolutely say for certain that I did not fire Angleton because he was a Soviet agent."

Angleton's resignation was announced by Nelson at the morning staff meeting. "There was a shocked silence," recalled David Phillips, chief of the Agency's Western Hemisphere Division. "Angleton impassively lighted another one of his filter tip cigarettes." After Nelson had explained that there was no connection between the resignation and the *Times* article, Angleton spoke. "It was what some in CIA called his 'nature of the threat' speech—dire predictions, grim warnings and suspicion of détente," Phillips said. "It was a gloomy forecast. We were uncomfortable. . . . When the meeting was over we all left hurriedly, almost as if escaping." That evening as he was leaving for home, Phillips encountered Angleton in the parking lot. "I thought to myself that I had never seen a man who looked so infinitely tired and sad," he recounted. "We shook hands. And I got into my car, backed out of the parking space and drove toward the exit. In the rearview mirror, I could see Angleton's tall, gaunt figure growing smaller and smaller."

Burnt-out Case

"Do you know what you've done?" Angleton hissed at Seymour Hersh, the reporter who had unearthed the facts about the CIA's illegal surveillance of domestic dissidents. "You've blown my cover. My wife, in thirty-one years of marriage, was never aware of my activity until your story." Talking to other reporters, Angleton said he had always told his wife he worked for the Post office—which was not entirely untrue given his role in the CIA's mail-opening program. But the story was preposterous. Cicely d'Autremont Angleton knew precisely what her husband did for a living. Post Office employees did not have autographed photographs of Richard Helms displayed on their mantels. The truth was that Angleton's vocation was known to anyone who had taken the time to read Kim Philby's book *My Silent War*, which was published in 1968 and which identified Angleton as his chief CIA contact and mocked him for having been so easily duped. For those who missed the book, an account of it in the Washington *Post* highlighted Philby's description. Angleton was so incensed by the story that he terminated his friendship with Ben Bradlee, the *Post*'s executive editor, although he remained close to a number of other journalists: Joseph Alsop, James Truitt of *Newsweek*, Charles Murphy of *Time*, Benjamin Welles of *The New York Times*—none of whom was under any illusion that Angleton worked for the Post Office.

Even if Angleton was not the well-kept secret he claimed to be, he was the personification of everybody's fantasy of a "spook." "If John Le Carré and Graham Greene had collaborated on a superspy, the result might have been James Jesus Angleton," a profile in *Newsweek* began. Overnight, he became a media cult figure—accessible enough to feed the public curiosity, remote enough to remain intriguing. He served as the model for the protagonist of a novel called *Orchids for Mother* and was the subject of a full-page portrait by the chic photographer Richard Avedon in *Rolling Stone*. He subscribed to a press-clipping service to stay abreast of all the stories about himself, and he installed an answering service on his telephone to keep track of all the calls he received from reporters. Each reporter thought Angleton was his own special source, when in fact he talked regularly with at least a dozen journalists, playing them off against each other. With no more spies to run, reporters may have seemed the next best thing.

A few months after his retirement, Angleton returned to the CIA to receive the Agency's highest decoration, a ceremony conveniently scheduled on a day when Colby would be out of town. The award was recognition that however badly his career had ended, there had been better days. But Angleton was not satisfied with mere recognition. He sought vindication, proof that his conspiratorial vision was the true one and that Colby was a fool or worse.

Although the *Times* had been alerted to the domestic spying scandal by a source in the Justice Department, Colby, by his own acknowledgment, had confirmed the essential elements of the story for Hersh. Without that confirmation from the Director of the CIA, the *Times* probably never would have printed the story. It did not require a particularly conspiratorial mind to suspect that Colby had given Hersh his scoop as a means of ousting Angleton. Beyond that, the story had set off an orgy of White House, congressional, and media investigations that threatened an unprecedented revelation of CIA secrets. Had Colby intended that as well? Angleton

and his aides had had their suspicions about Colby ever since the
1960s when he had failed to report to headquarters his contacts
in Saigon with a Frenchman of uncertain loyalties. To suspect that
Colby was a Soviet agent bent on destroying the Agency by getting
rid of Angleton and spewing its secrets into the public domain
required a breathtaking—but not unprecedented—leap of logic.

In his conversations with reporters, Angleton never intimated
anything sinister about Colby. His complaint remained simply that
Colby's naiveté was playing into KGB hands. A case in point was
that of Sanya Lipavsky, a Russian neurosurgeon and Jewish dissi-
dent who had volunteered his services to the CIA in 1975. With
Angleton gone, there was no one to expose Lipavsky's approach
as a KGB provocation, so the CIA readily recruited him as an
agent. Two years later, when he publicly revealed his CIA activities
and denounced his roommate, Anatoly Shcharansky, and other dissidents, it became embarrassingly clear that Lipavsky was a KGB
plant who had cleverly discredited, at least in Russian eyes, the
human rights movement.

Angleton may have felt vindication on a grander scale in 1979
when Russia and China agreed to hold preliminary talks aimed
at easing the bitter rivalry between them. Was the trap that Golitsin
had warned about some sixteen years before finally swinging shut?
To anyone not steeped in the Golitsin doctrine, these first tentative
signs of reconciliation looked like nothing more than an oscillation
on the fever chart of history, most likely brought about by the
normalization of relations between the United States and China,
an event that had radically altered the superpower equation. But
for Angleton, history was conspiracy. In 1978, when Israel's army
occupied southern Lebanon in retaliation for a barbarous PLO attack on a busload of Israeli citizens, Angleton told a friend that
the operation was being used as a cover to build an underground
channel that would divert the waters of the Litani River into the
parched Jewish state.

Very little of what Angleton told reporters ever found its way
into print. Most of the plots and machinations he spied were simply
too bizarre and too unsubstantiated to be presented as news. When
it suited him, however, he could leak a tiny nugget of hard and

valuable fact almost as if it was a reward for listening to his byzantine scenarios.

On a Saturday afternoon in 1978, a senior member of President Jimmy Carter's National Security Council staff looked up from his lunch in a popular Washington restaurant to see the instantly recognizable form of Angleton walk in. The senior official and Angleton were not on speaking terms, so he simply watched as the deposed counterspy proceeded straight to the back of the restaurant and into the men's room. "I wish he'd stay in there," the senior official remarked to his luncheon partner. "He's still blowing our sources."

The biggest news story in the seemingly endless stream of revelations following Hersh's original exposé was leaked not by Angleton but by President Gerald Ford, who during an off-the-record session with editors of the *Times* let slip the fact that investigation of the CIA could expose its involvement in assassination plots. With that lead to go on, it was not long before Bill Harvey was rousted from the obscurity into which he had slipped.

After a brief try at practicing law in Washington, Harvey had gone home to Indiana as the Midwest representative of a small investigative outfit known as Bishop Service, which counted several CIA alumni among its employees. "The reason I gave him a job was he needed one, and I'm the kind of guy who's willing to go an extra mile for a guy who's worked for his country," the head of Bishop Service, himself a veteran of the OSS, explained. "I had not been told that the guy had a massive drinking problem. . . . The fact was that he was sort of incapacitated most of the time."

People who had not seen Harvey for many years were shocked at how obese he had become. In 1973 he returned to Maysville, Kentucky, for the first time in nearly twenty years for the funeral of his first wife, Libby. "I was really horrified when he came here," Libby's sister said. "The change in him was unbelievable. He was a very thin young man when he married Libby." Like Harvey, Libby had never been able to free herself from alcohol. She had died by her own hand.

Such private tragedies attracted no public interest, and Harvey remained a man of indeterminate past and no future. When he applied to Bobbs-Merrill for a $9,000-a-year job as a law editor, "Bill said nothing at all about his CIA employment," said Dave Cox, head of the firm's law division. "He used phrases like 'having worked for the government' as if I was supposed to know something independently." Cox got the message when a friend of Harvey's called. "The friend said that Bill had really put in his time . . . that he had served his country well," Cox related. He did not know any more until the spring of 1975, when Harvey was publicly identified as the man who had directed Johnny Rosselli in a plot to poison Castro.

Harvey had known that reporters were onto the story ever since 1967, when syndicated muckraker Jack Anderson wrote that "President Johnson is sitting on a political H-bomb—an unconfirmed report that Senator Robert Kennedy (D-N.Y.) may have approved an assassination plot which then possibly backfired against his late brother." Anderson's column glossed over an enormous amount of complex and ambiguous detail, but there was no doubt that he had been given the essential ingredients. "Top officials queried by this column agreed that a plot to assassinate Cuban dictator Fidel Castro was 'considered' at the highest levels of the Central Intelligence Agency at the time Bobby was riding herd on the Agency. . . . One version claims that underworld figures actually were recruited to carry out the plot." The story had been brought to Anderson by Washington attorney Edward Morgan, apparently as a signal to the government of what the consequences might be of prosecuting his client Rosselli for an alleged card-cheating scheme. Harvey urged the Agency to block prosecution, but the Justice Department went ahead with the case, and Rosselli was convicted of violating interstate gambling laws. In 1971 Rosselli himself started talking, first to Anderson and then to a California court in an effort to win a reduction in his sentence. When Anderson's associate, Les Whitten, called Indianapolis to confirm Rosselli's story, Harvey acknowledged knowing the gangster, but little more. "This is a long story," he told Whitten. "I don't think it ought to be printed."

Harvey did not tell his long story until 1975, when he was called to testify before the newly created Senate Select Committee on Intelligence. Harvey surprised the committee with his willingness to talk. "We'd heard so much about what a tough customer he was that we were afraid we wouldn't be able to get anything out of him," one staff member recalled. "As it turned out, we could hardly shut him up." Some of the staff members thought they detected a subtle whispering campaign by the CIA designed to discredit their star witness. They heard so many stories about Harvey's three- and four-martini lunches that they briefly considered discounting his testimony about events that took place in the afternoon. But Harvey's ability to recall thirteen-year-old events in precise detail stood out in sharp contrast to some of the other witnesses, whose loss of memory sometimes strained credulity. "All these big shots from the Kennedy administration came slinking in, worried about their reputations," one committee investigator said. "And then came Harvey—the assassin himself—saying, 'Yeah, I did it, and I'd do it again if ordered.' "

Harvey's only worry was about having his picture taken. His testimony was heard in closed session, but hordes of reporters, photographers, and television cameramen waited outside. Matching the name with the face would stir up too many operations still alive, Harvey warned the committee. That was probably an exaggeration, but it was certainly true that anybody who saw Bill Harvey once would recognize him a second time. "Harvey made the greatest impression on me of any man I ever met in my life," one committee staff member said. Harvey was the only major witness to testify before the committee who managed to get in and out of Washington without having his picture taken. Rosselli went to great lengths to avoid photographers but saw his picture on page one the next morning. Fourteen months later his body was found with its legs sawed off, stuffed inside an oil drum floating in Miami's Dumbfoundling Bay.

Harvey and Rosselli, the CIA's odd couple, were the only two witnesses to command the attendance of all eleven senators on the committee—a rarity for a secret session that offered no chance for public exposure. After all the stories they had heard, the senators could not resist asking Harvey whether he still carried a gun. No, Harvey said, he was not carrying a gun, but he did have a tiny device that would erase the tape recording that was to be the official transcript of his testimony. He withdrew a small object from his pocket and slapped it down on the table in front of him. The stunned silence in the room was broken by Harvey's chuckle as he removed his hand to reveal a cigarette case.

Nowhere did Harvey cause a greater sensation than at the Bobbs-Merrill offices in Indianapolis where he worked. Everyone suddenly noticed the bulge under his jacket and decided that he had started carrying a gun for self-protection. Wisecracks such as "Don't take any candy from that man" began to circulate. When Sam Giancana, the Chicago mobster who had participated in the early attempts to kill Castro, was found murdered in his home, one law editor quipped, "Where was Bill Harvey on the night Sam Giancana was killed?" Executives at International Telephone and Telegraph, the parent company of Bobbs-Merrill, were aghast at the prospect of being linked to yet another CIA scandal. ITT collaboration with the CIA in attempting to block the 1970 election of Chilean Marxist Salvador Allende was already the subject of one congressional investigation, and the story of how ex-CIA officer E. Howard Hunt had donned a red wig and used a speech-alteration device to interrogate ITT lobbyist Dita Beard about her firm's involvement in the funding of the 1972 Republican National Convention had provided one of the more ludicrous moments of the Watergate affair.

Harvey was about to be fired. "The fact that Bobbs-Merrill is a subsidiary of ITT had some bearing on it," Dave Cox acknowledged, but the main reason was that "his drinking started to get out of control." The termination form landed on Cox's desk with a box labeled "Intemperance" checked off. Cox asked Harvey's supervisor what it was all about and was told that Harvey "had been gone for days at a time and that his work was not at all satisfactory." Cox called Harvey in for a talk. "I've drunk heavily all my life," Harvey told Cox. "I just can't handle it anymore. It's out of control. I just have to realize I'm an alcoholic." Convinced that Harvey intended to reform, Cox refused to sign the termination form, citing ITT's policy about the rehabilitation of alcoholic employees. Harvey began seeing a doctor regularly, and according to Cox, "got squared away on the booze problem." Cox said that "after Harvey got back . . . he came over to thank me for giving him a second chance. He said he couldn't guarantee the treatment would work. If it didn't, he said, he could forget about leading a meaningful life."

Harvey awoke with chest pains at five-forty-five, Tuesday morning, June 7, 1976. By seven o'clock he was in the intensive care unit at Methodist Hospital. On Wednesday he underwent open-heart surgery. For four hours surgeons worked to implant an artificial valve that might somehow overcome the toll taken by obesity, cigarettes, and alcohol. When he regained consciousness the doctors told him the operation had failed. "I've never lost a battle in my life," Harvey said with more bravado than accuracy, "but I'm prepared to lose this one." He died, holding his wife's hand, at ten minutes past two in the afternoon of June 8.

"Bill was 60, too young to go," his wife wrote in a letter to his colleagues at Bobbs-Merrill. "He had many plans ahead. He had lived a very full and satisfying life by his own estimation. He said few men were blessed with the opportunity he had to serve his country." She had received more than three hundred letters of condolence from people all over the world, she said. She had also received some unexpected callers—two attempted break-ins at the Harvey home. "They're after his papers," she said, "but I burned everything." At the funeral home she took people over to view the body and told them how he had "stemmed the tide in Berlin." She said he had been station chief in Berlin at the time of the airlift, which was not true. She could not talk about the things he had really done. She proudly announced that he would be buried wearing his favorite boots and silver belt buckle. Then the bitterness broke through. Standing beside the casket, she launched into a tearful tirade against "that awful Frank Church," chairman of the Senate Select Committee on Intelligence. She was entitled to her rancor. It was unfair to leave Harvey stranded in the public record as the CIA's hit man. He had been that, but so much more—the nemesis of Philby; the foreman of the Berlin tunnel. He had been the CIA's point man in the secret war, and although he had never heard a shot fired in anger, he was a combat casualty, a burnt-out case who, as one officer put it, "was asked to do things that nobody should have been asked to do."

What had happened to Harvey was in part what had happened

to the CIA. It, too, had been asked to do things nobody should have been asked to do, been given secret powers no one should have been given. The CIA had risen above its station in life. It belonged in the back alleys of espionage, not in the corridors of power, just as Harvey belonged in a tunnel beneath East Berlin, spying on the enemy, not across the table from the President's brother, planning a coup. Nothing, of course, was clear cut. Even when the CIA stuck to its primary mission of espionage, the record remained ambiguous, as with Harvey's Berlin tunnel, which had been blown to the Russians from the start. However badly abused and misused from without, the CIA always seemed to carry the seeds of destruction within.

For Angleton, the seed had been sown early and spread its roots wide. Whether or not the KGB ever succeeded in penetrating the CIA, it had at the very least infiltrated Angleton's mind. Hadn't two of his chief mentors been Kim Philby and Anatoli Golitsin? Angleton had created a world of deception and disinformation that for him became the only world. Even his severest critics acknowledged that he had not created this world from thin air. "It wasn't just insanity," a longtime Angleton observer said. "There were precedents one had to take into account," precedents such as Philby, who had secretly served his Soviet masters for fifteen years before he was uncovered, and Golitsin, who for all his ravings had displayed an uncanny knowledge of secret NATO documents. With such precedents, it was certainly not madness for Angleton to suspect the existence of a mole. But he had taken suspicion and turned it into reality. For Angleton, every CIA misadventure was by KGB design; for that matter, so was every CIA success, since it was merely setting the stage for the disaster to come. Under Golitsin's spell, he had even come to doubt the bona fides of the invaluable Oleg Penkovsky. Locked in this world, Angleton had become his own worst enemy. With every new KGB conspiracy that Angleton spied, Colby became more determined to get rid of him. Colby didn't believe Petty's analysis of Angleton's career any more than he believed Angleton's analysis of the KGB. Colby would have had to believe in Angleton to believe that he was the mole. Angleton would have appreciated the irony of that, but Colby never told him. The mirrors had played their final trick.

Afterword

From the death of General Walter Krivitsky to the firing of Angleton, riddle had piled upon riddle. Could the KGB really manipulate events with so callous yet hidden a hand, or were the fates that had befallen Krivitsky and Angleton merely the breaks of the game? Either way, the game was a vicious one, but it was important to know whether or not the wounds were self-inflicted.

Was there a mole? If there was, he must surely be gone by now, forced into retirement by advancing years and recurring personnel cuts. But the question still demands an answer. The KGB penetrated the intelligence services of other Western countries. Why not the CIA? Surely, sometime, somewhere, whether through ideological empathy or simple blackmail, the KGB succeeded in recruiting a CIA officer. But did the mole ever attain a position from which he could do real harm? The answer to that lies buried somewhere in the maze of counterintelligence cases surrounding the defections of Nosenko and Golitsin.

After both Angleton and Petty had withdrawn from the field, the CIA tried again to find the answer, this time with separate panels under the direction of two retired officers who had spent their working lives outside the double-cross world of counterintelligence. The panels—the one on Nosenko headed by John Hart and the one on Golitsin by Bronson Tweedy—concluded that both defectors were genuine. The CIA has adopted the findings as the final word, but they carry no more weight than all the other analyses that went before and do nothing to allay the fear of penetration, since to believe in Golitsin is to believe in the mole. It is possible, of course, that even a genuine Golitsin could simply have been mistaken. But what about Goleniewski, "the best defector the U.S. ever had," who was so certain that the KGB had found out about him through a leak in the CIA? Was he wrong too? And how did the Russians discover the CIA's plan to recruit the Polish intelligence officer in Switzerland, and where did they get a transcript of the CIA's debriefing of the defector Deriabin?

The mists of suspicion can never be burned away, no matter how intense the light. The resulting uncertainty is profoundly dissatisfying. It frustrates the longing for clear-cut solutions and leaves hanging questions about the existence of a high-level penetration agent. But if no amount of scrutiny can pierce the veil, it can at least reveal the mole hunt for what it was—the single most corrosive episode in the CIA's history, more so by far than the blatant yet easily eliminated excesses for which the Agency has been publicly pilloried. Assassination was contemplated by such a handful of men and kept so isolated from the rest of the CIA that it did not corrupt the mainstream of intelligence collection and analysis. The mole hunt, with its attendant fear that all the Agency's clandestine sources on the Soviet Union were compromised and transmitting nothing but bogus data, went to the heart of the CIA's business—the production of reliable intelligence about the motives and methods of the Kremlin. At the beginning, in 1947, Clark Clifford had warned Harry Truman that without reliable intelligence on the Soviet Union the United States would be "at the mercy of rumors and half-truths," and that is precisely what happened during the hunt for the mole. Whether by KGB design or CIA misadventure, that was the ultimate corruption.

While such tactics as assassination and mail opening can be

summarily banned, the dilemmas inherent in counterintelligence are not so easily resolved. The CIA has made a fresh start, but the secret war remains as devious and deceptive as ever, and no amount of well-intentioned "reform," whether dictated by Congress or generated from within the executive branch, is going to change that. The KGB would have it no other way. And if the CIA had such trouble holding its own against the KGB when there were virtually no constraints on the tactics it could employ, how will it fare in this new era?

The CIA's war against the KGB is undeniably just, but the reality is absurd. The careers of Angleton and Harvey were mired in absurdities, not the least of which was that they habitually violated the democratic freedoms they were sworn to defend. The futility of the first thirty years, the expense of spirit and the burden of shame, was staggering. The wonder was that Angleton and Harvey stuck with it for so long, stuck with it for too long, stuck with it until absurdity became the only logic they knew. Immersed in duplicity and insulated by secrecy, they developed survival mechanisms and behavior patterns that by any rational standard were bizarre. The forced inbreeding of secrecy spawned mutant deeds and thoughts. Loyalty demanded dishonesty, and duty was a thieves' game. The game attracted strange men and slowly twisted them until something snapped. There were no winners or losers in this game, only victims.

Author's Note

Although I accept full responsibility for the accuracy of the facts and the validity of the opinions contained in this book, there are several people who were absolutely indispensable to me in transferring the complexities of espionage from my reporter's notebooks to the printed page.

My father, Joseph W. Martin, was a tremendous source of encouragement and a very tough copy editor who could somehow display as much enthusiasm for the latest rewrite as for the first rough draft. Since my father worked for the CIA for twenty-three years, I need to make one specific disclaimer about his role in my work. For his entire career he was an intelligence analyst far removed from clandestine operations and had no involvement in or knowledge of the events portrayed in this book. He was not a source of information, and with one minor exception, neither were his friends. Mike Sniffen of the Associated Press spent days of his time reading my various drafts, going over them with me line by line, sharpening the language, warning against pitfalls, and suggesting avenues of inquiry that had never occurred to me. His reward invariably was another draft to read. Irving Wechsler, a man I respect and admire above all others, and his wife, Marion, read the final drafts of the manuscript and besides making numerous improvements in the text were able to articulate themes I had been wrestling with for the better part of two years but could never express.

Then there was Mel Elfin, my boss at *Newsweek* and one of the class acts in Washington. To paraphrase another prominent Washingtonian, Mel gave me unlimited time off to work on this book, and I exceeded it. Mark Lynch of the American Civil Liberties Union and Jack Landau of the Reporters Committee for Freedom of the Press were both extremely helpful in pursuing requests under the Freedom of Information Act. Elizabeth Jones at Carrolton Press assisted me in using that firm's unique catalogue of declassified government documents. At Harper & Row, Buz Wyeth bought the book on the basis of a five-minute conversation and from then on treated it as though it were his life's work. Burton Beals put this manuscript in its final form, which given my penchant for last-minute changes, must have felt like a life's work. My agent, Theron Raines, friend to English bulldogs and unpublished authors, led me by the hand through the publishing jungles without a false step.

Finally there is my family, beginning with my wife and children, to whom this book is dedicated, and extending to a network of relatives, my parents and hers especially, who have given so much of themselves to my obsession. I visited all the torments of authorship on them without sharing any of the satisfactions. My wife, E.D., was pursuing her own studies in medicine at the time, yet she always pretended that my work was more important and pressing. Truth is, the most important thing is the life we have together with Cate and Zach.

Index